A Well Misspent Youth

BY
BEN E. NEELY PE

I dedicate this book to my father, Harry L. Neely, the bravest man I have ever met. He took his family to sea on a thirty-two-foot sailboat and sailed to Hawaii. The boat was not a good sea boat, and weakly built, so we sold her in Hawaii. The family bought a thirty-six-foot steel haul and finished her on Magnetic Island off the coast of Townsville, Australia. Then we sailed the Skinnie Linnie through the South Pacific and back to San Francisco. That trip made me the man I am.

TABLE OF CONTENTS

CHAPTER ONE

Alley Cat plunges into a twelve-foot curling wall of water. The Pilothouse windows turn completely white with an explosion of foam. Foam blocks out all other sights. White water has buried us... again. Instantaneously, our speed drops from eight knots to three. Sliding forward, I almost pitch out of the seat and onto my butt. The only thing that saves me is bracing against the RADAR monitor.

Watersheds aft, leaving the bow shining, a reddish glow on the port side, and a greenish light to starboard. Alley Cat buries her bow into the bottom of the swell she just busted through. Spray shooting out from her bow reflects the red and green of the running lights. Sitting in the pilot's seat I'm deep in thought; wishing... wishing there was something better than instant coffee to drink. A Coke would be nice, but there aren't any aboard. Cokes cost money, you know?

I'm on one of two fishing boats. We're beating into a forty-knot nor-westerly blow, gusting to fifty knots. The boats are fifty feet-plus with a sixteen-foot beam. They're built in a northern troller style. The pilothouse is as far forward as aesthetically acceptable; both are less than 5 years old. Which means they are *brand-new boats.*

We left Moss Landing, California, five days ago, heading north, chasing Albacore. Right now, we're about a hundred miles off the Oregon coast. The time is just past midnight, the year is 1973. I am all of nineteen, and this is my first season on a troller.

The VHF radio crackles, "Hey-hey-hey, The Douggers, Douggers, you on this side?"

The voice is using the same inflections as Yogi the Bear, the cartoon.

Standing up and grabbing the mic, "Good morning, Stormy. The Douggers just went to bed, can I do anything for you?"

"Hey-hey-hey, Benjy, you'll do just fine." Stormy's disembodied, Yogi the Bear's imitation replies. Occasionally, Stormy slips from his assumed persona of Yogi the Bear, but not this night. Stormy is always Yogi, the Bear; except when he ain't.

"Hey-hey-hey... I've got this new kid over here. Nick is his name. Hey-hey, he's just a little jumpy tonight. He didn't think it would be rough out here... not in the summer time... any-whos. So... anyways, I was a-thinkin Benjy? Maybe you could call over here when he is on watch.

Kind of keep his mind all busy, he broods too much. You know what I mean, just keep him laughing and happy. Hey-hey, that way, he won't be waking me up every fifteen minutes. He woke me up four times last night; he was just asking dumb questions."

"What kind of questions Stormy?"

"Hey-hey-hey, you know Benjy, the kind every greenhorn asks. How do I know if the running lights are still on? What do I do if a ship comes upon us... in the dark? Do whales ever attack fishing boats?"

"I never ask questions that dumb, do I?"

"Hey-hey-hey, some of us are greener than others."

"I'll be glad to talk to this guy. But I really don't know what to say to him. We've never met. It's kind-a-hard, striking up a conversation with someone you've never seen."

The VHF crackles again, "Hey-hey-hey, Benjy, you just tell him a few jokes. You know, crack him up."

Shaking my head at the radio, "I'm not Bill Cosby, I don't know any jokes."

"Here, here are a few, write-um down."

The next ten minutes are spent with Stormy using his fertile imagination and creative mind. Me, I'm scribbling madly on a notepad. Between gales of laughter, Stormy arms, me with four jokes to tell Nick.

During the joke telling, Stormy slips from his Yogi the Bear voice.

"I'm going to get Nick. You wait about ten minutes, so he can get a cup of coffee. Then call him up and tell him our jokes."

A wave crashes into the port bow. The greenish glow of the RADAR lights that side of the helm area. It's sweeping a ten-mile radius every thirty seconds. Alley Cat is on autopilot, the wheel searching port, trying to hold a course in the gusting wind. The pilot chain groans and creaks. Our bow rises into an oncoming comber; the bell dings once, lightly. Then, the reassuring throb of the diesel engine changes in pitch as the prop cavitates. While waiting the prescribed ten minutes, the weather is intensifying. The rigging is vibrating the whole boat. The wind moans, and then howls. Every wave is sending spray over the flying bridge.

The night sky is filled with brightly shining stars. This is just a little summer blow, not a storm, not really. Without warning, the stars disappear. A large mass is blocking my view. Grasping the arms of the pilot's seat, I am forced back as the floor rises under my feet. A shot of adrenaline begins in the pit of my stomach and spreads to my limbs. This is one steep monster. If she's a curler,

3

she could be coming through the windows at me. We climb for a minute, or minute and a half; yep, she's a rogue. A fluorescent line of white rushes toward us. She's a curler! Instinctively turning my head to the side, I take a breath and hold it. White water blocks out all other sights for a long, long, time. Slowly, the stars return, shining through the quarter inch of safety glass.

For the second time in ten minutes, the pilothouse of the Alley Cat has been buried under the sea. I am on stage, this is my backdrop.

Puffing the adrenaline out of my system by taking two deep, cleansing breaths, I pick up the VHF mike. "Hornet, Hornet, you on this one?"

The VHF comes back with a breathless voice.

"Yea, this is the Hornet, what do you want?"

"I was just getting a little, aah-hum, sleepy over here. Thought I'd call you guys up, and you know, visit some."

"Well... we're all right, at least so far, but my God, it's rough! Where are you calling from?"

In a relaxed, easy going, happy-go-lucky voice, I click the mic button, and sounding like a highliner, 'at least in my own mind?'

"I'm off your starboard about a mile and a half, this is the Alley Cat. We're running with you."

The excited voice crackles through the VHF speaker again. "Oh good, we have someone out here with us? I didn't know that, oh good, oh good! Is it as bad over there as it is over here?"

Grinning into the mike, ad-libbing a little joke, "Oh, it's really nice over here, flat calm, and glassy slick."

"I don't believe you! It can't be calm just a mile away. If it is nicer over there, maybe I should head over that way. Is it really nice over there?"

My little jokes are falling on deaf ears. This isn't going so well, is it? I sure as heck don't want Nick to aim the Hornet at us. She's fifty-seven feet of steel, and thirty tons of fish.

Changing tacks, I launch into Stormy's material. "Did you hear about the fisherman who was taking out a waitress that worked at the coffee shop in Moss Landing? *'I throw in the line about Moss Landing, to make it more relevant to our life's. Stormy didn't even give me that one.'*

"Being serious, he decided he better bring his wild and rotten sons in. She needed to get a look at-um, before things got even hotter and heavier; if you know what I mean?

Now, these boys have been raised on a fishing boat. Angels, they ain't. Outside of the restaurant he stops his boys, lecturing them on the perils of using obscene language. All the booths are full, so Dad and the boys belly up to the counter. Dad introduces his boys to the hot little waitress. The eldest boy is seven. The next in age is six. The youngest is five.

The waitress says,

"My, my, what cute boys. They must be little angels."

She asks the eldest,

"What would you like for breakfast, Honey?"

The oldest boy, looking over the menu, glances up. "Give me some of those fucking pancakes."

Whack! His ol' Dad backhands him off the barstool. The little guy picks himself up off the floor, sniffling back sobs. The waitress doesn't know what to do. Befuddled, she asks the middle boy, what would he like? Well, this little guy has been concentrating on reading the menu.

He says, "That sounds good, give me some of those fucking pancakes too." Whack! Dad backhands the miscreant, and he goes flying off the barstool.

By now, the waitress is really disconcerted. The only thing she can think to do is ask the smallest child what he would like. The five-year-old, he pays attention to everything. His two brothers are sitting there, trying not to cry, and he sure doesn't want to get what they got.

He tells the waitress, "I don't know, but you can bet your sweet ass, I don't want any of those fucking pancakes."

Releasing the mic button; I listen for the appreciative laughter.

The radio is silent for a count of ten. Then, a wholly unexpected reply comes.

"What's wrong with you? Are you some type of deranged prankster? Are you crazed? We could die out here! And, and, you're telling me jokes? Do you have any idea what it's like over here? Well, do you?"

This isn't the happy-go-lucky laughter I expected. On top of being unexpected, this is a social blunder on the fishing grounds. Weather that you are caught in is never, ever rough. Weather can be a little snotty. It's OK to say there are a few sheep around. In a Force 5 hurricane, a captain can tell a close friend, who is still in port,

"You're just as well-off where you are."

If you're in the weather, it is never, ever bad or lousy or rough. Declaring this is admitting that you, or God forbid, your boat, is not up to the weather that you got yourself into. This conversation is turning a little uncomfortable.

However, I am nothing if not tenacious. "Well, don't worry about the seas. As long as you can see the stars, the boat is afloat. That Hornet is one hell of a sea boat. Besides, if anything were to happen to one of us, the other boat is out here to take care of things."

Releasing the mic key, I grab a spoke on the wheel, steadying myself.

Static fills the air between the boats. No response from Nick forces me to continue.

"That reminds me of a story." Glancing at my crib sheet, "There was this guy who people were worried about, and he was being sent to a psychiatrist.

The doctor, concerned with his sexuality asked, 'What would you think of, if you

were to see Raquel Welch bared to the waist?'

The man said, 'Well, I'd be thinking about a windshield wiper.'

'A windshield wiper?' the psychiatrist asks.

'Yep,' the man says, 'cause, I'd be going like this.'

Bending back and forth at the waist I am making smacking sounds with my mouth.

I am trying to sound like a man kissing one breast, then the other. Of course, Nick can't see these gyrations. The Alley Cat's motions make my movements even wilder. All and all, this is too much for me, I crack up at my wit. This joke ends with me regaling my audience with mad sounding laughter.

The VHF crackles, Nick's angry, breaking voice booms, "Man, are you nuts? Did you just tell me another joke! I can't believe it. If you had a brain, you'd take it out and play with it. We're about to die, and I have the village idiot telling me jokes."

Nick is committing just one social faux pas after another. At nineteen, I'm not sure how to tell him that he's embarrassing his boat, even if it is an honest appraisal of the situation.

"Well, you're on one hell of a sea-boat over there. It's brand new. Ya-got the latest of everything. Man, just kick back, and enjoy the ride. We don't get weather this rough all the time, when it's calm these night runs are real tedious."

"Tedious! Tedious! OK Man, OK man, now I know that you aren't even out here. You're on the beach somewhere just screwing with me. Come on, admit it."

Rubbing the fine blond hair on my jaw I fall to thinking. *"'Here I am, doing my best to allay this guy's fears. My jokes sure don't seem to be helping much. Old Nick here, he just don't know good humor when he hears it."*

Here he's had the wisdom of my nineteen years. Three of those years spent on small ocean going-vessels. I've got the feeling that everybody is looking at me. I don't like talking to this scary-d-cat. Gee, what if someone thinks this guy is my friend?

I am torn, there's my obligation to keep Stormy's deckhand calm, but, but, I've got a feeling that Nick's lack of fisherman's protocol is painting me as a nervous nelly. After all everyone can overhear our conversation. What to do; what to do?

The weather is abating a bit. The gusts seem to have disappeared. It's a nice steady breeze of forty knots that's puffing through the rigging.

Pushing the mic button again, "Well, I was just trying to keep from falling asleep, somehow... I'm not very sleepy now. So, I'll catch you later, OK? If you want to

hear any more jokes call me. I've got two more over here. That is, if you get tired, or ...anything."

Hanging up the mic, I scan the overhead; it is crammed port to starboard with hi-tech electronic equipment. Bolted to the overhead are; two VHF radios, a VHF radio direction finder, and a single-side-band radio. Behind my back is another bank of electronics, such as; a paper graphing depth finder, a flasher depth finder, a LORAN, and an old AM set. Scanning this twenty-thousand-dollar array of gear, guilt surrounds me like fog on an Oregon winter's night. Stormy needs to get some sleep, he's got a green hand onboard, who is more nervous than a whore in church, and I've let Stormy down.

But, talking to this guy is like poking yourself with a fishhook. It's not that much fun when you are doing it, and it sure feels good when you quit. Gazing at the VHF, I'm sipping my cold instant coffee. *I'll tell The Douggers to call Nick when he gets up. Yea, that's what I'll do. I'll tell him Nick really likes jokes.*

***

Doug relieves me at zero four hundred hours. I'll get an hour of lay down time before our eighteen-hour day begins. My eyes have just closed when I feel Doug's hand on my shoulder, he's shaking me awake.

Climbing over the foot-high leeboard of my bunk, my feet hit the floor. There is very little to do in preparation for my day. I've slept dressed except for my socks, boots, and raingear. Donning footwear, and rain gear, I head out the back door.

This is the beginning of my workday, no coffee, no washing, no teeth brushing. My only grooming is running my fingers through my hair. Forty-knot winds make the effort useless. Our deck is tilting port and starboard, while she's pitching fore and aft. The motion makes my commute to work an interesting chore. Jumping from bin-board to bin-board, I'm balancing on, up-right, two by twelves amidst this chaos of sound and motion.

Each leap brings me closer to the stern.

There ain't any safety-lines onboard, deck hands are cheap, you know?"

I'm within three feet of the stern, the only thing between the deep blue sea and me is thin air. A loop of half-inch nylon line hangs off the boom, just over the gaff hatch. One last lurch toward the stern, and my hand finds the loop. It halts my upper body motion. Feet swinging out from under me, I drop into the gaff hatch.

Looking forward, toward Doug, I grin. I grin big, I love this life.

Throwing out the first albacore jig, I start our day. The Douggers is grinning back. You can't do this job for long, not if you don't love it.

Each jig is finding its rightful place off our stern. I fall to thinking. How did I ever become a fisherman? It wasn't for lack of opportunities. My father owns a successful earth moving company. I could have been a partner, but I've always wanted to work on a small vessel in the open ocean. Going to college is open to me. If I elect to go, my folks will cover the cost. Money never was a concern of mine. Not until I became a fisherman, anyway.

Leaning against the hatch I contemplate my lot in life. The Alley Cat is charging into heavy seas. Spray is running off my raingear. The deck is awash with sea water. The smell of brewing coffee blows past my head. Still; I stand here and remember, remember how it started. It doesn't seem like it, but it was just over a year ago...

***

Sitting in the swim team's locker room there's only a month left before graduation. I'm slowly getting out after practice. Another swimmer is taking his time getting dressed too. We're both tired out after our workout. Just to make conversation I ask the other guy, "Marty, what are you doing this summer?" Turning Marty blinks at me, his voice like his manner thoughtful and pedantic, "Oh, I'll go up to P.C. and commercial fish dories, I always do." POP, my eyes open wide, and my mouth gapes. Marty and I have been on the same water polo and swim teams for three years. In all that time, I'd never known that Marty fished dories. I love dories. I've read Captains Courageous. It's the best book Kipling ever wrote. I read another book about a couple of men rowing a dory across the Atlantic Ocean. Great book; great boat. I've got plans of a cape dory; her lines are etched into my mind.

But man... Marty knows how to take a small boat and wrestle a living from the sea. Not just a small boat but a dory, a dory. This same boat took George Washington across the Delaware, my leg begins to bounce, eyes shining with the light of a new convert in a religious cult. A thousand questions flood my mind. They all boiled down to just one.

"Who do I have to kill to work on one of these boats?"

However, I've watched my father buy equipment and make business deals my whole life. Playing it real cool, "Well Marty, how did you start fishing dories?"

Marty scratches the sparse chin whiskers he's sporting. "Well, my dad fished dories as a young man. We've been going up there every year since I can remember. My bro and me, we just got a new boat. New gear, new motor, everything is new but the flashers and spoons."

I don't know what a flasher is, but using an old spoon to eat with shouldn't be a problem.

"Oh yea, what are you doing with your old boat, Marty?"

"Well, Dad is going to sell it. Man, Ben, you don't want that boat. Ben it's a piece of crap. It's old, the motor is old, she's Fallin apart man, no way man, you just don't want that boat."

I'm hooked, I've got to take a look at this boat. The high bow, the sheer amidships the up swept stern, it's a dory. A real seagoing vessel, I want this boat.

Marty is doing his level best to dissuade. I'm sure he is using a new sales technique, but then again, Marty is the sole of honesty. He wouldn't lie to anyone, not even a white lie to a young lady. Not even to receive sexual favors from her.

"Marty, what's she built of?"

Marty doesn't want me to buy his boat. However, it is his boat, and pride of ownership shows through in his description. Marty describes a boat almost twenty years old, plywood on two by four ribs at twelve-inches in center. She's a good sea boat in need of some tender loving care. With some paint and elbow grease, she'll be shipshape. The old Kisutch can be had for a thousand dollars. As it so happens, one thousand dollars is just the amount that I have in savings.

For that grand I'll receive a fine dory, a thirty-five-horse outboard motor, to push her with, and a Jeep to launch the boat through the surf. What a bonus! Getting the boat into the sea is a little adventure every morning, launching through the pounding surf. At the end of the day; you get to land the boat by running her back through the surf.

What a way to start the day; pushing your very-own boat through the cold Oregon surf; first thing in the morning. Man, life is good.

"I've got to look at your boat. Don't sell her to anyone else, not until I get a chance to make you an offer." We agree with a shake of our hands.

While we're shaking, I scrutinize Marty. Standing six feet tall his shoulder length brown hair has a greenish hue. Broad powerful shoulders taper to a skinny waist, Marty has very little facial hair, hailing from an American Indian heritage. He's wearing braces, which makes him shy around girls. He's a big, good-looking guy who doesn't know it… yet.

Only two small problems remain. One, convince my folks this is a good idea. Two, I need a partner. Every sea story that's ever been written, has a partner. Someone who is a best friend, true and loyal; preferably someone who's life you've save. Besides, someone has to hold the boat in the surf while someone drives it.

13

Heading off for home in my sixty-five Mustang I'll have to see if that thousand- dollars is mine. Driving along, Clayton Road recedes into the background. The red hood of the Mustang becomes the high swept bow of a dory. The wheel under my hand is driving a boat through breaking surf. My right hand pushing the throttle forward: we need more power. My hand is resting on the gear shift knob, *"OOPS."* I just shoved the car out of gear; better pay attention here. If I get in an accident Mom will be pissed at me. She's not too pleased with me and boats anyway; last summer I blew it. It was just one of those things, that could have happened to anyone. Slowing to a stop at our intersection I reminisce a bit. It was July of last year. My dad had, *'I do mean had'*, this scruffy little rubber boat, or rather half a boat. You see, I tied old Scruffy too far after one time while we were down in Australia. She hung her stern up on a pile and got her ass ripped out, ripped out real good. Dad, being a child of the depression knows how to squeeze a buck. So, instead of buying a new boat he had a canvas maker sew a tractor inter-tube in the stem. Scruffy looks like a real boat from the athwart seat forward; and like a canvas makers' nightmare from there back. But... it floats.

It seems like a good idea to take scruffy white-water rafting. Two buddies and I head up to the American River and throw her in. Way up in the Sierras somewhere; we have no idea of what we're up to. Lots of other boats on the river, so no big deal. Right? Unfortunately, we didn't get on the river until everyone else was getting off. I didn't know it then, but this is not a good thing, not a good thing at all. The sun low in the west cast long shadows across the river. It was wonderful, just wonderful. Off we paddle; the first rapid is a little bouncy, bubbly jog. Easy, so was the second and the third rapids. After an hour of these little splashy rapids we're getting mighty board.

There was an old guy on the beach; he must have been fifty if he was a day. He griped and complained trying to talk us out of setting off.

'What was it that old man griping about? Where is that gorge, he was bragging on anyway? This ain't nothin'. I sure hope something interesting happens soon.'

It's good dusk now and I think we found the old guy's gorge. He told us, "Don't go, don't go; once you reached the gorge, you'll have two hours of river left. It'll be dark by the time you get through the gorge. It's class three and four rapids all the way."

We don't know what classes three and four means, but we're about to find out. Up ahead a scary roar is coming back toward us. It sounds like a water fall crashing onto rocks. What did that old guy say? Something to do with big standing waves, large holes in the water, and white. He kept saying white water, lots and lots of white....

The river narrows and speeds up. A slick V shape draws us in; yep, this is the way to go. OH GOD! Water drops out from under us in a cascade of white. The boat hesitates, and then drops into the flow. We're at the bottom of a big hole covered by water. White water pours over the sides filling the boat. Paddling like hell the boat is acting like it's a led slug. She's starting to climb from the hole the boat flips over backwards. We're all swimming. The rapid spits us out; after running us through the spin cycle for what seems a vast amount of time. Me and my buddies all end up on a rock downstream more or less together, Scruffy is now a tattered wreck. The canvas has rotted from sun and salt. The inter-tube is floating away, gone into the dark. Now we have to walk out of this canyon and try to find the road.

Five hours later, we find the road. It's another two hours and we're back in the car.

We're still three hours from home; being teenagers we decide that if we call this late, waking everyone up, we could be in trouble. It's about eight o'clock Sunday morning when I drive into our driveway. It's been a full twenty-four hours since I left with a boat. Here I am, beat and battered, cut and scraped, without any kind of boat. *'I maybe in trouble here?'*

Walking in the door, there stands my mother. Tears streaming down her agonized face she strides to me and hits my butt as hard as she can. She's so mad at me she can't speak, which is fine by me. Her face contorts as she finds her voice.

"You're grounded! You left here yesterday. Where have you been? You're never leaving this house again!"

"Well you see... we kind of, of..."

"Oh, shut up, I don't want to hear any excuses. Have you been out getting drunk?

You better have a good reason that's all I have to say."

"Uh, no. No good reason for being out all night, but we lost the boat." Dad saunters into the kitchen, things are going from bad to worse. His eyes read mad, very-very mad. Wait until he hears about me losing the boat. He was pissed enough to bite a ten-penny nail into when I screwed the boat up the first time.

"Well, what the hell happened?

"Everything was going fine and we would have been OK, if? If...if we hadn't hit that class four rapid. Old Scruffy she kind of fell apart. The boat was fine going into the first big rapid, and only half a boat came out at the bottom."

Dad gets that light of humor in his eyes; a smile plays across his lips. Dad, he loves adventure as much as I do. Here's my out. Taking the cue, I go into hand motions to show how the raft bounced through the first few rapids. "Old Scruffy did just fine until she filled with water in the bottom of the hole."

Raising my hands I cascade us into the class four hole. "Then she just came unglued. Water was pouring in on us, the innertube shot out from under my ass; leaving me with nothing to sit on but some rotten canvas. After that we were all swimming."

My body jerks around the kitchen showing what the washing machine action was like in the white water. I swim out of the rapid through the dining room. Describing the rock we all ended up on, I breast stroke into our living room, where I flop down, my feet on the coffee table.

My Dad is sniggering, I won't get a beating. My Mom is still pissed, but I am alive and whole, so a few days of grounding, "No Car," should teach me. But, it don't. When a person has the adventure bug it never goes away. The only thing that saved me from being in real trouble was a near drowning.

***

Walking into the house, "I'm home, anyone here?"

Skinny, my little sister, comes around the corner. "Hi Ben-jo," she greets, "what are you doing?"

"Where is Mom and Dad?"

Linnie and I are friends. She's in eighth grade and is a good kid. Tall and reed thin, there is a small hint of the budding beauty she is becoming.

Seeing my mom down the hall I can't help asking, "Where is Dad?"

I've worked out a strategy, get both parents together, and then present this idea of mine. It isn't much of a plan, but it's better than no plan at all. My father, the born-again adventurer, will be the easiest to convince that spending my life's saving on a twenty-year-old plywood boat is sensible.

My mother is the keeper of the passbook. She is also the sensible one in the family; however, she spoils me rotten. They just have to understand what an opportunity this is. I've got to get my thousand dollars. Someone may steal this great deal.

Mom smiles, her face glowing, "Dad is working late. He'll be home in an hour or two. Are you hungry? I can cook you a stake now if you want."

I just swam five thousand yards, most of that distance sprinting. I'm ravenous.

"No that's all right," smiling back at her, "We'll wait until Dad gets home, that way we can all eat together."

Mom touches my face, "You're a good boy, it's nice of you to wait for Father."

Wondering down the hall I grab my books and do homework.

When Dinner is called, I'm ready, ready to make my pitch. We eat stake almost every night. My father grew up a migrant farm worker. Many nights, there was not enough to eat, when he was a child. Never, and I mean never was there meat on the table. Now that he is a successful earth moving contractor, our table is a cornucopia of good food. My mother is a great cook. She buys the finest ingredients, adding consummate skill, she creates a banquet every night.

My father asks the table in general, "Well, did anything happen in school today?"

This is my opening, "Dad, you remember that book we read about the two men who rowed a dory across the Atlantic Ocean?"

A look of concern crosses Mom's face; Dad's interest is peaked. Seeing how the wind is blowing, I address my pitch to him. Three years ago, he loaded the bunch of us into a thirty-two-foot sailboat and sailed to Australia and back. We were sailing for two years.

A dinner conversation that includes: boats, adventure, and ocean, is right up his alley. On the other hand, my mom was frightened most of the time at sea. The ocean, when it's angry, is not adventurous, it's death on a stick to my mom.

Rubbing a large hand over his bald head, Dad rejoins, "Yea, we still have that book somewhere around here. Don't we?"

"I think so. Anyway... I was talking to a friend of mine today. He has a dory, that he fishes commercially, and it's for sale."

The light of adventure comes into Dad's eyes, "That's interesting, how much is the boat?"

"Oh, only a grand."

"That's not bad, not bad at all."

"What are you two thinking about", mom is shaking a fork in my general direction, "neither of you have even seen this boat. It could be a twenty-year-old scrap heap, as far as you know. You don't know, it may leak at every seam."

That comment makes me a little nervous, after all she just zeroed in on Marty's description *of my new boat.* "Ah, Mom, you know how pretty a dory is. How can a boat with an up swept bow be anything but beautiful?"

Her fork stirs the air, "Don't you understand, you could drown.

Going out to sea in an open boat is dangerous. Lots of other men have died, you could, too. Life is not just some big adventure."

My mind rejects this assertion, life should be a big adventure. But I can't say that, can I? "I don't want to buy the boat; I just want to look at it, see if it's worth a grand. I'm just going to spend this one summer fishing. If it doesn't work out, I'll sell the boat."

There it is, my new dream, out in the open; buy a boat and spend the summer commercial fishing in Oregon. The argument continues through dinner with my dad and I battering at Mom's logic. By the time dinner is over, we have agreed. My father and I will take a look at Marty's new dory. We'll just see what she looks like. Then, I'll take my time and decide if I should make an offer on his old boat.

Dinner over, my father and I trooped over to Marty's home.

***

Dad and I are standing at the door of a house in a Concord suburb. The door swings open. The man standing there is about five-eleven, with large arms, and a barrel chest. His hair is salt and pepper gray. He's wearing a full beard and a big grin. This is Nole. Nole is Marty's father. Expecting us, he offers a beer to my dad.

Harry, my father, declines the beer, "I broke my drinking thing a few years ago and have not been able to get another."

Nole is a college professor at the local Junior College. He teaches biology, mostly to young nursing students, eighty percent of his class is female. Nole enjoys his job, however, he needs a break from the nubile creatures that stare up at him with rapt attention during most of his days. Hence, Nole fishes in the summer time, that way the glassy eyed stares comes from dead salmon, not university hotties. Adjourning to the back yard we view the new Kisutch. She's twenty-two feet long with an up-swept bow. Her flat bottom is five feet wide. The sides are four feet high and flaring. An Oregon Dory is eight feet wide at the gunwale. The flared gunwale makes for a good sea boat. Her stern is wide, unlike a Grand-Banks dory.

The wide stern allows the boat to pack a larger horsepower motor and achieve planning speeds on the ocean. The outboard motor is in an inboard well; a plywood flap allows the outboard to come up, while keeping most of the ocean out… most of the time.

In a short time, the four of us; Nole, Harry, Marty and me, are lined up on the side of the boat, staring at the far gunwale. Leaning on our forearms, we're looking out over the boat, contemplating it like a group of sages. In less than five minutes the lines of the Oregon dory won us over. No sales pitch is necessary, the boat sold herself. However, this isn't the boat I'm buying. I'm not even buying her older sister; I'm buying her great-grandmother.

Even though we promised my mom that under no condition would we make an offer on the dory, I did. My father, a full grown adult, allowed me to break that promise. It just goes to show a man like a boy, loses what little sense he has when faced with the beautiful lines of a fine boat or lovely girl.

***

It's a Friday night, and I'm looking around for a seat at the basketball game. A raven-haired beauty named Claudia glides along beside me. Unfortunately, she is not with me, the way I want her to be with me. Her boyfriend has dumped her again, and I'm her booby prize. When the guy she has been with since seventh grade dumps her, she calls me. I hang around her like a hungry hound dog at the butcher's back door. I am hoping against hope that one of these times she will get mad enough at her boyfriend to give me a whirl.

Claudia and I have been friends now for a couple of years. But she is maddeningly loyal to her boyfriend. Here it is, the onset of the sexual revolution, I'm well-armed, my weapon loaded and cocked. It just seems there are no targets of opportunity available to me. My hope is this doe eyed beauty will relieve me of a curse, my virginity.

At the top of the bleachers, not too many people around, there's a place to sit. This will give me a chance to rap with Claudia. Claudia and I are leaning back taking up about six spaces, our legs touching and our feet entwined. Man, I'm really making progress tonight. I know she's not a virgin, she told me so. This could be my night. We're holding hands looking deeply into each other's eyes. Talking about what a rat her boyfriend is, all systems are go. Her soft brown eyes give me a slow come-hither blink.

Man, this is it; I'm going to score.

Headed straight toward us is a guy and a gal. I know this guy, what's his name? Mike, Mike something? We were lab partners in... Marine Biology? Yea, that's right, Marine Biology. He has his girlfriend in tow. Looking at all the space we've bo-guarded they decide to join us.

Standing above me, Mike is looking down at us, "Hey Ben, mind if we sit down?"

Weighing alternatives in my mind; one, we've taken up enough space to seat the whole basketball team. Two, Mike's lady friend is kind of easy on the eyes, in fact she is a bona fide Goddess. Three, Mike and I always talk about diving, and he's good for a laugh. Fourth, talking about the rat boyfriend is becoming annoying. And five, I'll look like a jerk saying no.

"Yea, have a seat." Peeking over at Patty, I add a conversation starter. "Been doing any diving lately?"

"Un-hum, I went last month down in Monterey, how about you?"

Mike and I pause, as we watch Claudia cross her long, shapely legs. Claudia chooses this time to begin playing footsies with me. Claudia has one of the best set of legs in the school. To show them to their best advantage she wares' miniskirts, short tight miniskirts. She rubs the inside of my calf with her shoeless foot. Me, I am trying to remember where the heck I went diving last.

"Ah, ah, Salt Point Ranch, I think", my husky voice croaking out the answer?

"When did you go?" Mike is leering at me. He can see that hormones have relieved me of the ability to speak.

"Last weekend?" My vocal cords straining with the testosterone driven utterances I'm making.

Claudia lays her hand on my thigh in a natural way. It's as though rubbing my leg is an everyday occurrence. Man, this is going good, real good.

Mike makes another try or two at small talk, all to no avail. My mind can't handle Claudia playing Love Me Tender on my inner thigh and forming words.

***

We're sitting in silence. We haven't spoken for twenty minutes or so.

The Clayton Valley Eagles are getting plucked again. There is no chance our guys will come back. Claudia gives my thigh a break from her tender ministrations and my brain reengages into gear. Coming from my gland induced stupor I remember... '*Mike? Mike, I should talk to Mike?*'

Turning to him, "What are you doing this summer?"

"Going to Hawaii again, I guess, picking pineapples. What are you up to this summer?"

"I've bought a commercial fishing boat. Up in Oregon, I'll go north this summer... and fish her."

Mike's eyes glaze over, his hands tremble, a small spittle of droll forms at the corner of his mouth. Mike is hooked, like I'm hooked. I didn't know I was trolling for converts, but I have one.

He blurts out, "So, how did you get involved in fishing in Oregon?" He's sounding like me, when I was talking to Marty.

The basketball game is forgotten. I'm relaying what little I know about commercial fishing to Mike. Relaying everything I know, about the business I just sunk my life savings into, takes all five minutes. During the rest of the game, Mike and I rehash every detail I don't know about fishing.

By the middle of the third quarter, Mike is my new partner, in a boat that neither of us have seen.

***

It's pushing midnight; Claudia and I are rolling around on her living room floor. Her blouse and bra were left up on the couch, along with my shirt, over an hour ago. Claudia's lips cover mine in a tender yet passion-filled kiss. My body trembles with the yet unknown delights that I'm on the threshold of experiencing.

Sighing happily, I bend to my task of kissing Claudia's breast. Her nipples taste like honeydew vine water, sweet and tender. My muscles are strung bowstring tight, I've never had so much fun.

"God, I want you." I murmur into her ear.

Claudia clasps my face with both hands, "I want you too. My parents left for the weekend. It's just my sister and me in the house. I'd planned to seduce you tonight. I've changed the sheets on my bed and everything. I even bought a new nightgown. I've been planning to seduce you all week. But now? You're leaving, going to Oregon. It just wouldn't be right to begin a relationship; if I knew that you were going to be around, it would be different. For right now, we have to remain just friends. We should get dressed. You have to go home, I'm sorry, so so sorry."

I gape at her horror stricken. I want her. I'm a virgin for God's sake. My mind won't work. My chin dropping to my chest, I mumble.

"All right."

25

What a silver-tongued devil I am. With this type of savior faire, I'll be a virgin my whole life.

Walking out of Claudia's door, buttoning my shirt askew, I fall to thinking. *'This is some fun, I want to do it some more, wonder when?*

***

My little old sixty-five Mustang is flying down Highway One. We're cooking along at fifty-five miles an hour. The car is stuffed with teenage boys and gear. It's the Saturday following our Thursday graduation. We're on our way. Going to Oregon via Fort Brag, California. My Mom, an ever-practical woman, found us a sixteen-foot house trailer. Up in Fort Brag, it belongs to a family friend. Like our new boat it's twenty-some-odd years old.

We're riding along; Mike, me, and a kid named Scott. Someone, I don't know who, told him that if he could catch a ride with us to Oregon, he could stay with Nole for a month. So, here is this kid I don't know; Mike, my new partner whom I really don't know and me. We're all speeding along the coast highway.

At the pit stop, Gowan's Apple Farm and Cider Emporium; my father told us, "Speed ahead, go get us some abalone for dinner."

They're driving a pickup and camper. Their progress through the coastal mountain roads will be much slower than ours.

Harry started me diving at the tender age of nine. He needed a float tender, so he made me one.

'He could have used a five-pound lead weight and a string, but he didn't, he put me in charge of the five-dollar float. My job,

was to follow him with his diving float, and put abs in the game bag.'

This, symbiotic relationship worked well for about two years. Then I got my first abalone.

Harry, my dad, and I were diving near Fort Brag. *'We were at the Albion River and RV park; you will hear a lot more of this little hot spot in my next book.'*

Back in 1962 as I lived it; I was tending float, when Harry came to the surface.

"There is one right below us in about ten feet of water. You go get it."

I went to the bottom and saw the ab. My ab bar slid under it like a hot knife through warm butter. Pulling up with all my might the ab shot upward, about three feet. It started to float back down and I clutched it with both arms. Kicking toward the surface with all my energy, my lungs were crying for air. I could hear moaning as my diaphragm worked up and down trying to suck in air. The surface was ten feet above me, then five, then two feet, finally, my head broke through. Blowing out with all my might I clear my snorkel, and suck down new air. Oh, how I needed that air. Taking two more deep breaths I am back in control.

Handing the abalone to dad, he puts it into the game bag. "Good job," spitting out his snorkel, "here hold the float, I'll go get another one."

He pushes the dive float toward me.

Pushing it back toward him, I gurgle past my own snorkel, "You hold the float; and, I'll go get Another One."

That was the last day I tended float. Dad didn't mind it's a part of life. So, being sent ahead to get dinner seems perfectly natural to me.

Turning into Albion Flats we're going to get our dinner. Driving down the steep, winding narrow road that leads straight to the beach. Grabbing our diving gear, which is stuffed into the back seat on each side of Scott we fall to dressing. Dressing, we discuss our plan of attack.

"Do you see that reef out there about a half a mile, the one off the south point?" I'm pointing to a large group of rocks.

"Yea." Mike says.

"Well that's not real good diving, too much fresh water."

"Yea?"

"Yea."

"So, where are we going," Mike is struggling into his wet suit top?

"Past the reef you can't see it from here. The point extends out another mile or so. The water is deep just off the point. There's a shelf, it's thick with abs." I state with the assurance of an nineteen year old.

Scott looks at us, turning his head back and forth so that he can focus on us through the thick lenses of his glasses. "Are you guys nuts? It's getting dark. The wind is blowing, and man those are big waves. I don't think you guys should go out."

Mike and I are finishing up dressing in our wet suits.

Looking at Scott; Mike mumbles, "You worry about finding a camping spot. We'll worry about getting the abalone."

Then going into an imitation of Donald Sutherland, the part he played in Kelly's Heroes. "Like man, we don't need no negative waves. You're always making with the negative waves."

Scott stammers, "But, but, but what if it gets dark?"

I want to be funny also, so I mouth; "That's why God made Lighthouses. They guide lost seafarers into land. Don't worry, my mom will worry enough for all of us."

Walking backward into the surf Mike and I wave to Scott. He is a poor forlorn looking creature. Turning to belly into the surf we high five each other, then swim out to sea.

The Dive goes like clock-work. We swim out on an out-going tide, the Albion River pushing us along at about two knots. Taking turns diving, we collect four abs. It's enough to eat and not any more. Starting for the beach we find the tide has turned. We're riding the current and waves in at about two knots. The current carries us into the mouth of the Albion River as good dark falls. Mom and Dad have camp set up and are ready to clean abalone. The dive went well, I trust Mike, we respect one another. This is going to be a good summer. I've found a partner, he's easy going and doesn't get nervous, we work well together.

CHAPTER TWO

"FISH-ON! Whiskey Line!"

Pulling me from my reveries, Doug's voice is cracking with excitement. Old Douggers loves to catch fish. The snubber rubber over my head just sprang straight out. It's stretched out six feet long, out from the usual eighteen inches. Peering around I'm looking for my nippers. Two pieces of motorcycle innertube cut into circles two inches in width. My nippers are in the jig box; I slip them on. They fit just behind my fingers and over my palms, protecting my hands while I pull albacore. Grabbing the gaff hook to extend my reach; I swing it toward the whiskey line, catching it, I pull it down to me.

Breaking out with another horse yell, Doug bellows, "Fish on, longline, hotline!" This information is given to me for impetus to; work harder, pull faster, get them fish aboard. There's money on those hooks, get it, get it.

Alley Cat plunges off the top of a twenty-foot swell, at the bottom, she buries her bow, scooping up two tons of water. Stopping her forward motion in the process and slamming me into the forward bulkhead. Arching my back, if this albacore gets slack in the line he's gone. Arms milling in a wild motion, I'm taking in line as fast as I can.

Pulling in the line, hand over hand; I'm letting it drop onto the deck of the gaff hatch. The six-hundred-pound test line is cutting into my palms. The nippers are rubbing my sore and cut-up hands with salt water. I'm fighting a steady fifty pounds of line pull. An albacore hits a jig at twenty-two miles an hour, then it sounds, straight down swimming at full-tilt boogie.

The water washes aft, buoyancy lifting the bow. Alley Cat shutters, as the wave travels the length of the vessel. I'm still arching when five hundred gallons of water washes over me. The wave slamming me into the gaff hatch combing. Losing my footing; I collapse. Coming to rest on the hatch combing, I'm still pulling on the albacore. I've got to keep tension on the line, or we'll lose this six-dollar fish.

Salt water running out of my hair drains into my eyes and mouth; tasting strong on my tongue, and stinging my eyes.

The wave washes over the bulkhead, sea water pours into the gaff hatch. Water is above my knees, slopping port as the Alley Cat rolls in that direction then washing back to the starboard. I am maintaining my footing, somehow, while still pulling on the whiskey line fighting both the sea and the fish.

The Douggers yells at me, "Two more just hit, you get um, I'll put the boat into a circle."

Oh God, a circle? Glancing forward toward the Dutch door my eyes are pleading. Too late, Doug has gone to the wheel. The boat begins to turn. An albacore troller must accomplish two things to be successful. One, find the fish, two, stay on-um until they're in the hold.

In calm weather a circle is a fine device to stay on the fish. A nice leisurely circle lets the gear work without tangling too badly. A school of fish working bait is attracted to the wake. On a calm ocean, the wake looks like bait breaking the surface. Albacore are followers, if one fish shoots toward the surface going for a jig other fish will follow. All and all, a circle can be very productive.

In rough weather a circle is hell on the deckhand. The seas and wind changing directions whip and blow the lines. Tangles are a certainty, two or three lines will have fish on, generally in one huge tangle, trying to pull three albacore is a Herculean task.

The Alley Cat is turning port, and I'm losing the protection I've enjoyed from the pilothouse. The starboard lines begin to sway toward the gaff hatch with each wave.

The albacore is at the stern bending over close to the water I lift carefully, like picking up bubbles from a bubble bath. The albacore makes a stiff-bodied shake as he clears the water. Coming over the stern the fish hits the deck in front of the gaff-hatch. Sliding my hand down the line my palm connects with the hook. Lifting, I turn my wrist and the hook breaks free. It's one smooth motion as I turn and throw the jig back into the sea. The albacore begins a death dance, flopping on the deck. Setting up a constant tapping; tap... tap tap tap, tap...tap, performing this straight-bodied flop until it's over.

The whiskey line is slow going back out. The line is a series of snarls, caused by the knee-deep water swirling around the gaff hatch. Clearing tangles, the line slides through my hand. Now, the boat is broad side to the wind and seas; our starboard lines whipping around my head. Pulling the longer tag lines down to control their movement, I tie them off. Reaching for the hotline the pulling begins again.

Douggers voice comes from the Dutch door, "Keep gettin-um Ben, you're do-in good."

The hot line is behind the boat steadily coming toward me. I'm pulling it with a constant pressure. The boat is now directly down wind and sea. If we were going down wind all day long, we wouldn't even think that this is rough weather.

The Alley Cat settles into the bottom of a large wave, the next swell rushing toward the stern. The swell is a deep, deep blue. The blue of a young lady's eyes when she's in lust. Like a soul of a saint; deep and translucence, the water is so clear that you can see through the swell. The albacore is swimming down into it; swimming for his very life, trying to shake the hook. Traveling in the approaching swell; the speed of the fish becomes so great it pops from the wave. The albacore on the hot line tumbles down the face of the wave, falling, flipping, and skipping along the surface of the water. Me? I'm pulling the line as fast as my arms can take it. The line must have some tension on it, or we'll lose the fish. Our stern is rising to an on-coming wave as it caps. White water is tumbling towards me; the morning sun glinting off it, a shimmering sliver, like a snowcapped mountain peak.

The ol fish is back below the surface now. Line pull has just gone from zero to sixty pounds. The free ride I received for the last twenty seconds is over. The albacore deep in the wave is swimming down for all he is worth. Me, I'm pulling for all I'm worth.

Douggers calls out his voice cracking, "Get-em Ben, pull boy pull!"

Alley Cat is swinging in her circle. The port side is up wind now. Port side lines are blowing toward the boat and into the gaff hatch. The Starboard lines are still tied-down close inboard. Port side lines are crossing over the starboard. Already, they're in a tangle. Wrapping the albacore line around my right hand I reach over with my left to untie the starboard lines before they all tangle. Jumping into the gaff-hatch with me Douggers grabbed a line on the port side. Looking over at Douggers, I grin; letting the starboard lines go, they fly out and away from the stern, pushed by the wind pressure.

Unwrapping the line from my hand, I return to pulling the fish. Swinging the albacore over the stern, our second fish of the day drops onto the deck. The hotline is feeding out through my hands. The line is bouncing up and down, twisting back and forth. It's running free over my palm. Bringing to mind a curvy coast road, I'm watching it fly out, just like the coast road outside of Pacific City, Oregon. Yea ...yea, that's just what it looks like...

I can see the little twisting road right now. I can almost see Pacific City, the store, the gas station and all.

***

My Pony addition Mustang is dragging its tail mighty low as we pull our twenty-year-old trailer into Pacific City, Oregon. It has pulled this trailer over six hundred miles up the coast road. We all need a little R and R. But we aren't going to get any. It's a real stretch to call Pacific City… a city. The entire town consists of one bar, one grocery store, and one gas station. However, the town of Woods is just up the road and it consists of one park, that's it, just a city park, no town at all.

According to Marty's directions we turn left in the center of town. There is only one stop sign in Pacific City, that's our landmark. It's a left over the old wooden bridge and north to Cape Kiwanda.

Swinging into the trailer park, we're here to rent ourselves a new home; a space for our sixteen-foot trailer. The sign in front of the Cape Kiwanda Park is obliterated by rust and blowing sand. We think it says welcome? Although, it kind of looks like the sign at the Bates Motel.

Mike, Scott and I unbend. We're stomping around heavily, just outside of the trailer park office. Mike nods at me and we enter the office together. Opening the door a lady of about forty looks up from her TV program. Standing she smiles a welcome, opening her mouth to speak, and her false teeth drop out of their own volition. Staring just above her head I look neither left nor right. If I look at Mike, I know I'm going to lose it. Turning, Mike disappears out the door. He's running for the beach to roll around on the sand and laugh until he pukes, or busts a gut, whichever comes first?

"Hi." I say, stoned face. "We're looking for a space. We've got a sixteen-foot trailer."

Putting her teeth back in her head, she smiles demurely. "Will that be for the day, weekend, or the week?"

I can't smile back I'm barely under control now. If I smile I'll regale her with laughter.

Using my utmost serious tone, "All summer, if the price is right."

"Oh, a fisherman," she says in a husky voice, "we have special deals for young fishermen."

"That's great." I respond to her, by lowering my own voice. "How much a month is it?"

"I'm Uness, and I am very happy to meet you." She's whispering to me.

It dawns on me she is being sexy. Oh my God, what do I do now?

"How, how much will that space be?"

"For you, a hundred dollars a month." She is fluffing her hair now.

Mike walks back through the door. His face is red, but he is in control of his sense of humor.

Looking at him I'm smiling, just a little. "We can have a space here for a hundred dollars a month."

"Sounds fair," Mike grins back at me.

The deal was made; we hauled out our first month's rent. Walking outside I consider telling Mike that I think Uness was making advances. No, I must be mistaken, what would a forty some odd year-old woman want with an eighteen year old boy; what, what indeed?

Pulling the Stang down to our new space, we pull to a stop. Getting out, Mike directs me back. This is no mean feat. I go ahead with a trailer real good. I don't back a trailer worth a damn.

Mike starts giving me directions. "Come on back a little left, that's going right, no go left, you're going right, left, go left, wrong way. Stop. STOP!"

Pointing the way I should go, Mike is giving me this advice. "OK, pull up and try again."

Pulling straight ahead, I start backing, again. Pointing, he yells. "Left, go left, back right now left, try and go straight Ben."

After three or four more tries we get the trailer in our space, kind of. The edge of our siding is on the line. Rain hitting the east side of our trailer falls onto our neighbor's space.

Our neighbor is Archie Bunker. Well, he's a conservative Archie Bunker. Archie is wearing a crew cut, and an old tee shirt, which says, "Love it or leave it," stretched tight over a beer belly. As Mike and I are going through our marathon trailer parking session, Archie stares at us. Disgust at our lack of skill is plain on his face. He doesn't say a thing, but his expression speaks volumes. I'm sure he thinks we parked on the line to piss him off. We didn't. I was running low on gas and the trailer parking could have gone on all night. We stopped because the trailer was almost straight. Archie grunts and goes back inside of his trailer.

Edith Bunker comes out and begins visiting with us. "Well, where are you nice boys from?"

Mike is shy, looking at her he grins. This is just too much like Hollywood.

Archie Bunker married to Edith Bunker here in Oregon. It just can't be so?

"We're from California, we just bought Nole's old boat. We plan to fish here all summer."

"Oh, isn't that nice, you came here to fish, how exciting for you." Edith gushes her voice quavering up and down the scale.

"I'm Ben, and this is my partner Meathead, I mean Mike."

"I am Virginia and my husband's name is Joe. Happy to meet you boys; I know we will be just great neighbors. Joe, oh Joe, come out and meet the boys. "

This turned out to be a prophetic moment. From this time forward, everyone in Pacific City calls us, "The boys". Mike and I are a unit; we're The Boys.

Virginia goes back into her trailer, turning to Mike. "Sorry about that Meathead crack. I just couldn't help myself."

"That's OK," Mike scratches his chin, "I'd have said it, if you hadn't."

Camp made; we walk next door into the boat yard. It's filled with Oregon dories. Their bows sticking high into the air like fine stallions ready for a race.

Wondering around the boat storage lot, we're looking for our new boat. In the corner of the lot, one boat seems to be the right color, but it's so old. The paint is mostly pilling off, so maybe this isn't the boat. The old boat, that is the right color, also has the right horsepower motor on it. The old boat has an old, old, thirty-five-horsepower motor on the stern. Could this be our boat?

But it's so old, old and small, smaller than all the other boats. The old, old boat that's kind of the right color has an even older Jeep parked in front of it.

Marty's sales pitch floods back to mind, "Ben, it's an old boat with an old motor, it is a piece of crap. Ben you don't want that boat."

Now I understand this was not some kind of reverse psychology. Marty was just being honest old Marty.

An old man of about forty-five saunters by. Mike nods in the direction of the old guy, "Excuse me, do you know if this boat belongs to Nole?"

Interrupting his saunter, he reflects, "Not anymore. I heard that Nole sold it to a couple of greenhorns from California. Just young kids, they shouldn't have been let out of the house with their allowance, if you ask me."

Mike looks at me then back to our "new" boat, "What do you say, let's name it the Bloody Wog."

I look at Mike and then back at our *new* boat. "Sounds good to me."

The old stranger smiles and saunters off. Mike and I also saunter off toward our sixteen-foot home. Tomorrow will be a big day.

Sighing, "Well, it's not as bad as Marty said it was."

Mike glances my way, "Well, that's right, but nothing could be as bad as Marty said it was."

"Yep, that's about right."

"No, not as bad as it could be," replies Mike.

"It has two by four ribs. Did you see that?" I continue thinking out loud. "Not those funky one by fours like Marty and Albert's' new boat."

Turning toward me, Mike's speech becomes more animated, "Yea and her bottom is narrow too, she'll cut through the chop better."

Facing Mike, moving my hand in a motion like a boat breaking through the surf. "The low sides won't matter that much with the big flare she has. She'll still be able to take a big sea. And, her bow has one of the best rakes in the fleet, did you see that."

Mike grins at me and says, "Yea, she won't be too bad of an old boat."

When the Bloody Wog became a she in our conversation, she became a boat, not just a pile of wood. She also became our boat.

***

It's seven o'clock in the morning. The trailer door swings open, revealing Marty and Nole,

stepping in, Nole grins, "Come on boys, get up. We're cooking breakfast. We have a Trollermen's Association meeting this morning. We may be on strike."

Rolling out of our beds, we slip on clothes. Mike sleeps on the Kitchen table made into a bed. I sleep at the other end of the trailer in the one full-time bed.

Blinking sleepily, I ask, "What's for breakfast and where is it cooking?"

Nole replies, "Follow me in your car. It's pancakes, with my brood, we would have to own a chicken ranch to be able to afford eggs."

Changing his mind, Nole turns to Marty. "You hang out here and bring Ben and Mike to the house when they're ready. I'm going back and help your mom with breakfast."

***

Walking into Nole's summer rental, I agree with his appraisal. A man would have to own Fosters Farms to feed this brood on eggs. Dawn, Marty's Mother, is cooking pancakes on all four burners. Setting at a large table is a huge group of boys. In the far corner is Albert, Nole's eldest son. Marty is a year younger than Albert, next to Al is Robby. Robby's father is a teacher that fishes. In fact, his Dad was my high school math teacher. Rob is the same age as Marty they're seniors in high school this year. Next to Rob sits Buzz he is in seventh grade. Then there is poor Greg. He's eight; small for his age and he's got three older brothers. That's a tough life. Seats are saved for us next to Greg.

Sitting down, Mike and I dig in like the rest of the crew. To request more pancakes, butter, or syrup one need only grunt and nod at the required item.

Nole advises, "Eat, eat, eat if you like it… eat some more. It's going to be a busy day. We're going to the Dorymen's Association meeting. Then Marty will help you get the outboard started. You guys can take your new boat for a spin down the river. The jeep may take a little work."

Scott, whom we have not seen since we arrived, wonders in from one of the bedrooms, his red hair in disarray. "Good morning," he yawns.

All the mouths in the room are full of fried dough and syrup, except for Dawn's. She replies to the room, "Good morning, Scott; how are you today."

Breakfast over; Marty, Albert, Mike and myself all load into the Stang. Nole loads everyone else into his family station wagon. We're all headed back to the Cape Kiwanda Fish Company.

Marty and Albert fish a boat together named the Kisutch. Nole will fish his boat, the Noles' Ark, with the help of his two younger sons, Buzz and Greg. Robby is looking for a job boat pulling.

He may try to lease a boat this summer. We all have a vested interest in what will be decided today. I do know, that I don't know, enough to express an opinion on what happens.

The relationship between the fish buying company and their fishermen is a close one. It's somewhat like a pimp with his stable of working girls. The more girls out on the street, the more profit for a pimp. The more fishermen dragging their hooks around the ocean, means more profit for the fish company.

In a working girl society, the pentacle of success is being a hundred-dollar-an-hour call girl. In the fisherman's hierarchy, this equates to being a highliner, they go out early, stay late and always, I mean always, catch fish. About five percent of the fleet are highliners, and they catch about thirty percent of the total catch. Then there is the twenty-dollar a trick street hooker. These girls stand on the street corner and yell at passing cars. They are equivalent to good fishermen. A good fisherman will go out early and stay late, and they catch fish when the fish are on the bite. Good fishermen catch a few fish most days, even when they are not on the bite. Thirty percent of the fleet could be called good fishermen. The good fishermen catch about fifty percent of the total catch.

Then there are the wasted druggy chicks with no teeth and a small sunken chest. Their bony little legs stick out of their dirty miniskirts. These girls have to wait until the bars close on Saturday night and catch the real drunk, real horny guys. And, then, they charge minimum wage for their tricks. These are the rest of us. The remaining sixty-five percent of fisherman split the remaining twenty-five percent of the catch. You may go out early and you may come in late but if you ain't a good fisherman, you ain't a good fisherman. Only time, experience, and the fish knowing that you deserve to catch them makes you a good fisherman. Mike and I didn't know it yet, but this year, we're a part of the remaining sixty-five percent.

The Dorymen's Association is having their meeting in the packing shed. This is the only building big enough to hold all of us. The dory fleet representative tells us we've been offered thirty cents a pound for silvers and fifty cents a pound for king salmon. The king salmon price is fine. Fifty cents a pound is good money. Thirty cents a pound, well, it's just too low. So, we're on strike. We're on strike for a… nickel?

Knowing nothing of the fishing business, I keep my thoughts to myself. I know striking workers make nothing at all. Thirty cents a pound seems like a lot more to me than zero cents.

Turning to Nole, "So, how long will we be on strike?"

We'll be fishing a long time before you have your boat ready."

Frowning in puzzlement, "Gee, that's good to hear?"

***

"There ain't any battery in this battery box." Head down, my butt up; in the ostrich defense position.

Marty looks over the stern where he is working on the lower unit. "Better go buy one from Hogie."

"Where is Hogie's?" Straightening, I groan at Marty.

Mike has his head under the steering console, a curse rumbles forth. "This flippen thing is a ball of rust."

"Over at the fish company. We can get you some WD 40, Mike, you might as well come along and meet Hogie."

"Who is Hogie?" Mike and I chorus.

"He owns Cape Kiwanda Fish Company. Hogie is cool."

Marty wipes his hands off and throws the rag at me.

Albert walks up, "You guys about done with Marty. I need his mechanical ability on our boat unless he is really into something groovy over here."

Al is the same height as his father, five-eleven, with light blond hair. He works out a lot and it shows. His arms are not as big as Nole's but they will be someday, like his father he has a barrel chest. There are a lot of girls at school who think Albert is really cool.

"We're going to the fish company, want to come?", Marty asks his brother.

"Sounds good."

Al yells over his shoulder, "Hey Robby, we're heading to the fish company. You coming?"

Rob jumps from the Kisutch, where he is helping Al, and heads our way. We string out into a line five guys wide and start a slow saunter toward the fish company. Looking at us from a distance, a person would think that we're on our way to the gunfight at the OK corral, not going to buy a battery and a can of WD 40.

Walking in the front door, a little brass bell jingles at our arrival. A counter spans thirty feet of the store. A small office is at one end. Behind the counter is a pretty girl with long, auburn hair and a tight little body. She's wearing blue jeans that fit her lovely curves like they were made for her.

Behind the pretty girl is a wall covered with fishing gear, big flashers, little flashers, medium flashers, spoons, hooks, hoochies, anything and everything to catch a fisherman's eye. Do they catch fish? Only a highliner knows for sure.

Marty turns red, speaking to the lovely young lady; he's truly in love.

"This is Mike and Ben. They bought our old boat. They'll need to be set up with a tag."

"OK," the longhaired beauty smiles at us, "what's the name of your boat?"

Being quick, Mike spouts proudly, "The Bloody Wog", He named her after all.

Me, I'm lost in lust. Carefully printing Bloody Wog on a receipt book, the beauty asks, "What can I get you?"

Finding myself staring and trying to control my lust, I look down at my feet. Marty elbows me in the ribs. Looked up, and into a set of deep blue eyes, stating way too loudly.

"A battery," the words rattle around the room for a while then a silence follows. "And, a can of WD 40."

She smiles showing perfect teeth, "I'll get Hogie for you." What a beauty.

Hogie walks through the door of the fish house. He's tall and thin with large forearms. He's the jokester that made the comment about not letting me and Mike out of the house with our allowance.

Hogie grins, "Well, how's it going, boys?"

Grinning back, we nod; how true last night's comment was. "Good," I reply, "we need to buy a battery for our boat, how much do they go for?"

Setting down on a stool, Hogie rubs his bristles. "Twelve dollars for a car battery, you don't need a marine battery for a little thirty-five horse outboard. You aren't going to put an electric gurdy on the boat, are you?"

"No? No, I don't think so?" I don't know what electric gurdies are but I only have two hundred dollars left. Mike is broke. We ain't buying nothing that we don't need.

Hogie stands and turns. "Follow me; I'll show you where the batteries are." Leaving the other guys talking over fishing gear with the auburn-haired beauty, we follow Hogie into the cavernous packing shed. Climbing a ladder to the roof over the refer room, we're confused. There are nets, longlines, buoy bags, and sundry other fishing gear stored on the refer room. Stacked on a pallet in a comer are about twenty batteries. Hogie gestures with his head. "Get it down and bring it to the store front. Did Debbie start you a book?"

"She sure did," Mike nods at Hogie.

"Good, we'll see how you do."

Turning, Hogie heads down the ladder. Hogie continues to work; he glances up at us every now and then.

Mike and I have a conundrum. We're up two and a half stories and we have a thirty-pound battery to carry down a ladder.

"I'll hand the battery down the ladder to you. You hold it on your shoulder, I'll sneak by you, then you hand it to me."

Mike nods at my plan; "Don't go any lower than my waist, I can one-arm it to your shoulder, but it might get away from us if we try to go too far."

"Cool, sounds good to me."

As with most of our team efforts, this plan goes off without a hitch. Mike gets as low down the ladder as I can reach. Lowering the battery to his shoulder I settle it there. Moving to the side of the ladder he lets me climb past him. Sneaking by him, I stop two steps lower down the ladder. Using one arm Mike lowers the battery to my shoulder; while he's holding the rung with his other hand, climbing past me, we rub shoulders.

I lower the battery to him. Passing the battery back and forth we climb down two steps at a time.

"Hogie where's your WD 40?" Mike inquires.

Straightening, Hogie grins, "This way."

Going on a tour of the fish buying facility we're in awe. Hogie points out different items of interest, while we're walking around. Finding the WD 40, Hogie hands a can to Mike. Looking around we find ourselves on the backside of the front counter.

Albert is rapping with Debbie. Marty is looking over hoochies and Robby is drinking a coke. Parading to the right side of the counter, I set the battery down. Pulling out our book Hogie writes down the purchases. I reach into my pocket for my wallet.

Hogie looks like I've insulted him, "What are you doing?"

"I'm paying for the battery and the WD 40."

"No, that's not the way it's done. If I think that you'll catch fish and will pay your bill, I give credit on future catches. If I think that you'll lay around all day, run up big bills, and then run out on what you owe." Shaking the book in the air at us. "Then you'll never get one of these."

I'm a little startled, "How aah, how do you know that we'll be able to pay you back?"

"You will," Hogie says, "maybe not this year. There's a learning curve to this business. Next year, you'll pay me off. Then you'll make money, for me, and for yourselves. All I want from you is to buy your fish. And, I'll pay the going rate."

Mike opines, "Seems fair?"

Hogie grins at us. "Most of my fishermen use the forklift to get a battery down. When I saw you two performing that maneuver getting the battery down the ladder I knew we had a couple of go-getters. Welcome to the fleet."

Mike shoulders the battery, and we all walk out.

Albert gloats, "I'm going to get me some of that."

"Some of what?" Glancing past Marty I'm eye-balling Al.

"That, man, that little Debbie. She's packin one fine little body."

Marty, the practical one of us says, "Debbie is not going out with one of us.

She is dating some guy in the Air Force, for God's sakes! Why would she go out with a fisherman?"

"You watch. By the end of this summer, I'll get me some of that."

"Bullshit," Marty says with feeling.

I know what Marty means. Both, he and I, are big time in lust with Debbie. I've just met her; Marty has known her for a year. But, we see her just alike. She's not just a lay, just a piece of tail. Debbie is in class.

***

The sun is setting. The boat storage lot is empty except for Mike and me. The Day has not been productive, but it has been a busy first day. We tore the outboard motor apart. We know we aren't mechanics enough to get it running. I've been working on it, Marty giving direction to my tools and hands. Marty is the only one of us who truly understands the workings of an internal combustion engine. That knowledge makes him a God when drifting toward a lee shore with a dead motor. The whole bunch of us pay homage to Marty's aptitudes.

The Jeep is also beyond our meager mechanical abilities. We think we have analyzed the problem correctly. It won't run.

We have Two hundred dollars to our names. Two hundred dollars won't buy: a dune buggy, an outboard motor, fishing gear, gas, bait, food and sundries.

I am putting the outboard motor cowling back on. Mike is installing a rubber sleeve over the sweep ores we bought from Hogie today. The sweep ores are the only means of propulsion that will perform their function on our new equipment.

The sweep ores are ten footers. Standing on the bow about six feet in the air, Mike is trying to roll the sleeve down the ore to the correct position. He's over the ore pushing straight down with all his might. He's been at this job for fifteen minutes.

I am watching him work, "Come on Mike, let's call it a day. We've been at this for thirteen hours."

"I want to finish these ores first. They're the only things on this piece of crap that works."

"Well; I work," I mumble to his back, hoping that he can't hear me.

The ore slips and Mike disappears over the bow. He's pushing down with all the force his one hundred and fifty pounds can muster. Then the ore slips giving him an initial impulse downward. He disappears from view in the blink of an eye. Watching from the stern, I'm astonished. Mike is pushing one instant the next instant he is gone. Just gone from sight, but only for that instant.

There's a loud "hum-rump," as he hits the ground. Before the sound can travel to the stern Mike is back standing on the bow cursing. He's back, pushing the sleeve into place with all his might. Had I blinked at the moment of his slip, I'd never have known he was gone.

"OK... You rat firkin son of a buck. You crack sack-en, craven, dog humpin'!"

With one mighty shove, the sleeve is in place in less than five seconds. This is my first insight into Mike's speed and ferocity when he's angry. Mike is faster than anyone I have ever seen, EVER. Grabbing the other ore, he rolls that sleeve in-place within another five seconds.

Spinning on me, he growls, "What do you want?"

"Think you can pull-start that Jeep when you are like this?"

"Yea... but not tonight," Mike grins, "I'm tired."

Walking across the boat storage lot, we're beaten but not broken men. Opening our door, we're assailed by rock music. Marty, Albert, Robby, and Scott are crammed around our kitchen table, two cases of Winehart's beer between them. All four of them have a beer in hand. I step through the door a beer fly's into my chest. I grab it with both hands, stepping in behind me, a beer flies toward Mike's head; he snatches it from the air.

Opening our beers with a church key, we find a place to lean. Mike and I haven't eaten since breakfast. The cold beer draining down my throat, hits my stomach. I have very little experience with alcohol. Beer tastes good, I like it. My head feels a little light with just one good gulp. Man, I'm hungry. The beer comes up, and another swallow slides down my parched throat.

Albert inquires, "So, what's the old Bloody Wog look like? Think you're going to get her running tomorrow?"

"Are you being a smart-ass?" Staring into his eyes I can see the question is an honest one. "I think the engine is frozen up. I can't get it to budge with a twelve inch crescent wrench."

Tilting the beer, I drain more Wineharts out of my bottle.

"What have you done to her?" Al asks, over the top of his own beer.

Describing our travail with the outboard engine in torturous detail. All other conversation in the trailer stops during my pathetically self-indulgent monologue.

By the time my monologue is complete, I'm drunk. For the first time in my life, I'm truly drunk. I'm not so drunk as to be a fool, but now I know why people drink. You feel better. Your problems diminish in stature and complexity. The guy that sold you all your problems is your new best friend.

Marty slurs, "We got-ta get you nother engine, that's all there-is-to-it, engine that's the answer."

Albert throws an arm around Marty's shoulder and slurs, "Absolutely, absolutely right, that's the only answer, new motor."

Marty and Albert are leaning against our kitchen cabinets and stove. Robby and Scott are stretched out at our dinette table taking up four seats. I am sitting on my bed leaning forward.

Mike, leaning against the door shakes his head in assent, "Right on man, a new fucking motor."

Leaning over Scott, Mike pulls out the six remaining beers. Passing out beers as he opens them.

Raising my new beer, "To a new motor. One that runs first time and every time." The smell of propane gas filters out behind Albert. "Albert either you got funny smelling farts, or you turned on our stove."

It's a little later when our uninvited, but most welcomed guests, stagger out our door heading for home.

Marty yells over the top of their launch vehicle. "I'm going to talk to my dad, you'll see, we'll get you guys a new motor."

They all pile into the heap and drive away in a cloud of blue smoke.

Walking back into our trailer we strip down to sleep. I am still hungry, but way too light headed to cook. Crawling into bed I turn out the light. I'm waiting for Mike to do the same at his end of the trailer.

"What's the time?"

Looking at my watch, "Bout five till twelve, why?"

Mike is swaying, "Cause... I'm trying to set this damn alarm clock."

"Don't set the damn alarm clock, I don't want to face oatmeal at six-thirty in the morning, after all we've had to drink."

"OK," putting down the offending item, Mike drunkenly shrugs.

"Benjy? Ben you awake? Ben!" Mike's insistent voice intrudes on my almost a sleep mind. I am about to drift off to some very nice sleep.

"What?"

"There are two girls over there, they're flashing a red light at me."

"No; no, they aren't, you're drunk! Go to bed. Don't you know, girls don't flash red lights at guys, not at midnight."

Mike's hurt voice responds, "I may be drunk, but there are still two girls flashing a red light at me."

I reply, "No, there aren't any girls flashing red lights at you. It just doesn't happen that way. You're drunk!"

"I'm going over there; they're flashing me and I'm going."

Groaning, I throw the covers off me. "OK, OK. I'll go with you. Just to prove they're not flashing us."

We're walking toward a twenty-six-foot trailer; Mike is right. There is a girl and she has her hand in front of a flashlight. She's blinking her light in our direction. A red glow emulates at each blink. As we walk up to this young nymph of the night, she continues to blink her light.

Using his hippy voice Mike queries, "Like, why are you making with the red lights? Are you like making with the red lights, to like get some attention? Like aah, we like girls who make with the red lights."

Adding my wit to the conversation, I snigger and grin like the village idiot.

The two girls turn out to be from Portland Oregon. Their fathers own a boat together, which they fish on weekends. The girls came out to the coast last weekend. Their fathers left them here and to their own devices. Left to their own devices, the young ladies have broken out the beer and red lights. We came to Oregon, but have arrived in nirvana, women, and free beer fall on us like manna from heaven.

"You guys want to come in," the skinny girl asks?

Finally finding my wits, "Cool, sounds good."

The trailer is richly appointed, with thick carpet, real wood paneling, and the stove, sink, and refrigerator are full size. This trailer has all the comfort that can be crammed into two hundred square feet.

The two girls blink with a come-hither look,

"You guys want some beer?"

My mind reels with a negative reaction; I sure don't need more beer, "Cool, sounds good."

The taller girl hands out a round of beers. She is nice, long silky black hair falls to the middle of her back. A nice figure fills out her sweater and Levi's, at least, as far as we can tell. There is only one dim bulb lighting the trailer.

"Our Dads own a dory together. This is the first time that we have been allowed to stay here by ourselves. We're having the best time."

The slender girl says, "We watched you guys working today. How come your boat is so ugly?"

Ugly? The Bloody Wog, ugly? My beer-fogged brain tells me we have just been insulted. However, there is a sexual tension that fills the room. And, she's right, it's an ugly boat.

"We like ugly boats and pretty girls, that's why we like you."

The young lady I'm speaking to is about sixteen, small in frame maybe five foot one or two. She is slender to the point of skinny, with hardly any breasts. Long, silky brown hair frames a very pretty young face. The silky crown ends just above a round and very pretty butt. She is wearing a red black and white flannel shirt, the top three buttons are undone. Tight Levi's caress her slender frame.

Stepping close, "Do you think I'm pretty?"

"Oh... I, I think you're very pretty."

She rubs herself up and down against me, she is looking up and her lips are pursed. There is an expectant look on her face. I bend and kiss her, her passion surprises me.

Pulling at my neck, she is thrusting into me as we embrace. I've gotten hold of a piece of dynamite. Her intensity scares me as she pulls me toward the lower bunk. Staggering toward the bed, she's unbuttoning my shirt. *Wow!* Flopping on the bed, I'm on top and caddie corner over her.

As though on cue, the raven-haired girl takes Mike by the hand, and leads him to the upper bunk. Climbing the ladder, she pulls him up after her, kind of like a spider with a fly.

Falling to the bed my brown-haired beauty pulls my head close. Putting her mouth near my ear she whispers, "I'm a virgin."

Those three words tell me volumes. They tell me, that I am welcome to keep doing what I'm doing. I can put my hands on her lovely young body. Those words also tell me what I don't get to take from this encounter. What I do get is the memory that there are girls who shine red lights into the Oregon night. But, there will be no relief from my cursed virginity. It seems more than a fair deal to me.

It's four in the morning. Walking outside, the stars are bright overhead. A sea breeze is blowing the smell of salt marsh to us. The bell buoy at Cape Kiwanda rings a bearably perceptible chime. Strolling back to our trailer, in two hours, another day begins. That's just fine by us; sleep is for the tired. We're eighteen, fishermen in Oregon, and masters of our own destiny.

***

Now, as predictable as the sun, Nole enters our trailer. He's all good humor and beaming, at seven in the morning. Mike and I are up. I'm putting oatmeal on to cook.

"Might as well come to my house to eat, pancakes are on. Then we'll run your boat up to Tillamook and have Jerry take a look at the engine."

"What?"

"Jerry, best outboard mechanic in Oregon," Nole grins. "Marty came in our room last night, where did he get the beer anyway?"

Looking back and forth at one another Mike and I are not sure of what to say. How mad is Nole, really?

Shaking my head, "I don't know. He had it when he got here."

Nole grins, "Are you guys hung-over? You should be."

If Nole only knew, if he only knew, "Not too bad, but I could use some sleep.

How about you, Mike?"

"Naw, I'm fine. A little beer never hurt anyone. What about this Jerry guy?" Scratching his beard, Nole replies. "Oh yea, Marty came into our room last night. Drunk as a skunk, told his mother and me about your decision. Anyway, Jerry has a shop, up in Tillamook, he'll get you going. After breakfast, we'll hook the Bloody Wog up to your Mustang. Haul her to Jerry's shop. You should be able to bring it back today. Fired up and ready to go."

Swinging the Stang to the right, we pull off of Highway One. We are headed toward a big red barn. Nole's station wagon is kicking up dust just ahead of us. The Bloody Wog's weight pushes the stern of my Mustang to the left. The sound of the crunching gravel under the breaking tires is loud. Dry rock dust blows into the windows.

We've pulled the Bloody Wog up the coast to the outskirts of Tillamook. This is where the renowned Jerry Live's, his shop in the big red barn. He will lay hands on our engine and resurrect it like Lazarus; from the grave.

It seems to me that it takes a crew to get anything accomplished here in Oregon. Mike is riding shotgun in the Mustang, Marty and Scott in my back seat. Nole, Albert, Robby, Buzz, and Greg are in the station wagon. Apparently; it takes a lot of manpower to deliver a thirty-five-horse power motor to a Shaman of the Evinrude cult, here in Oregon?

Clambering from the cars, we stand around in a cluster. We are awaiting our bellwether, a leader, to move in one direction or another. After milling around a short time Nole saunters toward the barn's double sliding doors. A beam juts out from the center of the door, a large block and tackle hangs down about ten feet.

Walking through the cavernous opening we wait until our eyes adjust to the dim light.

Out of the darkness comes a short, round man with quick jerky movements. He is going bald, what little hair he is swept over the top of his pate as only the innocently vain will do. I am sure he thinks no one will notice that he's only got five hairs.

Jerry is about thirty and round from top to bottom. Not fat, just round, a round head, rounded shoulders leading to large round arms. His arms lead to large round hands and fingers, which hang down by his round hips.

"Jerry; I want you to meet Mike and Ben, we brought the boy's engine to you. See what you can do with it, will you?" Nole places a hand on my shoulder as he describes our plight. "I'm sure you can get it going."

Jerry wipes excess grease from his hands. "Oh, yea sure, sure, no problem, there isn't an engine alive that I can't fix. Where is this little hummer?"

"On the back of our boat, outside." Mike jerks his thumb toward the double doors.

"Back her in here and we'll take a look at the little hummer."

Mike's eyebrows shoot up and down at the back-her in request. I am the designated driver and my trailer backing skills have not improved.

My shoulders slump forward. Slowly walking back out to the car I'm like a condemned man. For a teenager, death before humiliation is the proper motto.

The dang motor turns over and catches. I had a vain hope that it wouldn't start; then someone else could back the boat between those two doors. From where I sit they look like the rift into the entrance of hell.

I have to back down a driveway, then around a curve, and through set of doors with about three feet on each side to spare. Sweat is sticking my shirt to my back, as I begin my test by backing. Mike is in his usual place of support. At the stern of the boat he's ready to point the direction it should go. Both, Mike and I know that I'm about humiliate us, our families, and long gone friends, with this display of backing.

"Come on back, take her left some," yells Mike. Damn, the boat is going the way Mike is pointing. "Straighten her out."

Following the boat, somehow, I get her going straight? Almost. A little more, she is going down the driveway. Wonder of wonders I can back?

Mike's expression is one of delighted surprise. Like a kid on Christmas morning when he sees a new bike under the tree. It takes only three pullups, and I get the Bloody Wog where Jerry wants her.

Nole walks up to the stem of the Bloody Wog, "We're going to town. See you back at P.C. tonight? Come by for dinner."

Mike rubs his belly, "We never say no to food."

Mike is able to distend his stomach so that it looks as though he is carrying an extra twenty pounds of beer gut. Mike is a long-distance runner, and wrestler; he's hard as a piece of oak. He enjoys deceiving the unwary with his instant beer gut.

A toolbox rolls up beside the motor. Parts and pieces start forming a line on the bench behind the stern. Part after part falls into Jerry's waiting hands. A monologue pours forth from Jerry's round mouth.

Talking to the bolts that hold our engine together; Jerry has his first conversation with the Wog. "Well, think you're tight? There how's that, can't take it, eh bitch?" Soon the starter drops onto the bench top, "Want a little breaker bar do ya?" The first head bolt starts out. "Come on, come on just like your sister your coming too." Jerry is becoming intimate with our motor; maybe a little too intimate.

Jerry walks off into the cavernous barn whistling a little tuneless song. Mike and I look at one another. Mike shrugs at me, "Should we follow, or should we leave?"

"I don't know, let's wait here and see what happens."

Mike's eyebrows bounce up and down, "Jerry is getting to know our motor. They may want to be alone?"

"Naw, I think we should chaperon them. After all she is our engine. I don't want just any stranger putting his hands all over her. Not without us watching."

Jerry walks out of the darkness, an outboard wiring harness in hand. "Here it is, this

little baby ain't getting any juice. We'll hook her up. You'll have a real hummer on your hands."

These are the first words that Jerry spoken to us; since he told me to, "Back her in." So far, Jerry has only spoken to our motor.

Throwing the wire harness on top of the motor, "In Nam if we had a little problem with a hummer like this, we'd throw it away."

I'm still not sure that he's talking to us, "What?"

Jerry fixes one of the wires to a spark plug, "Nam man, the big V... used a lot of these engines in the Delta."

Mike inquires, "You were in Vietnam?"

"Oh yea, I spent a lot of time patrolling the Delta."

Mike hands Jerry a wrench, "What was your job?"

"Job, job man I did everything, worked on the boats, ran the boats, shot the commeies, I did it all."

Jerry is grabbing parts off the workbench. Some are re-attached other parts are thrown on the floor. The logic of what is being used and what's discarded escapes me. Jerry plugs the last spark plug into the new harness.

"Lets light this baby off, and listen to her hum."

Jerry's innate shyness has evaporated; he is talking to us like long lost buddies. It seems to me that if Jerry likes your motor, he likes you.

***

The setting sun pours light in through the double doors, hanging just above the tree line to the west. The shadow of the block and tackle is being cast into the doorway and falls across the bow of the Bloody Wog. If viewed with the right frame of mind it looks like the Bloody Wog is being hung. Parts from our engine, and parts of three other similar engines, are strung all over Jerry's workbench. Jerry has been working on the Bloody Wog since we drove up this morning.

"Well, well, well, looks like the engine is frozen up after all."

Nodding I shrug, "Well, what do we do now?"

Jerry runs a flat hand over the long hairs, partially covering his bald spot. "I have an engine just like this one, low hours, I can hang it on your boat for five hundred dollars."

Glancing at one another, Mike and I both raise and drop our eyebrows.

Mike rubs the stubble on his chin. "Give us some time to think things over.

Do you mind if we leave the Bloody Wog here tonight?"

Jerry rubs his own stubble, "Naw... Make it easier to install the new motor if you go that way. Really, a new engine is the only way to go, a new power head will cost over a thousand dollars."

"That's as much as we paid for this whole lash-up."

Jerry jerks his head around to face me. "You paid a thousand dollars... a grand, for this, this, pile of, pile of... equipment?"

Shrugging, "Yep, we got a jeep with her, also, but it don't run either."

Dipping his hands into a can of hand cleaner, Jerry begins to rub them furiously. "I love old jeeps what year model is it?"

Glancing at Mike, "Nineteen fifty-two model."

Jerry nods as he wipes grease and hand cleaner off, "Great year for jeeps, great year."

***

The Mustang is cooking along at sixty miles per hour. She's hanging onto the coast road as if it were a long-lost lover. The front windows are down and a cool ocean wind is blowing around our heads. The car smells of ocean marsh, pine trees, grease, and oily gas. Michael and I are sitting in silence. We haven't spoken of our plight since we left Jerry's shop.

The little Stang is cornering left hugging the double yellow line. "How much money do you have left?"

"I've got twenty three dollars in my wallet and two dollars in my bank account." Mike and I have split the cost of everything so far. I know how much I've spent. Slipping my wallet out of my back pocket, I hand it over to Mike, "Count it." Mike pulls out a wad of cash, mostly ones and fives, "Two hundred and seventeen dollars."

"Yep," I say, "there's also a twenty under the spare tire."

Mike looks up from his counting. "What's it doing there?"

"Well... Dad told me, always hang onto a little cash, for emergencies. Looking under your spare tire for money, it's got to be an emergency."

Slowing the Mustang down, we're entering Woods. "What do you say, we'll offer *Jerry two* hundred and fifty dollars, our outboard motor and our Jeep, for the used motor he has."

Mike sighs, "It's all we have. You can't offer more than that."

Pulling up into Nole's driveway, we skid to a stop. Getting out we stroll into Nole's house for dinner, without knocking.

***

It is seven fifteen in the morning. I'm standing next to the small four-burner stove. The pan handle is burning my palm; water is on the boil. Shaking salt into the pan I'm trying to estimate a quarter of a teaspoon. Mike reaches past my head opening up one

63

of the overhead cabinets. He's taking boxes out of the cabinet, holding them in one arm. Then, Mike replaces the boxes into the same cabinet. Opening the next cabinet also right by my head, he begins the same procedure. Boxes and bags are coming out and being shifted into his empty arm. To my confusion Mike replaces them in the same cabinet. Sliding past me, he opens the cabinet nearest my bed.

"What in the heck, are you doing?"

Mike glowers, "Taking stock."

"Taking stock of what?"

"Our food supplies," Mike, continues loading food boxes into his arms. "What the heck for?"

"We're about to offer all our money, and everything that we can quick sell, for a used motor. We're on strike. We don't know how to fish. We don't know how much money we're going to make when we do start fishing. We don't know where our next meal is coming from. I'm taking stock of our food stores. It may be a long time before we get more."

"Oh." Pouring oatmeal into the pan, but not as much oatmeal as I would have three seconds ago, "How do we look?"

Looking pained, "Well, we have two boxes of Bisquick, a five pound bag of pancake mix, and two bottles of log cabin syrup. A can of bacon grease, some very old crackers that came with the trailer, and a dented can of Dinty Moore stew."

Stirring the oatmeal thoughtfully, "And, oatmeal."

Mike agrees, "And oatmeal."

"How long until we make some money, do you think?"

Sitting down at our table Mike mumbles, "I'm not sure, two weeks?"

"Maybe longer? We can go out and spear bottom fish, eat-um, maybe sell them? There aren't any abalone in Oregon we can poach. But, there are rock scallops... Maybe we can find a bed. Maybe sell them too."

Mike grins, "It ain't desperate 'til its desperate. Even then it ain't as desperate as you think it is. We have food and water and a means of getting more food. It isn't too bad, not yet."

Taking the oatmeal off the stove, "And, a brand new, used engine. Man, life doesn't get any better than this. I read somewhere, anything above enough to eat and a warm place to sleep is all ego and excess."

***

The little red Mustang pulls up to the big red barn. It is eight twenty in the morning. Clambering from the bucket seats, standing there, we eye-ball one another over the top of the Mustang. I'm nervous, I've never tried to make a business deal with a real-live adult before. We bought the boat from Marty and Albert, they made our deal with Nole.

I signal Mike and we walk toward the barn to make our offer.

This conversation will tell us if we're out of business. Striding purposefully into the barn we pass our Bloody Wog, God... what an ugly boat. She is half on and half off her trailer. Her stern is plopped on the greasy dirt.

Jerry is off in his cavernous shop somewhere, we think? "Jerry! Jerry, are you around?"

Gazing off into the darkness, I am intently looking. Nothing stirs in the outer recesses of the barn, and then our round savior appears at the double doors. He is wiping his mouth, a tiny round napkin in hand. Ah, it was breakfast; that is what kept our hero.

"Well, well, well, boys how's it hanging this morning."

I am our elected spokesman, "Good, good, we're doing good, ah, Jerry we were wondering...?"

I should have worked out this conversation in my mind, before we got here. "Jerry, we don't ah, have ah, five hundred dollars. What we do have is two hundred and fifty dollars." Jerry's face takes on a grim appearance. Hurrying on, "We also have that Jeep we talked about yesterday, and this old motor you can used for parts."

Placing my hand on top of the old stripped-down motor hanging on the stern of the Bloody Wog. Not much there to trade.

Jerry's face still looks grim. "Well, I don't know boys? I've got to make a profit. Have you got any more money, at all?"

Gazing over at Mike, then searchingly back to Jerry. "Two dollars we were going to save for emergencies."

Jerry's face breaks into a grin, "Well, that's all right you can keep your two dollars. I'll just have to take a loss on this deal."

Mike and I sigh together. I had no idea how important making this deal was to me, to us, we're back in the fishing business!

***

The setting sun is nearing the tree line on the ridge across from Jerry's shop. The shadow from the block and tackle stretches across the bow of the Bloody Wog. Somehow, it doesn't look like she is being hung today. It just looks like a block and tackle, hooked to a boat. The new used engine is on the boat, along with a new shifting mechanism. The new old engine, and the old old engine, can't be shifted with the same shifter. Jerry threw that in. Everything seems to work now. All we have to do is take her out and make her pay.

***

My little red Mustang pulls our twenty-foot Bloody Wog into the Cape Kiwanda storage lot. Out in front of the fish company are two gas pumps, both pump regular gas. The Kisutch is in front of pump number one. Marty has a gas nozzle stuffed into their fuel tank and he is waving us over.

Skidding to a stop, we pop from the Mustang and saunter toward Marty. We both have a burning desire to be invited to dinner; we're starving, pancakes for dinner just don't sound that filling.

Marty keeps the nozzle stuffed into the tank, looking over his shoulder, "We're going to the mouth of the big Nestucca River. Fish for crab, have a crab feed."

Looking over the top of Marty's boat, we can see Albert in the Fish Company rapping with Debbie.

"Let's go. We need to test our new motor anyway. Hey Mike, let's bring our diving gear. Maybe, we can catch some crab?"

Walking off, Mike mumbles, "I'll get our gear, and grab our tanks too."

Hanging the Stang in gear I swing a big arc, pulling the Wog next to the unoccupied pump.

Finished pumping, I walk into the fish company.

Albert has a hold of Debbie's hand. "Come on, Deb, it's just a little crab feed.

Your Dad won't care if you go down with us."

Debbie looks at me and pulls her hand away, "Is that all you want, or is there something else I can do for you?"

Looking down at my feet, I don't want to stare. Debbie is wearing a skintight top that stretches around her every curve. It conforms to her so well that I can make out the lace in her bra. Bending to her task Debbie writes down the amount in our book. Glancing up she catches me staring again. To cover myself, I gape at my feet. I'm so cool.

She overlooks my cool and sticks our tag book under my face to sign. "Here, sign this, would you?"

Turning to Al, "If only there were other girls going, I would go, but, but, just me and six guys? I would feel funny."

Al reaches for her hand again, "You would be with me, not six guys."

On the way, I sign my tag book and leave.

The wheel of the Bloody Wog is under my left palm. We're following the Kisutch down the river. Marty on my right, Mike is on my left, they are hanging onto the davits.

'Davit' this is a good time to describe a couple of things I talk about, but; someone not of a fishboat background may not know of what I speak. In general; *a davit is a steel pipe configuration built with plumbing fixtures that a gertie can be bolted to. A Gertie is a device that raises and lowers the fishing spreads from the bottom to the top of the Pacific Ocean. It is a spool built of plastic with a*

68

handle attached that is used to crank up or down stainless-steel wire, that a spread is snaped to.

***

Swerving to the outside of the bend, we're skimming along at eighteen knots.

Marty points to the shoaling water on our right by jutting his chin. He pointed out the shoaling water just twice so far. He's grown up on this river; running it every summer. He has observed the changes from year to year; sand bars disappearing and reappearing according to the winter flows.

When we left the launch-ramp Marty watched me looking for shoaling water. Moving the boat were the current runs the swiftest. Most other teenagers would be telling me; where and when and what. They would have loved showing their superior knowledge. Marty being Marty, keeps his expertise quiet, and lets me pilot the boat.

Feeling a growing confidence, I spout out one of the many random thoughts pervading my brain. "What do you say, let's run the bar and take the boat out the mouth."

"Nooo-way man, just no way, that's one man-killing bar."

Looking directly into my eyes, Marty wants me to understand that he is not kidding.

"Ah, come on, Marty, what's a little bar?"

Marty floppes his head back and forth, in an attempt to persuade me. "Let me off on the beach; and, give me yours, and Mike's address. We'll need to know where to send the remains."

His hart-felt warning has an effect on me. But, looking at Mike, I can see the wheels in his head grinding.

Asking the world in general Mike says, "Has anyone made it across?"

Marty looks past me to Mike, "One guy, an old-timer here, he did it on a flat slick, oily calm day, at high tide."

Mike shrugs, "Then we can, today."

My stomach tightens. If Mike intends to go across the bar, then, I'll go with him? But, but, man I don't want to go now? Another twenty minutes of flat out running brings the bar insight. Twelve-foot combers are breaking out a quarter of a mile. Turning into a series of two-foot rollers.

It's low tide. At the mouth, thin layers of water flow over a sizable bar. Waves rush over the bar and into the river; they're a foot and a half, or two feet deep. Then the bar goes dry, and then another two-footer sweeps the bar. Trying to cross the bar would cost us the boat. Our prop, lower unit, and boat would be mangled. Then we would just be washed back into the river. We can't even attempt to cross tonight. Thank God!

***

Perched on the gunwale of the Kisutch, I'm hot. Both Mike and I are in our diving gear. Sweat is running down my back and dripping from my hood. My hood is two sizes too small, and is choking me. The tank on my back is over balancing me toward the river. My flippers are splayed at an uncomfortable angle; and Mike is standing on top of them. If he moves there is a fifty-fifty chance that I'll flip over backward.

Spitting into my face mask, I dip it into the river; grabbing just a little water in the bowl of the mask. Using a gloved hand, I smear the concoction around and around. I shake the mask vigorously; I hate spit and salt water in my eyes.

As I balance on the gunwale, my wet-suit restrains and constricts my every movement. The quarter inch of rubber neither lets my arms hang down, nor allows me to lift them easily.

Mike spits into his face mask and hands it to me for a dip in river water. Dipping the mask and grunting I hand it back. Sticking my regulator into my mouth I suck. Air feeds to me; accompanied by the sound of valves opening, air rushes past my ears. Tiny little valves click open and close, delivering the correct pressure. Exhaling, a different octave of sounds surges by. Assured that everything is working I grunt toward Albert, who is running the boat.

Picking up a gunny sack, Al throws it at me. Gunny sack in hand, my other over my face mask, I fall backward. The world turns white, bubbles and salt water closes over me. Water, cold salty water runs down my neck and back, filling the air voids around my torso. Water seeps up from my feet finding the small air pockets around my knees, seeping further up my legs. Finally, it finds the large space

around my groin area. The water is around fifty-five degrees. It shrivels every part of my body it touches; I am lying at a slight angle head down about ten feet below the surface.

Fighting with the gunny sack; *where is that opening?*

I'm trying to keep it open so that crabs can be thrown in. This doesn't look like that it's going to work too well. The twenty-two pounds of weight on my weight-belt is slightly off center, rolling me to the right. Releasing the gunny sack letting it float, I've got to pull my weight-belt around and center it. There, tightening it for good measure. The gunny sack floats next to me, sinking slightly. Bending at the waist, kicking my feet up, I head on down.

Another ten feet down brings me to the sandy river floor. Visibility is good, around fifteen feet. Crab are scurrying away in every direction. Kicking forward, reaching for one, the crab turns to fight, claws up, snapping at me aggressively. The crabs are Dungeness about six to eight inches across the back. Their claws are four inches long and two and a half inches across. A Dungeness crab cannot break bones. If one grabs you, they can crush a fingernail like a blow from an eighteen-ounce hammer; but that is all the damage they can do.

Flagging the gunny sack in the crab's face I reach around behind. Picking the crab up from behind, the crab reaches for my hand to pinch an offending finger. My fingers seem to be just out of the crab's reach. Shoving him into the bag, I turn him loose and scan the bottom for my next victim.

Drifting along with the incoming tide, I'm grabbing crab as the opportunity arises. It hits me; I'm comfortable. The fifty-five-degree water has warmed to body temperature. My hood is no longer choking me. The weight-belt is riding comfortably above my hips. A small amount of water has leaked into my face mask. Tilting my head, I blow air out my nose, purging air and water out the bottom. Life is good; life is very good. Crab after crab is falling victim to the waving gunny sack and the hand that sneaks behind. Crab after crab falls into the perilous darkness of that sack. The sack is dragging the river bottom. Three quarters full of live crab.

It's time to come up; that's the name of the game when diving. Those that don't come up are out of the game.

Surfacing, I look around. Albert is at the controls of the Kisutch, he spots me, and guns her around. In seconds, I am alongside; Albert has another gunny sack in hand ready to change an empty sack for a full one.

Lifting the sack toward Al I spit my regulator out. "I'm coming aboard, if Mike has what I've got, we have plenty to eat."

Albert reaches down, grabbing my tank by the "J" valve. He hauls it over the gunwale. Releasing my weight-belt, I hand one end up. He hauls the weight-belt over the side, "Think you can flop aboard Ben?"

"Get back, I'm comin aboard."

Grasping the side of the dory I give three powerful kicks. Over I flop, and into the crab, my head and face sliding into the gunny sack. My arms are down at my sides, I'm unable to get them under my chest; can't seem to get a purchase here. Arching my back, I get my face as far away from those crabs as possible. Crab, are running sideways out of the opening. There's a two-inch space between their backs and my nose.

Having held my arch as long as I can; I flop forward. My facemask creates a traffic jam for the crab. It was kind of scary watching them tare by with two inches between me and their exit. Being their exit is worse yet.

Their last shred of dignity has been assailed by this new development. They seem angry all out of proportion, to the injustice that they are suffering. After all it's my head they are using as an escape route.

A hideous scratching sound emanates from their pointy little feet. They're running sideways away from us. Thirty irate crabs surround us, pinchers in the air as though they're about to attack. Making their little clicking sounds, the threat apparent to both of us, grabbing my arm, Al hauls me bodily out of harms way.

Mike chooses this time to surface, looking to be picked up. Al makes for the wheel, kicking crab out of his way. I am standing in the middle of the deck, gazing around, I'm not sure of which way to move, Al guns the motor, going for Mike. Al's gunning of the engine flops me over my flippers; I am down among the crab... again?

Since I'm down, I reach for my flippers and slip them off. My face mask comes off next, then I regain my feet, my lips are puffy and blue from grasping the regulator. The too small hood is choking me again.

Al swings the Kisutch alongside Mike. Mike hands a gunny sack up to me, fuller than my own. In the fishing vernacular, "We're in-em." Mike's tank and weight-belt come aboard next.

Pulling my hood off, I shake my head, looking down at him, I warn, "Watch it; when you come aboard. A couple of crabs got out of my sack."

Grasping the gunwale, Mike gives two kicks and rolls aboard, and into about thirty irate crab. Sixty pinchers click their undiminished anger at anyone near them. Being faster than double geared lightning, Mike is on his feet, even before he hits the deck.

Standing next to me, he opines, "There are more than a couple of them on the deck."

Tilting my head I bang it, trying to clear water from one ear, "Well, I didn't have time to count-um."

"Oh, I see... shall we catch them... again?" A crab scurries over Mike's flipper.

Al looks over his shoulder, "Naw, we'll see what Scotty can do with them."

This is one mean trick to play on a flatlander from California.

***

The drift wood fire licks up around the two-gallon stainless-steel pail filled with salt water. The water is at a hard boil, steam pouring forth, mixing with the smoke. The saltwater steam and smoke mingle creating an unforgettable aroma, something like the ocean on fire. Sand still warm from the afternoon sun conforms around my body in a grainy caress.

Marty grabs a crab from a sack. Holding it above the boiling water, he drops it with a flourish. Another crab follows the first, and another, and another, salt water is splashing over the top, into the fire.

Marty glowers at the full bucket. "Well, it's a beginning, I was hoping to get two apiece in there for us."

Raising my head, "I'm so hungry... I could eat a dozen. But, beggars can't be choosers?"

Robby jumps down from the bow of the Kisutch; two loafs of French bread in one hand, and a pound of butter in the other. "Carbos, and crab meat saturated in animal fat, the dinner of champions."

Rubbing his belly Mike says, "I love a meal, any meal."

Marty is still trying to fit one last crab in. He flops on the sand instead, the crab still in hand. "Are you having a bad day?"

Marty is holding the crab about six inches in front of his face. The crab's claws are working like mad trying to reach his nose.

"You know if this was happening to us, we'd be mad as hell."

"Yep." Al says, "You're be-bopping along, going over to a buddies for dinner.

A one-eyed monster grabs you by the back of the neck and stuffs you into a sack."

Propping up on my elbows I throw my head back laughing. "Seeing your buddy... the Craw, grabbed. The monster starts after you. What do you do? Old Cyclops, one of his steps is equal to fifty of yours. Escape is not an option."

Marty rubs the sand from his hair, "You get mean, mad crab mean... ready to fight. You scream at your tormentor, *'Come on, I'll take you on and that other big blimp at the same time. I'll kick your ass! I'll kick your big brother's ass too!'* The monster he don't care. To him you're nothing but protein, ya see, you just taste good, dipped in butter."

The crab clicking his claws is trying to tear Marty's face off. Marty roars at the crab. The crab stops all movement, then he begins the clicking and leg waving again.

"It's all got to do with karma, sometimes you make it to your buddy's for dinner; sometimes you end up being dinner."

Marty; moved by the crab's plight, a light of kindness showing in his brown eyes, pets the crab between his eyes. He must be oh so careful as the front of the crab is where the claws reside.

Rubbing the blond fuzz on his chin, Al reflects. "You know Marty, if your boat sinks off the mouth of this river, you're going to end up crab dinner, too. Only it'll be the crab dining this time."

Marty scratches his own sparse chin whiskers. "Ah, that's a point, it's a circle. Karma completes it."

Robby is slicing bread with his buck knife, "Nope, life just ain't fair. That crab in your hand, he didn't do anything that the other crabs haven't been doing for years. Heck, he may be a Christian crab. Getting down on his little claws every morning, he prays. He prays that he won't get caught today. Today, his prayer just wasn't answered."

Marty turns the crab to get a better overall view. "Does this Christian crab deserve to be released? Wouldn't that be the Christian thing to do, and what karma demanded?"

Shifting in my sandy bed, I look at the crab. The sun is setting into the Pacific Ocean and a golden glow hovers to the west. The driftwood fire is producing more light than the setting sun.

"No-way that crab is a Christian crab. I think he's a Viking Berserker. Here, he is confronted by a giant predator two hundred times his size. He's not said prayer one; this, this... mighty mite's been trying to rip Marty's face off. Those aren't the actions of a piece loving crab. He sure ain't turning the other claw. That is one tough, self-reliant, warrior crab, asking no quarter and giving none. Release the crab, but release him for his bravery. Not because of something he may have done. We don't know what he's done... or not done?"

Marty shoots a finger into the air. "Ah, that's the reason for karma! We don't know if this is the one good crab in these two bags. Should he be released, karma knows and karma says the crab goes free."

Marty gets up from the fire. Stepping to the water's edge he sets the crab down. The Christian, Viking Berserker, good karma, crab runs sideways into the river.

Mike's using a gaff-hook to pull cooked crab from the pail. "Marty, you turn any more of our hard-earned food back to the sea and I'll eat your share. All Ben and I have to eat is pancake flower, and you just let a pound of meat go." Marty grins at Mike, "Don't worry about that. I promised Dad that we would bring some crab home."

***

The bell over the door rings lightly. Mike pushes his way into the fish company's store and office. We're here for the free hot chocolate. Turning, Mike holds the door for me, as I clear it, he releases the door to the spring. We head straight for hot chocolate; Mike pulls a couple of Styrofoam cups off the stack. He lugs two chocolate packets from the box, tearing both of their tops off in one smooth motion. A packet of chocolate goes into each cup, then Michael reaches for the hot water.

Hogie is kicked-back in his over-stuffed office chair, "Did you guys hear the strike is over?" Hogie's voice is low and mellow like the surf pounding a gravel beach on a calm day.

Mike hands me a cup of hot chocolate, "No, when was it settled?"

Nodding in his relaxed manner, Hogie hands me his Styrofoam cup for a refill. "Late yesterday afternoon, thirty-five cents a pound for Cohos and fifty-five for Chinooks."

Pouring coffee into Hogie's cup, "How is that price, is it fair?"

Hogie leans back, taking on the air of a wizened old man, "It's fair, if there are fish around, if there are no fish the price will go up anyway."

Hogie puts his hands behind his head and drawls, "I saw Jerry come in and get your launch vehicle, was that part of your deal for the new motor?" Taking a sip of chocolate, Mike drawls back, "Yep, we didn't have enough money to pay him off, so he took the Jeep as part of his payment."

Hogie sips coffee, thoughtfully musing, "What are you going to launch with?"

"My Mustang."

Hogie's face takes on a concerned expression, "No... I, don't think that'll work, you'll get stuck every time you launch. You'll destroy your car, the saltwater will rust your fenders off. Ben, that's a nice little car, don't do that to it."

Glancing over at Mike, then back to Hogie, I opt for the truth. "We don't have any money to buy another vehicle. We're broke."

Hogie shrugs his shoulders, "Look around. See if you can find an old launch vehicle. I'll front you the money."

Marty pushes through the door, the bell calling attention to his entry, "Good morning."

Hogie nods his greeting, "Morning, Marty. We were just talking about Ben and Mike's launch vehicle situation. Do you know of anyone that has an old beater for sale?"

Marty looks up at the ceiling, deep in thought, "Yea, The Fiddler has an old car out by our summer rental. It's parked in the weeds it hasn't moved in a couple of years."

Hogie leans forward in his high-backed office chair to make his point. "Go see Fiddler, he's a wheeler and dealer. Offer him half of whatever he asks for the car, if it runs."

The three of us trooped out the door the bell ringing its salutation at our exit.

The Fiddler is standing in his dory, "The Fiddler," and is laying out troll gear. The dory has artwork scrolled up and down both sides. A cat playing a fiddle and dancing adorns the gunwale from bow to stern; notes of music float off the stern. Mike, Marty and I swagger up to the aptly named *Cat in the Cradle*.

"What's happening, Fiddler?" Marty is our spokesman.

"Getting ready, Marty, strike's over, did you hear?"

Nodding his agreement,

"Yea, we heard; Fiddler… this is Mike and Ben, they own our old boat."

"Good to meet you-all."

Fiddler is around forty. A three-day growth of beard adorns his sunken cheeks. Brown blood-shot eyes shift from one to the other of us. Jet-black hair is greased back under his Greek fisherman's cap. Fiddler has a soft, southern, raspy voiced draw. It's obvious Fiddler is well acquainted with Jack Daniel's whiskey and cigarettes.

No one speaks for half a minute. Clearing his throat, Mike intones, "Ah-hum, we heard you got an old beater? In the field, beside Marty's house?"

"I do? Oh, yea I do" Fiddler grins, his mouth is empty of any teeth. Pink gums flash at us, "Is it in your way?"

"No; it's OK. We were wondering what you would take for it? We need a launch vehicle."

"A hundred bucks," Pink gums flashing.

"We'll give you fifty if it runs." Fiddler and Mike are eye-balling each other.

"OK, but I don't have time to mess with it, you guys get it running."

"We'll go take a look at it, see what we can do" Fiddler shakes hands all around. The three of us saunter off toward Marty's launch vehicle.

***

Marty is on the bench seat beside me. We're in a nineteen fifty Ford station wagon the steering wheel shaking uncontrollably in my hands. The car is filled with the sound of vibrating metal. The rusty hood thrashing about is bouncing up and down two or three inches; the hood threatens to fly up and off at any moment. The rear bumper of Albert and Marty's launch vehicle is twenty-four feet ahead of my front bumper.

Both cars are flying down Interstate Highway One. The towline stretched tight just below my field of vision.

Marty sticks his head out of the passenger side window. "Faster Mike, tell Albert to go faster. We need fifty miles an hour or she'll never start."

Mike sticks his head and upper-body out of the passenger's window. "WHAT?"

Waving his arm in a large circular motion, "FASTER, GO FASTER!"

Blue smoke pours from Albert's tail pipe, as he puts the pedal to the metal. The speedometer creeps toward forty-five, the steering wheel vibrating so hard that it blurs my vision. My eyeballs are rattling around in my head from the jarring; joining my teeth in their chattering.

Pulling his body back inside, Marty yells, "What's she... do-ing, Ben?"

"For-ty-six," my voice unable to form whole words. "Is this fas-st en-ou-ght"?

"Get her up to for-ty nine, any-way," Marty wants fifty miles an hour; anything less just won't do.

"She is do-ing fifty," I dare not take my eyes off the road.

Through clenched teeth Marty blurts, "Do it now, she'll go or she won't!"

Dropping the automatic transmission lever from neutral to low, wide, slick tires grab the asphalt with a screech. The motor coughs, she wheezes once, and roars to life.

Big Bertha Butts, our brand new launch vehicle is pulled off Interstate Highway One, behind Marty and Albert's Ford. Jumping from the passenger's side Marty unties the towline. He throws it into the trunk of his car. Gunning Bertha's motor, I'm trying to keep her running. Marty jumps back into Bertha sliding her into drive, I gun the motor. Bertha lurches back onto the highway. She's careening down the road after being unconscious, in a coma, for two years. Taking her first breaths of clean Oregon air, she emits a foul bluish gas from her tail pipe. Bertha is gasping and wheezing, clutching at life for all she is worth. Like Lazarus she has arisen, she'll not be laid low easily.

"I'm going to tell the Fiddler that we'll take her."

Mike flashes me an OK sign as I accelerate past Albert's car. My foot is stomped to the floor. Bertha's mass is gaining velocity, six miles an hour, then seven miles; creeping, creeping up to eight, eight miles an hour. She's no powerhouse, but she can drag the Bloody Wog to the beach.

Bertha slides to a stop alongside 'The Fiddler', hollering out my window, I gun the motor, trying my best, to keep her running.

"Hey Fiddler, we got her going. Tell Hogie you got fifty coming, he'll put it on our bill."

Fiddler lifts a flasher to his hat brim and grins. Fiddler ain't about to complain, not with Bertha on the prowl. Gunning the engine, we crawl away. I'm pumping the gas pedal like I'm riding a bike.

Bertha has an ever-so-lovely habit. Exhaust fumes leak into the car. It's not just the pristine Oregon air that's fouled. The driver and passengers are fouled along with the coastal air.

Pulling into Nole's driveway in a cloud of blue smoke, and gravel dust; I skid to a halt. Crunching gravel is barely audible above Bertha's roar. Pressing the gas pedal to the floor, the engine roars in protest. Fumes of unburned oil and gas pour out the tail pipe, gas fills the car's interior through the gaps in the dashboard. Killing the engine amidst this discordant chaos of noise and RPMs, I'm not sure what I'm doing, or why?

Marty has told me this is good for the battery. It gives a small shot of juice to the battery, just as the engine dies. He never mentioned what I was doing to the engine with all these un-used RPMs.

My plan is to use Marty's tools to pull the plugs on old Bertha and clean them up.

The screen door squeaks open, Nole's smiling face pokes out, his baritone professor voice booms.

"Ah, Mike, Ben, glad you're here. The strike's over. We'd better go to Hogie's and buy you boys some gear."

Albert and Mike pull up behind Big Bertha Butts. Bob drives in beside me as I step out of Bertha. His plain white Ford pickup truck, adds just a touch of class to the heaps littering Nole's driveway.

Everyone starts to migrate toward Nole, our undeclared leader. "I thought we could get our fishing gear together. Perhaps, we'll have a gear tying party tonight? Mike and Ben need all new gear. My boys and me need some replacement gear. What say you, we'll go to Hogie's and buy what we need?"

Always agreeable, Bob answers for all of us, "Sure, we'll meet you there, Robby, let's go get our gear."

"Ah Dad, I want to ride with Ben and Mike in their new car."

Our new car is about three years older than Robby. Bob shrugs, "OK, see you there."

Al bends over to view the bluish haze within Bertha. "I'll go down to Hogie's with you, I want a ride in Bertha too."

When nylon tires are set in one position for an extended period of time, they'll take a set. That is to say; the material will retain some memory of the flat area. It will not become circular without heat and working. These flat spots caused the excessive vibration Marty and I underwent. The small amount of driving just completed, has reduced the vibrating significantly.

Mike moseys up to Bertha, hands in his pockets, bending over Mike inspects the blue gases escaping out of the windows.

"How does she handle Ben?"

Tossing the keys at Mike, "Like a porcupine in heat, you can handle her but caution is advised."

Mike; snatching the keys in mid-air, "That's funny it doesn't go fast enough to be dangerous, what does she do, put you to sleep while you're driving?"

Marty and I eyeball one another. "No, falling asleep isn't the problem. She vibrates like a motel bed with twenty dollars-worth of quarters in her."

Mike swings open the driver's side door, "Let's take her for a spin."

Scott bounding out of the house, pushes past Nole. Nole steps forward catching his balance just before he falls off his porch. Over his shoulder Scott bawls.

"Sorry! Hey, I want to go. Man, you guys got it started real quick. Have you tried it on the beach yet?"

We're cruising down Highway One. It's the direction we just came from. Big Bertha Butts is chuck-a-luck full of teenage boys. The whole California crop over sixteen is riding in her.

I'm holding forth on the adventure of getting her started. "She was vibrating like a woman of the night, having a religious conversion in my aunt's church. I couldn't see past the hood; the steering wheel was shaking me hard. And, Marty is yelling for more power,

"Scotty, we've got to have warp nine."

Peering my way, Mike kicks' back in the driver's seat. "We could see the hood jumping up and down, we thought she was going to throw you guys off. She's not handling to badly now, though, the steering is a little lose."

Mike works the wheel back and forth to show us how much play there is. Suddenly, Bertha careens to the left. Tires squeal as she skids sideways down Highway One on the wrong side of the road. Mike corrects the wheel right. Bertha swings madly right, tires still in full choirs, squealing in agony as their outer layer is peeled off. It's a grim reminder; the life of a rubber tree is not an easy one. Mike corrects left, Bertha's steering wheel spins out of control, locking left. Mike, Scott, and myself all slide to the right, they pile up on top of me. Marty, Albert and Robby are making the same moves, locked in the same dance, in the back seat. We end up out in the sand dunes, a cloud of dust and noshes fumes surrounding us. We're facing the wrong way with the sound of escaping air unmistakable in the background. The six of us scramble out of the car, happy to be alive.

Marty takes out his Buck knife and starts picking gravel out of the rim on the front left tire. All four tires are hissing at us from gravel being lodged in the rim, breaking the airtight seal. Following Marty's lead; Albert and I start prying gravel also. When all the tires are through hissing at us, we jump back in Bertha. Mike under the wheel we head back up the road toward Cape Kiwanda, hooting and howling about our close call.

Pulling into the parking lot, all four doors burst open. Hopping from Bertha, there's a sound of rusty hinges creaking and popping in the background of our raucous laughter. Running on the ragged edge of disaster sure is fun.

No big surprise, Nole and Bob are here ahead of us. Their backs to us and on the other side of a plate glass window. They're pointing at goodies on the back wall, ordering gear from Debbie. Ah, Debbie, so so lovely, she is so… so Debbie?

Hogie kicked back in his overstuffed office chair grins at us through the window. It's as though he's in on our joke, hands clasped behind his head he's gaming with the dads.

Trooping in randomly, we cover the bell's greeting with our back slapping good humor. Turning to the group Nole demands, "Where the hell have you been?"

Mike, being quickest on the up-take answers, "We took Bertha for a little spin in the dunes." It was the truth, kind of, but not the whole truth.

Debbie smiles at the crowd of horny young fisherman, knowing that we truly appreciate her. The thirty-foot long counter gives more than ample room for all of us boys to belly up. Mike and I crowd between Noel and Bob to get the best advice. Old fishermen are the best fishermen.

Looking from Hogie to Nole, Mike inquires, "Well… what do we need?"

Closing the deal to buy the Bloody Wog, Mike wrote a contract. We four boys signed it. It stated: "We will be taught how to fish."

Albert balked at this, he said it took years to learn how to fish, besides, fishing can't be taught; it must be learned; Mike relented. He wrote a provisor to the contract: three days of training will be sufficient.

We wanted and needed advice while buying our fishing gear. We wanted gear that would work; catch fish, lots of fish. If we only knew, if we only knew.

Nole points to a number 2 flasher. "Put twenty number 2 flashers on the Bloody Wog's tag."

Debbie lays a stack of flashers on the counter; it's all two inches high.

Scrutinizing the stack, I've got to ask. "How much apiece are they?"

Debbie smiles that beautiful smile of hers, "Two dollars each."

Her voice was soft, like the whisper of wind through pine trees, well-modulated with a West Coast accent.

Looking into Debbie's soft blue eyes, my knees feel weak with lust.

"Are you nuts? Two dollars for a lump of shiny flat steel?"

Debbie's smile disappears, "You don't want them?"

"We want them, we can't afford them… Ah heck, we'll take fifteen."

I didn't want to hurt Debbie's feelings, but; my God, forty dollars for flashers. Bertha just cost us fifty dollars, and she was a thousand times bigger than a flasher and she has a motor.

Nole drops a hand on my shoulder, "Give them twenty." He looks me square in the eyes, "That's just barely enough to get started."

Shrugging, "I guess we'll just go deeper in debt."

Bob joins in the fun of spending money Mike and I don't have. "Give them a bag of red hoochies and, some black ones too."

Mike takes up my side, "How much are the hoochies?"

Debbie realizes she's on shaky ground here, "Six dollars a bag?"

"Jeez-us, that's a-lot of money, what-da we do with that many hoochies?"

Marty leans forward on the counter to be able to see past Robby and Nole. His voice was mellow and languid. "You fish with them, you got-ta have something to cover the twenty-dollars-worth of hooks you're about to buy."

"How much is a salmon worth?"

"Oh, about three fifty," Nole answers.

"Three dollars and fifty cents a fish. How the heck are we ever going to pay for all this junk?"

Nole grins his big friendly grin, "Why you get a few hundred fish days under your belt, you'll be richer than an Arab Sheik."

"Hundred fish days, we'll be making three hundred and fifty dollars a day, man, that's good money. How many hundred fish days did you have last year?" Directing my question to Marty, he feels incumbent to answer.

Mumbling, "Oh, none." In a strong voice, he blurts, "But, we're expecting some this year... With the new boat and motor, this is going to be a better season anyway. And, that old Bloody Wog... she never did fish too good."

Silence, follows this statement of fact. Glancing over at Mike, I'm trying to think of something intellectual to say. Nothing comes to mind. Mike's eyes reflect a forgiveness for getting him into this mess that I don't deserve.

Nole claps a hand on my back, "Don't worry it's all in who's running the boat that makes it a highliner or not. You'll do just fine."

We return to spending money, on future earnings, from a very uncertain source.

***

The large crowd setting around the living room of Nole's house is in a jovial mood. Covering the old beater of a coffee table is; hooks, hoochies, swivels, and leaders. Everyone's gear is laid out more or less in front of the owners. Bob pulls some leader from our spool. Picking up a snap, he threads the eighty-pound test leader. Leaning toward Mike, he lays three small loops into the leader, then bends the end of the line through the eye. Releasing his thumb, allowing the loops to spread out, then Bob carefully pulls the knot tight watching the loops tighten down on themselves. As the knot forms he licks the line to moisten it cutting down on friction. Holding up the snap and subber with the barrel knot, it's a perfect little column. Bob pulls out three fathoms of leader; a fathom is a six-foot measurement. He snips it off with fingernail clippers.

Bob grins a challenge, "Let's see you do one."

Picking up the line Mike threads it through the snap. Mike ganders at the knot that Bob has just finished his brow knits in concentration; the room has gone silent as we wait for Mike to either fail or succeed.

Loops form one after another, the line snakes through the loops, Mike draws down the line on the snap. The knot looks almost as good as Bob's.

Bob hands me a subber and three and fathoms of leader. "Your partner just tied a perfect barrel knot; on his first try, now the pressure is really on you. Can you do as well?"

I grin as my stomach ties it's self into a barrel knot; I know that Mike picks things up much faster than I do. He is very good with ropes and was watching Bob when he tied the knot for the first time. I had just been pretending to watch. Now the pressure is on me, the rooms' gaze shifts targets; now I'm the focus of humiliation. Everyone in this room can tie a knot like this. Even little Greg at eight can laugh at me if he wants. I grasp the leader and line-snap. The leader is looking like a serpent ready to strike; I'm ready; yea, I'm ready for this?

From Mikes' display, I know I need to make loops. How many? Oh yea, three. One... two... three. Now, what do I do with this end? Through the swivel and then... oh oh, through the loops, yea that's it. Lick; and then pull slowly.

"There's the knot!"

Marty being a natural born teacher holds up a spread he just finished. "We are tying spreads like these. They consist of a; line-snap, surgical tubing as a subber rubber, a swivel, and a snap. A barrel knot is used on the swivel and snap. The line-snap is inserted into the surgical tubing thus."

Marty pushes the stainless-steel heavy gauge wire figure into the tubing. "The tubing is cinched up around the line-snap with Oregon leader, using a clove-hitch and a square knot."

Marty is in his professor mode, his voice slow and patient, after all, his students are especially dubious. The line-snap has a large bulbous end that fits into the tubing. The bulbous end distends the tubing. Marty wraps Oregon leader around the surgical tubing. Tying a clove hitch, he puts his foot on the spool. Using pliers to pull with, he's turning the subber rubber with the other hand. Turning and cinching, turning, cinching the line. Cinching it tighter than anyone would think possible.

Marty grimaces over a knot, "Do you see the knob on the swivel?"

Mike and I are nodding in unison like one of those dogs in the back window of a fifty-nine Chivvy.

"You do the same with that, only on the other end."

Stretching a subber in and out, Marty is showing us how flexible it is. Spooling leader off, he whips out a barrel knot. Measuring off three fathoms of a leader by pulling line across his chest, he grabs a tiny snap, and ties it on. Snapping one of our new flashers onto the tiny snap, he smiles. A hoochie is snapped on the other end of the flasher.

Marty holds the hoochie by the hook. Slowly the flasher and hooch begins undulating, it's a dance? Moving his body up and down, he slides across the floor; hoochie, flasher, and leader all moving in a three-dimensional sin wave. Marty begins biting at the hoochie, his mouth just missing the enticing treat.

Looking more and more like a salmon trying to corner an elusive bait. His dance circling the living room, Marty's little dance is a sideways slide, shuffle and stop.

Leader, flasher, and hoochie rise from Marty's grasp, the hoochie escaping his mouth, lucky Marty.

The room is filled with fishermen and want-to-be fishermen. We're watching in fascination, wondering will the salmon bite? Will this be the beginning of a big run? Is the snap on?

Marty jumps on top of the back of the couch. Balancing, his sideways shuffle continues, Marty is doing his salmon dance, undulating three feet above the floor. I lean forward to let Marty pass by behind my head.

"Marty!" Dawn steps into the room. "Marty, what are you doing?" Nole, how could you let Marty walk on the furniture? Marty, don't you dare bite that hook. We'd have blood everywhere! I can't leave you boys alone for a minute. Nole how could you let Marty walk on the furniture?"

We all return to making knots, we can't meet Dawn's eyes after being caught in this bit of foolishness.

Marty, keeping his eyes peering toward the old carpet, adds, "And, that's how you tie gear in P.C. Oregon."

We all keep our heads down and stare at the table, studying our gear with more intensity than any of us have ever done before. This tying gear is serious business.

CHAPTER THREE

Twang, another curling breaker, smacks our bow. Sounding like a fifty-five-gallon oil drum being whacked with a pipe wrench, glancing around from my fish, at the unexpected sound, spray hits me full in the face.

Eyeing me from the other side of the gaff hatch, the Douggers laughs; me... I'm sputtering out salt water, "Never ever look around when you hear a wave hit forward of you. It's only got one way to go, and that's aft."

I spit out one last bit of salty water while nodding at Doug's sage advice; bracing my knees on the after bulkhead, I return to work. "Doug, you've been fishing since the end of World War Two. Do you still get a kick out of it, or is it just a job?"

"Kick, Ben, definitely a kick. There ain't a job, one a workingman can do, that's as much fun as fishing in a bite. We've just made a hundred bucks in twenty minutes. You sure can't do that ashore."

Picking up my pace, I pull faster. Doug will think I'm shirking work to talk. I've got other questions to ask. Bending over I lift another albacore from the water, lifting carefully so the hook doesn't pull out. I throw him onto the growing pile of fish in the bins. Sliding my hand down the line, I lift and twist. The hook is free, turning I throw the jig deep into the wake. Pretending that I'm paying attention to my job, I glance at Doug. "Do you ever get afraid out here, like that guy the other night?"

"Naw... you can't do this job if you are going to be a Nervous Nelly. Now, that night of the Columbus Day Storm, we sank... *I* was swimming around out here in a hundred-mile-per-hour wind and wouldn't have minded a shore job that night. No-sir-re, that would've been a dam good night to be snuggled up to the old lady."

"You were on a boat that sank? Wow! Can you tell me about it? I didn't know that you ever sank a boat; that's, that's cool."

Doug glowers at me,

"You're talking too much; tend to business."

This is an unusual comment for the Douggers. He's one of the most even-tempered men I've ever met. I know that I've hit a sensitive spot, I don't know what, though. We're working in silence, I don't want to bring up another sore subject, that's for sure. Wonder what I said wrong?

Grunting Douggers pulls a fish over the stern, popping the hook free. He turns and throws the jig into the water.

"I lost almost everything that I owned... when that boat went down."

Ah, that's the sore spot, I stumbled into; Doug is tighter than bark on a tree, fair but tight. The jig I'm feeding out is back in place, reaching for another line I continue to gam. Uh-oh I haven't been paying attention.

The tag lines tied down beside me should have been released. As the boat completes another circle, the two longlines and whiskey line are all tangled. All with fish on them. Reaching for the whiskey line I begin pulling. It's a three fish tangle. One fish gives about fifty pounds of line pull. Three fish, oh well.

My arms and back strain against the force. Three twelve-pound fish are swimming straight down at twenty-two miles an hour. The Alley Cat is making an average of six knots over the ground, as the boat climbs from the trough of a swell to the crest she slows. Sliding down into the next trough she picks up speed. When the speed picks up, I just hang on. When the boat slows, I pull deliberately. My left hand is pulling toward my chest. Albacore line is cutting deep into my palm, '*get her in just a-little more.*'

Pulling with my right hand, I can feel my right arm weakening.

Douggers grins at my struggles, "You got to keep your mind on what you're doing out here, it's a dangerous place."

I grunt back, "Hum." It's all I can manage right now.

Doug gestures with his chin, "There's the Hornet." As; his hands are busy dragging in an albacore.

Peering into the mist, caused by all the breaking combers, she is barely visible.

When it's this rough, sea spray reduces visibility down to a mile or less. This close to sea level we're looking through ten-percent sea water. The wind has been picking up with the raising sun. Not an unusual occurrence, not at all. The wind is back up to fifty knots. Whitecaps are blown horizontally after breaking in this kind of weather. The spray staying air born, blowing from one wave peak to another. In truth, it's really not fishable. But, the Douggers is no sissy, so we're fishing.

The Hornet coming down on our circle is up wind. Raising up on a swell, her great bow ploughing, she's breaking the top of the wave apart. Even the Hornet disappears from sight at the bottom of one of these deep troughs. Reappearing spray shoots out from her bow thirty feet or more; jig lines are jumping up and down in a wild motion.

Grunting and groaning with each pull of my three fish tangle, leaning aft for a short rest, I'm trying to find the best position possible for my back and arms. It's hard with a hundred and fifty pounds of pull on me.

"Douggers you ever think of quitting, just pulling the plug? Selling everything and moving ashore?"

"Naw, Benjy. I was born to pilot a small boat into a rough sea. I love the feel of a deck rising to an on-coming swell, the spoke of a wheel in my hand, bracing for the on-coming roller.

There's a shot of adrenalin I get as we climb for the heavens. I love it when the bow punches through a capping swell. That empty feeling is in the pit of your stomach as the deck drops into the next trough. I love it all. You get those three fish aboard. I'm going to talk to Stormy on the VHF."

The Douggers at fifty-two years of age, and a little over weight grunts as he climbs out of the gaff hatch. The Douggers is one of those quite easygoing people who never toots his own horn. He is not a very tall man, but he is a big man on the coast.

The Douggers fought in the European Theater of Operation during World War II. He was with the Eighty-Second Airborne, the Screaming Eagles. Doug was in the Battle of the Bulge, held the town of Basigne. He helped to capture the bridge at Remagen. But, the part of the war he likes to talk about is when he and Sea-yak Jack captured the NAZI Officer's wine cellar. The whole Eighty Second Airborne was drunk for three days from the Colonel down to the lowliest private.

Stormy's voice booms over the deck-speaker, "Hey-hey-hey, the Douggers are you punishing Ben with that circle over there, or are you into a snap? You tight little bugger, you'd kill a good deckhand to make an extra five bucks."

Continuing to pull my guts out, I start thinking about that first-day fishing, is that why I'm out here? No, but it was a good day, yes it was...

***

Mike and I are at the breakfast table; it's four-thirty in the morning and still dark outside.

Throwing open the door, Nole grins, his big infectious grin, "Morning boys, morning. What a great day to start the season. Are you ready?"

Mike has the pan with about half our oatmeal in it. I have a bowl with the other half.

Neither he nor I have been able to eat much of the congealed mess this morning.

Reaching out with his pan, "Want some Nole?" Mike inquires with a playful lilt to his voice.

"No, that's OK, I brought sandwiches to eat later."

Standing I pitch my bowl at the sink. It rattles around the sink, spilling out oatmeal in a circular pattern before coming to rest.

Mike wipes his hands on his pants, "Well, we're ready to go."

Outside, we saunter toward Big Bertha Butts, our launch vehicle. She is hooked up to the Bloody Wog, ready to go. The three of us get into the front seat. I slide in under the wheel

98

because I am such a good trailer-backer-upper. Turning the key, I pump the living hell out of the gas peddle. Big Bertha Butts begins her grind; err-errr, cough choke, wheeze, VEROOM!

That's the ear-splitting roar we love so well. Bertha lives, after all she is blowing bluish gas at us from every nook and cranny in her dash and floorboard. The bluish haze filters toward us, we're heading to the gas pumps to fuel the Bloody Wog. Mike jumps out as good-old Bertha rolls to a stop, walking back to the Bloody Wog he hops aboard her, with one fluid motion. Joining him at the pump I hand Mike the gas nozzle. Striding off toward the fish company, Nole is heading straight to the giant coffee pot.

Stuffing the gas nozzle into the filler neck Mike pulls the trigger. It's a gas tank out of a pickup, one that's probably older than the boat. The full tank leaks gas from every orifice. The neck where the filler is attached leaks. The tube that feeds gas to the engine leaks. The electrical connection for the non-existent fuel gage leaks, it holds gas about as well as a sieve. Gas flows out of the tank and runs onto the deck, travelling slowly but inexorably toward the bilge.

Eyes glazing over in horror, Mike purports, "Hand me something to wipe this up... we could blow ourselves up here."

Having observed that fishermen are calm in all situations, I respond, "Well, at least we won't sink on our first day."

Mike takes the hint, "Yep... ya can't sink, if-in you blow yourself up first."

I nod in sage agreement with Mike but look in Big Bertha Butts anyway. I am stumped. There is nothing to wipe up gas with in Bertha? A few old tires, a hundred foot of hemp rope, but no rags. Pulling off my sweater, I hand it to Mike. He gives me a Do you really want to do this look then starts swabbing.

***

The ringing bell greets us as we saunter into the fish company. Nole and Hogie are by the coffee pot, each with a Styrofoam cup in hand. Steam rising toward their faces; cups of coffee partially raised to their lips; they're motionless. Part of the pleasure of a cup of coffee at four thirty in the morning is the aroma. It's the warmth in your hand, steam filling your nose. Strolling to the coffee pot, Mike makes us a cup.

Sniffing the cold in, I ask, "Where's Debbie this morning?"

Grinning at Nole, Hogie winks at me. "She doesn't come in until nine in the morning. You could hang out until nine if you'd like?"

"Oh," my head sags in disappointment, "well, we got twelve dollars' worth of gas."

Nole nods at Hogie, "They need two packs of herring."

Pulling out our book, Hogie writes down how much we owe for this day's expenses. Coffee in hand, we all tramp outside. Crawling into Big Bertha Butts, she roars to life, filling the pristine Oregon air with her blue haze. Bertha crawls out to Highway One. Creeping across it, she's gaining speed in the downhill section. We're charging toward the beach at six miles an hour, rolling onto the sand. Bertha's wide, slick tires are throwing sand onto the bow of the Bloody Wog.

The trip is a short one. The fish company is just across the Highway from the parking lot. Once on the beach, we head north about a quarter of a mile. Nearing the head at Cape Kiwanda we join the other dories; fishermen are readying their boats for the day. They're jumping to and fro, fetching and doing for their boats. Do the machines serve the men or do the men serve the machines?

Swinging our stern to the surf, we roll to a stop, all three of us climb out. Mike and I are going to learn how to rig the boat for fishing.

"You grab the pole like this and swing it around to the pole rest, then set it into this notch."

Nole has one of the poles that juts out over the bow in his hands, his arms raised over his head he carries it to a perpendicular position over the side. Continuing to prepare the Bloody Wog for the sea as he describes what we need to do. In about twenty minutes, the boat is set up, we're ready.

Mike, Nole, and I, are all wearing hip boots. The hip boots are folded down to our knees for ease of walking. Once under the wheel of Big Bertha-Butts, I crank her up. In the off-driver side Nole is there to guide me through our first launching. Shifting Bertha into reverse I back toward the darkness. Backing toward the surf I'm not sure of what I am doing but whatever it is, it seems to be working.

The golden glow of morning is cresting over the coast mountains. The ocean still in darkness, is behind us.

"Come on Ben, faster, get this pig going, or we'll never get her off."

Pushing the accelerator down a little further, her speed creeps up.

"Faster Ben, faster. Come on, we need some speed."

Slamming Big Berth's accelerator to the floor hard, the engine roars, and blue smoke gushes from her dashboard.

"That's better, but give her some more, get her up in the power bands."

We are hurdling through the darkness, toward the ocean, backward. Gripping the wheel hard my knuckles are turning white; adrenaline is flowing. I'm concentrating fully on my backing skills. Nole lifts his finger in the air, spinning it around and around in a come-on kid, speed it up sign. I stomp down hard. Bertha redoubles her efforts. The first wave strikes the Bloody Wog on the stern; spray covers our new, used engine, our recently freed-up steering console, and oh yea, Mike. Mike is in the boat to handle her now, that she's in the surf.

"Faster Ben, Faster; give her the gun!"

I glance at Nole, trying to reassure myself that he is still mentally stable. His big, infectious grin is all I can make out in the dark car. Returning his grin with an uncertain grimace, I back for all I'm worth. The next wave rolls past the front tires. Foam and water swirling in the headlights ahead of me; this can't be right.

"Hit the breaks, NOW!"

Lifting my foot from the gas peddle, I slam it onto the break. At this same instant, a breaking wave smacks the Bloody Wog on her stern. Another twenty gallons of salt water cascades into the boat and, of course, all over Mike. It's good to be the trailer-backer-upper.

The old Bloody Wog begins to slide aft off her trailer. Rolling ... she's rolling. Splashing into the ocean, she just lays there, helpless, beaming to the breaking waves.

Shifting Bertha into low, we pull forward, leaving Mike to care for our helpless boat. Ahead, I can see the breaker spending its energy on the sand. The breaker recedes. Pulling onto the dry sand, I'm looking for a place to park. It's got to be above the high tide line, somewhere, anywhere.

Nole opens his door, stepping out of the accelerating Bertha. "I'll get out here and show Mike how to handle the boat in the surf."

He tells me this as Bertha is accelerating out of the surf, Bertha sure as hell is not a speed demon.

Jogging toward the beach, which dark shape is the Bloody Wog? There she is, the fourth one from the head. I like the way she looks. Laying there, bowing into the surf, she's ready for work. At her stern, Mike is holding the bow into the waves. His hip boots are up around his crotch while he does a little dance.

Entering the surf, I stop and pull my hip boots up before wading out to the Wog.

"What's the haps man?"

Mike braces himself on the stern. A wave runs under the Wog, he lets the boat pick him up, and the wave never reaches the top of Mike's boots.

"Get a hold of the stern. Pull it around to bring the bow into the next wave. Just straight arm yourself on the stern like this."

Mike braces himself for the next wave, it slides under the Bloody Wog, "Walk sideways after every wave. To keep her bow poking into the breakers, just pull the stern south. Her bow hits the next wave just perfect."

Mike pulls the Bloody Wog aft towards the beach. I grab a hold on the other side, next to our new used engine, and he rolls aboard. Water flies from his hip boots as they clear the surf.

Grasping the stern, the next breaker lifts the bow. The stern drops and Bloody Wog rotates over the crest of a breaker. I stiffen my elbows, and the boat lifts my feet from the sea floor. The breaker rolls on past, as we settle back down, my feet find terrafirma. Side stepping south, I pull the stern with me. The bow swings into the next on-coming roller. This is easy. Old Bloody Wog lifts again, rising like a gallant steed. I feel the sand under my boots wash away, leaving me standing on tiny sand pedestals.

Mike drops the engine from the up position, pulling the crank. The engine is purring and sputtering next to my ear. Pushing the boat a little further out, we're through another wave. Following Mike's example, I roll over the aft gunnel.

Nole is standing next to Mike, hanging onto a davit giving directions as needed. At the helm, Mike punches it, as my boots clear the water. Bloody Wog accelerates through the next breaker, the bow thrusting straight up. She slaps into the next trough. One more curling roller and we'll be through them. Mike throttles back into the trough. Accelerating into the next breaking crest, up, up, we're through the last comber and onto the open ocean.

Nole points to Haystack Rock. "Head out to the rock. We'll sniff the air, decide to go north or south."

Mike guns the engine. Old Bloody Wog pops up, onto step, the cold Oregon morning blowing against our faces as we speed toward the rock.

We've been running north for thirty minutes. The ocean is a gentle rolling swell; swell height is five to six feet; the period almost a minute; throttling back to troll speed, Mike leans into the wheel. We're slowly rolling along; we are as slow as a dory can go.

Nole picks up a spread from a cheap ass Styrofoam ice chest that our gear is stored in; "OK, this is as good a place to start as the next."

Grasping the cannon ball, Nole grunts as it comes off the deck, lifting it over the side, he swings her into the ocean. He holds the crank handle tightly in one hand. Nole cranks the cannon ball below the surface.

"Always put the heavies in first. When it's rough that will help steady the boat. Hand me a spread."

Nole takes one of our new spreads from Mike. He snaps a flasher on, adding a hoochie. Nole snaps the whole mess to the seven-strand wire. All this junk is suspended twenty fathoms above the sea floor.

Using his professor voice, deep and authoritative, "Putting out gear; as the gear goes out, you watch, make sure that nothing tangles. OK? Now, you want to crank down to the next set of beads. Snap on the next spread. Here, Mike, here, take this a second."

Nole wiggles the gurdy handle to show Mike what he means. Mike grabs the gurdy handle not knowing fully what he is supposed to do. Nole whirls past me, standing at the steering station, I snuggle up to the rusted old Pontiac steering wheel with the broken plastic cover that don't work anymore.

Getting to the down-wind side, he grabs the davit and pukes. "Ra-uhff, ah eh ra-

Nole's eyes are red-rimmed and watery. Sitting back on our new, old engine; "uhff ah, that's better, good I'm good, OK. I get sick the first day ever season. It's a tradition and I wouldn't want to break it."

Mike's eyebrows shoot up and down. My own eyebrows answer back with their own vertical movement. We haven't said a word. But volumes have been communicated.

Nole gives one of his big, friendly grins. A slight breeze blows his longish hair about his face, "Might as well finish putting the gear out, Mike."

Mike grabs a spread from our new gear box. It's that seventy-nine cent Styrofoam cooler, I bought brand-new from Hogie yesterday.

'I am editing this in 2024, and believe it or not; Mike still has that Styrofoam cooler, and it has a lot of the original fishing gear in it. Fifty-two years later, and the eighty-cent cooler is still doing the job.'

About two hours have elapsed. We've ran the gear four times to re-bait the hooks, and nothing, just nothing. Running the gear, one of us cranks the thirty-pound cannon ball up eighteen fathoms. Stopping every two fathoms, he unsnaps and lays out a spread on the gear locker. Finding the bottom spread, then one of us slowly cranks the gear back down, re-baiting our hooks. After the heavies, we pull in the float lines. A float line cannonball is only twenty pounds. Easy.

Suddenly the spring on the port heavy is shaking, differently; nodding toward the port Nole opines, "Yep... that's a silver, time to go to work."

The spring makes a lazy stretch, up then down, shaking almost imperceptibly. Mike begins pulling the line. One spread comes up empty then another, and another, nothing, just nothing. There's a flash of silver off our port quarter. Bringing the gear up, Mike's arm is making a circular motion. With each crank of the gurdy, his muscles flex and strain.

A line-snap breaks the surface, another flash of silver, there's the fish. He's running up beside the boat. Getting a look-see we're amazed. It's about two feet long. It must weigh ten pounds.

Nole is excited by this first fish of the season. "Put the break on! On the gurdy, the gurdy!"

Nole's voice becomes low, a whisper, calm and slow. "Take the line in slowly. don't push him. Let the fish come to you."

Nole picks up the scoop net, brandishing it at the fish; I tried to keep him from buying it, it cost us eight bucks. I am happy just knowing we're using it already.

"When you get him close, I'll net him."

Slowly pulling the fish, Mike's face is a study of concentration. His soft brown eyes are cold with murderous intent.

The silver is still out about four feet. Nole leans overboard, scooping the fish from behind. The silver passes over Mike's head and smacks me in the shoulder. Finishing his trip from the Pacific Ocean to the deck of the Wog, in one smooth motion.

The fish hits the deck, flopping and smashing into everything. Net and gear are in a big tangle by his third flop. Hoisting our gaff hook into the air, Nole beats the whole Whalen pee-water out of him. Whack, whack, whack. By the third blow, our new fish just lies there, quivering.

The gaff slides under the fish-hook. Nole picks the fish up, while he holds the monofilament line back down along his body. Dropping the gaff hook toward the deck he jerks up and down once. The fish is free from the hook and clear of the net, all in one clean motion.

Gaffing the silver through the gill plate, Nole throws him into the fish box. "Now, you boys have a tangle to clear, if I try to fix that mess I'll puke again."

***

It's five thirty in the evening. We're rounding Cape Kiwanda, heading toward the beach. Reaching in front of Mike, Nole pushes the throttle to the firewall.

"We want to be at full-tilt-boogie when we hit the beach."

The Wog gains speed, our bottom pounds as we slap through the chop, wind cutting at us, we're obtaining top speed.

The swells approaching the beach pile up, becoming steeper and closer together; old Bloody Wog is pounding through wave after wave as we close on the beach.

My right hand gripping the starboard davit tightens, knuckles turning white. Glancing my way, Mike holds the wheel, his own knuckles bone white. The blood is forced from his hands by the pressure being applied to the wheel. I am just riding this disaster to the beach; Mike is driving us to our doom.

Nole clutches the port davit lightly his big happy-go-lucky grin leading us to our destruction. In his professor's voice he tells Mike, "Ride the back of a swell up onto the beach, even if you have to adjust your speed a little."

Approaching the beach, a wave is breaking ahead of us. Mike slows the boat, adjusting our speed on the wave, riding the white water up the beach. We're sliding onto the sand, a thin film of water running to the dry sand carries us with it. The Wog comes to a halt well above the surf, it is like sliding in on a magic carpet. A beach landing turns out to be nothing like I expected.

***

The Bloody Wog is on the trailer, and Big Bertha Butts is polluting the pristine Oregon air. Sitting in a line of waiting boats and rigs it is almost our turn to unload. Marty and Albert's rig is just ahead of us, they caught fifteen silvers standing between the rigs we're discussing the day's events.

It won't be long now, and we'll know how much we made today. Finally, it's our turn at the scales.

"Well, how did you do today?" Hogie dumps Marty and Albert's fish into a fish box. His wife, Marline, fills the head and belly cavities with ice. Her tiny hands were encased in

huge orange gloves. Marlean is a small, fine-boned woman with beautiful brown hair cascading around her shoulder in ringlets. Her hair and makeup are done to a tee. She is wearing new Levi's and a very attractive sweater. There is blood and fish gurry everywhere, except on Marlean.

"We got ten."

Throwing open the fish box, a captain delivering fifty tons of albacore couldn't have shown any more pride in his catch.

Hogie is waiting for us to throw our fish in the scale, "You got ten, not bad, not too bad for your first day."

I'm pitching them into a stainless-steel tray hanging from a large round scale. The fish landing gently, head first, flat, on their sides. The scale needle is bouncing toward a hundred pounds when we finish.

"Eighty-nine pounds," Hogie fills out our fish tag and signs the bottom.

Not bad, not too bad at all. We caught twenty-two dollars and twenty-five pennies worth of fish; it only cost twelve dollars for gas and four bucks for bait. Losing two spreads, at about four dollars each. On top of that Mike and I ate five of Nole's sandwiches, figure a buck a piece. Just a quick estimate of our standing: we lost only two dollars and twenty-five pennies if you don't count wages.

Now, I know why fishermen are always talking about this easy money.

***

The next day we got up at four and went out. We stayed out for fourteen hours and caught nothing. The day after that we did the same. The third day we caught nothing, absolutely FUCKING-NOTHING!

Following Nole and, Marty and Albert around like a puppy dog, they caught fish. We couldn't catch a cold.

Each day is a clone of the one before. Starting cold and overcast the sun breaking through at about ten O'clock, the rest of the day fine and warm, each day the Pacific Ocean, living up to her Spanish name. She's a calm ocean, a swell running from five to six feet, the period over a minute. Everything is just perfect... Except for one damn thing, we can't catch a fish.

It's the end of our third fruitless day. Mike and I are walking back to our humble abode, two very dejected souls. Standing out in front of her trailer is Virginia, our neighbor. Virginia is always happy to see us. We've been getting along swimmingly; at least, with half of our neighbors to the east, Archie Bunker, 'Joe,' has not spoken a word to us. He hates us. We're young you know, that makes us bad.

"Boys, oh boys, how are you? Have you been catching lots of fish?"

I shake my head, "No, we haven't caught a fish in three days."

"No, that's terrible, you're joking aren't you? Joe has been doing great. We've been making a hundred dollars a day, every day."

Walking up, Mike throws in, "No, it's the truth... We haven't caught a fish since the first day of the season."

"Oh my, oh my, I just don't know what to say. My oh my, how can you even afford to go out or even eat?"

***

It's dark, not quite four in the morning. We're sitting at our table, trying to force down oatmeal again. This meal will be our only food until dark.

There is a pounding on the door then it flies open. Joe, 'Archie Bunker,' sticks his head in, "You ain't catchin' no fish?"

Shaking my head, "Nope."

I'm nervous. He must be mad at us. After all, these are the first words that he has ever spoken to us. Ever.

"Here."

Archie Bunker throws a green and yellow hoochie on the table. Then the door is empty. It's as though he was never there.

Mike and I stare at one another, "What was that about?"

"That, my good friend Ben, was the hoochie fairy."

"That, my good friend Mike, is the ugliest fairy I've ever had the misfortune to see."

"They do seem to grow them ugly in this part of Oregon."

The hoochie is tied up, a hook and snap the whole deal, she's ready to go.

By our fourth day of fishing, we have our system down pretty well. No longer are we the white-knuckled launching duo. In fact, Mike and I are relaxed and professional in our demeanor and comportment.

A typical morning starts with a free cup of coffee, shared with Hogie and any other fisherman buying bait. There is always talk of yesterday's fish. Someone will give his opinion of which direction to go today. Armed with this straight scoop we saunter out to Bertha and head west.

The boat is gassed up the night before. That way, the leaking gas has a chance to evaporate. Coffee cups in hand, we drive across Highway One, heading north, up the beach. Exiting the rusty doors of Big Bertha Butts, hinges cracking and popping with each movement.

Once on the beach, we stand in the cold morning fog, for a while.

At the port side I'm preparing the Wog for launch. Mike is doing the same on the starboard, lashing poles into holders, setting davits. We're getting her ready for the open ocean. Mike jumps into the boat he prepares to pull start the motor. One mighty pull and the engine turns over half a dozen times. She coughs once, just once. Another pull and she repeats the first performance of the morning. Taking his jacket off, Mike pulls again, spinning half a dozen times, coughing twice, she burps. A puff of exhaust fumes makes a smoke ring, the ring lazily drifting upward.

Standing and watching Mike work, I shiver. My heavy sweater still smells of gas. If the smell doesn't dissipate soon, I may have to wash it.

Mike pulls on the starter rope again. This time, she only spins over three times before she tries to catch, with a cough, wheeze, and puff of smoke.

Mike places a foot on the engine cover, "OK, you son of an engine, you're going to start or bleed."

This time, he pulls with even greater effort. The engine pops to life with a ring-a- ding-ding-ding, pop pop pop sound. Judging that the motor is warm enough, Mike kills her, killing the engine with a flick of his wrist. The motor dies while he is still flat out on his back. On that last pull Mike trips over his sea boots, then he magically arises from the deck using levitation.

The mountains to the east have the hint of a golden glow. I love this life.

We no longer need to speak during launching; words are not necessary. Nodding to Mike I walk toward Big Bertha Butts, she is idling in the cold clear Oregon air, spreading her noshes vapors.

Sliding under the steering wheel, I grasp it in my left hand, throwing my right arm over the bench seat I back Big Bertha Butts with total aplomb toward the dark ocean. I'm at full speed, we're roaring backward, foam from a wave passes the gleam of our headlights. I slam the breaks; Big Bertha grinds to a halt, as the Bloody Wog slides into that cold wet sea.

Parking Big Bertha Butts, I trot toward the Wog. Nearing the surf line, I reach down without breaking stride. Up comes one boot, then the other. With the boots up, a feeling of anticipation wells up in me. Splashing into the waves behind Mike, he rolls aboard. I grasp the stern, pushing the boat into deeper water. I'm hopping at every wave; Mike drops the engine next to me.

It's time to do my little; hop, shuffle, sideways dance. Jerking on the pull rope, Mike pulls our little thirty-five-horse outboard to life. She purrs. Spinning to face the helm he throttles up. Rolling over the stern, I land on the deck facing skyward. The low clouds are rushing overhead as we gain speed; once again, the Wog's high-raked bow breaks through the surf. The pounding surf is small rivulets compared to our gallant vessel's bow. We're away, away from the beach, and so, starts another day living off the bounty of the Pacific Ocean.

Looking north, there's Albert and Marty in the Kisutch, waiting for us. As with every other morning this season, we follow them to which-ever fishing spot they choose.

When we bought the boat, no electronics were mentioned in the deal. She did come with a C. B. radio. There is only one problem: the radio puts out, but can't receive. Not a peep, not a scratch; nothing comes from our speaker except silence.

Information is the lifeblood of a fishing boat. Without information a fishing boat is like a blind man, a blind man searching through Death Valley for water. This realization is just dawning on us as we grope for some kind of success in this venture.

When Marty and Albert slow up, we do the same. When they put fishing gear into the water, we put fishing gear into the water. They're our mentors, our only link to anyone who can catch a fish. We follow them around like a lost duckling.

After running north for half an hour, we slow to troll speed, the gear is going out. At the third spread, I remember the green and yellow hoochie with the red eyes. The hook poking me through my shirt makes it easy to remember. Pulling the hoochie from my breast pocket, I smile, "A *gift? A gift from Archie Bunker, the hoochie fairy, whoed- a-thunk-it?"*

Un-snapping a hoochie from the next spread going down, I snap on the green and yellow hoochie. The rest of the gear goes out as before. Taking the wheel from Mike I grunt at him; Mike grunts back, then he starts his side out.

Mike has just gotten his gear in the water; my side is shaking with that funny shimmy motion, like when we had Nole aboard. It kind of looks like that first day, that day we could say "fish-on." Cranking up my heavy, thirty-pound cannonball, I have high hopes. Spread after a spread comes up empty, just like every other day this season.

At each spread, I stop cranking, reaching over the handle I put the break on. It's a circular wedge device; pulled tight friction holds the cannon-ball in place. Our breaks do not always work as designed. Sometimes, a cannon ball falls free and the break always has some drag. *Like, it's a real drag, man.*

Cranking up the forty pounds of lead and stainless-steel wire is heavy work. Getting to a spread, I apply the break, unsnap it and pull it in. Repeating this routine time after time; again, I get to the green and yellow hoochie with the red eyes. A ten-pound salmon is hanging onto the hoochie; a hook protrudes from his upper lip.

Pulling him in I replay Nole's words in my head, "Go slow, don't push him, let him come to you, get the net ready."

Then, my own words rush in. *"First fish in three damn days; don't lose him, don't lose him. If you lose him Mike will kill you. We may never catch another fish, what if he gets away? Oh my God, oh my God! Don't lose him."*

Mike slides the net under him, the salmon pops from the water, flying through the air, he tumbles onto our deck. The fish is everywhere, flopping, spinning, dancing.

"Mike! Where's the gaff, the gaff?"

"I don't know. We haven't needed it for days. Oh... lookup forward under my coat, my bear coat."

"What's it doing under your coat?"

"I was using it for a pillow."

"A pillow? A gaff hook?"

During this heated exchange the two-foot-long salmon is still flopping. Spinning himself in our net, chaos reigns supreme on the deck. I vault the fish-box and race to the bow. Picking up Mike's coat, I shake it. The gaff-hook falls, six-inches of stainless-steel hook, strikes the deck next to my foot. No big deal. It didn't penetrate the deck but half an inch.

Gaff in hand, I jump the fish box again, and, whack, whack, whack. This salmon is no longer causing any trouble, not on the deck of the Bloody Wog.

Mike's eyes meet mine, "Remind me not to get smart with you."

"Hey Mike, don't get smart with me."

We grin at each other, happy to have a fish aboard. It's been a long three days; a very long three days indeed.

The day is progressing; we're getting fish. Twelve fish, all of them off the green and yellow hoochie with the red eyes.

Landing the third fish of the day as Mike looking over his shoulder, mumbles, "Well, the Archie Bunker Super Hoochie strikes again."

"Hey, that's a great name for her. She's deadlier than a shotgun at point-blank range."

Howling out our laughter, we're our own best audience. The curse of the Bloody Wog is broken. We caught a fish. God, it feels good.

Since we couldn't hear anyone calling us, we never talk on our radio, and it would be like a deaf man having a conversation with a blind man. One shouting, one using sign language, there sure wouldn't be communicating going on.

***

Sliding up onto the beach, it must be around six o'clock. Marty and Albert are cranking the Kisutch up onto their trailer. Walking to their rig, I'm one "highliner" exchanging the news of the day with another. Right?

"So, Marty, how did you guys do today?"

"Oh, we got ten, not too good."

Marty and Albert have been feeling low, then bad, and yesterday they felt responsible for our lack of success. They've been under-playing their own catches, so we won't feel so bad. It hasn't been working.

"We got twelve, all ten pounders."

"Wow, that's great, twelve, man, you beat us, good going!"

Marty slaps a high five with me, his grin infectious making me feel even more successful than I did before, if that is possible.

"Yea we got us an Archie Bunker Super Hoochie, deadlier than a shotgun at close range."

Spinning on my heels, I walk away. Knowing, just knowing, they'll squirm like a worm until they can take a look at our new secret weapon.

Walking up to get Big Bertha Butts, I drop back by the Bloody Wog. Mike is putting the poles forward. He's looking at me with a; what is wrong question on his expression.

"I just thought you should know... we beat Marty and Albert by two fish."

Mike Looks over my shoulder at the Kisutch. Using my body to block their view, he put his hand out for a low five. I bring my hand down on his with a resounding smack and then walk away.

Maybe it's the soft sand, or maybe the flush of success. Maybe I've lost what little skill I have in backing up a trailer. Whatever is wrong, what I'm doing is not working. This is my third attempt at getting our old wooden trailer under the Wog. Each time I try to go back under the boat, the bow pushes off to the north. Old Bloody Wog is a little closer to falling off the trailer with each try.

This has never happened before. There is a possibility of losing the trailer and Big Bertha Butts in the bargain. That is, if we get stuck in the sand on an incoming tide.

Loading the boat on the trailer has been a cakewalk so far this season. It's easy: back the trailer up to the bow of the boat, make sure the aft roller and the bow is perpendicular, and then gun it. The boat rolls up the trailer until the stem clears the ground. Then Mike or I crank the Wog the rest of the way up.

When the trailer touches the bow, I gun Bertha backwards. Up the old Bloody Wog comes, then she falls halfway off the trailer. Pulling forward, I take another run at it. Again, the Bloody Wog loads on the trailer catty corner pulling out. I try again; for a third time.

One more time, "Jee-zus, this is getting worse the more I wool it."

The tide is coming in. Each attempt to load the boat is less successful than the last. Irritated by my own incompetence, I jump out of Bertha. Slamming the door, I run back at and begin cranking on the Wog. The wire on the trailer winch is much heavier than normal wire. It is a cast-off half-inch cable from a troller's anchor winch.

Using my full one hundred and sixty-five pounds of bone, muscle, and anger, I am going to force this boat onto that trailer. I crank and things begin to tighten up; the trailer winch groans, and I'm cranking with all my might. The hitch creaks a small popping sound comes from between my legs. It's going to work this time; I'll make it work.

The Bloody Wog slides over the rollers at an angle. The weight on the trailer is such that the force on the hitch is straight up. Our after-most roller is stuck in the sand. It ain't rolling, not a bit, not at all. Nothing wants to give, I redouble my efforts, by applying maximum force to the problem. SNAP!

The trailer hitch releases from the ball; standing straddle the trailer, I'm in the best position for this kind of work. The tongue rises up like a sperm whale breaching, striking me in the groin.

"Huff-OO-ah!"

Releasing the winch, I grab myself. It seemed like a good idea at the time. The old Wog starts to roll backwards… FINE! The rollers won't work going up; they roll just fine backwards. The winch handle is whipping around in a circle. The Bloody Wog pulls wire off the winch like a rabid dog at the end of a leash. In deep pain, I sway into the path of the winch handle. It catches me in the forehead, just above my left eye, cutting a swath up to the hairline. The blow knocks me backwards onto the sand. Luckily, I still have two good hands. So, I grab myself in both places that hurt, and boy, do they hurt.

It hurts so much that I want to run, but I can't get up. Running anyway, while I'm lying there on my side, my legs drive me around in a circle, my head drilling a hole in the beach.

"Hey, you look just like one of the Three Stooges, kind-a-like Curly going around in a circle like that," Mike comments. Then he lets out a deep-throated "nuk-nuk-nuk," followed by a high pitched "we-bee-bee-bee-bee." He entertains himself by playing all three parts of the Three Stooges for a while.

This strikes me as very funny, and I want to cry but know that I can't. I am supposed to be a man now, so I laugh, hard and loud, and Mike laughs with me.

Standing there, his fist on his hips, he watches me for a few minutes, letting me get my breath.

"Are you going to get out of the way? I need to hook this thing up. Or, are you going to lay there like a dead salmon?"

"Lay here like a dead salmon. Why?"

"Well, the tide is coming in, and we did just buy Bertha fifty bucks, you know? Roll over anyway. I don't want to drag the boat over you."

Groaning, "Ok."

Hogie walks up, peering down at me he opines. "Funny time to take a nap. Don't you have some fish to unload?"

Kicking a foot onto Bertha's bumper, Mike replies, "As a matter of fact, we do have fish to unload."

Sitting up, I'm looking through a red haze on my left side. Blood is running into that eye. "What are you doing here, Hogie?"

"The sand is soft today. Lots of problems loading boats. Lots of fishermen are getting stuck. Brought my rig down to pull guys out. Thought you guys were stuck. I didn't think Ben would be taking a nap, not in the middle of all this fun."

Hogie reaches down with a hand; I reach up with one. Pulling me to my feet he nods toward the fish company. "Let's get you loaded up. Then we'll clean that cut up so Ben here doesn't die of blood poisoning."

Pain shoots through my head and groin as Hogie pulls me to my feet. He did get me moving when Mike couldn't.

***

Bertha is pulling the old Wog into the unloading line. My head is pounding; the throbbing of my other wound has lessened to a mild roar. Mike is driving while I lay my head back and relax. Hogie beats on my window, trying the window crank and wonder of wonders, it works, the window is squeaking slowly down.

Hogie looks in at me, "Come on inside. I want to get that head wound cleaned up, maybe Mike should run you up to the hospital?"

"Naw, I'm OK, really Hogie. You're right you know, a blow like this could have killed me if it hadn't hit me in the head. You can't hurt an Irishman, not by hitting him in the head any ways?"

"Well, come on in. I want to look at it in the good light."

Blood still oozing down my face, we saunter into the fish company store. Debbie is helping another young fisherman who is buying hoochies. They aren't the Archie Bunker Super Hoochie. I'm relieved; our secret weapon is still a secret. It's just us, and Archie Bunker, who knows about the Archie Bunker Super Hoochie.

Glancing at my face; Debbie's smile of greeting turns to a look of concern. "My God, what happen to you? Are you alright? Come over here, sit down, we need to wash that cut out. Sit here in Hogie's chair."

Nobody but Hogie sits in Hogie's chair, but Debbie is being firm, so I mind her, she seems to be in charge.

Debbie walks from the room, Hogie shrugs his shoulders, "You're in good hands here. After she gets it cleaned up, I'll come take a look at it. I don't care what you and Mike say, if it's bad enough, you're going to the hospital."

My head hurts too much to argue, so I shake my head yes, '*I don't mean it. I ain't going to no hospital. We don't have enough money to eat, much less pay for a damn doctor.*'

Debbie walks back into the storefront. She's dressed in one of her skintight stretch tops, it clings to her perky little figure. Carrying a large bowl filled with water, she sways toward me, lucky me. A towel is thrown over her lovely shoulder, auburn hair, soft and shining, flows down her back, and her halo of auburn catches the setting sun. Beneath her stretch top is a tight pair of levis; they hug her round feminine curves and end in stylish flared bottoms. She looks sexy as hell. Hormones are making my head throb just looking at her, '*Her deep blue eyes express concern and intense what; longing, interest, no, no way, man, she just doesn't want you to die on her?*'

Wetting the wash-rag she places it above my left eye. This is so cool; my right eye is free to admire her tender young body.

The water is warm, and she is gentle in her ministrations; up close, she inspects the cut. A light sprinkle of freckles covers her cute up turned nose. She flashes me a smile, then returns to a concerned, business-like demeanor.

While she is washing my wound, I'm able to admire her young firm body.

"I'm not hurting you, am I?"

"No, it feels good... I like it."

"It's really not too deep. I think you'll be all right. How did this happen?"

"Well, ah, I'd hate to tell you the truth... it makes me look really stupid. I could tell you... Mike hit me with a gaff-hook. He went absolutely wild when we hit a bite."

"Did he... really?"

She might buy this, brightening for a second. No, I can't lie like that. Nobody would believe that Mike could go mad in a bite.

My voice takes on a sad quality when I speak, "No. No, like I said, I would just look like a klutz if you knew what really happened."

Debbie is busy ministering to me. Getting a glimpse down her top, every now and then, I see that she is wearing a black bra. Wow! A black bra! I've never seen a black bra before on a real girl. This is just great, just great.

To control my lust, I begin a conversation, my voice quaking with delight, "Debbie? Ah, ah, tell me about yourself?"

"Oh, I don't know. There isn't a lot to tell. I graduated from high school this year. I'll be going to college this fall on a scholarship. Pretty boring, huh?"

"No, not at all. I find you fascinating, truly fascinating."

Debbie brightens, "I won the Dory Derby Queen contest this year."

"Wow, you did? You're the first Beauty Queen I've ever talked to."

'I wonder? If I had money, I could probably ask her out. If I wasn't so shy that is. What if I just told her the truth? Just tell her

that I can't take her anywhere because I only have two dollars to my name. We could go for a walk on the beach. No, no girl would just want to go for a walk on a moonlit beach. Would they?'

Silence is pervasive in the room. It is stretching into an uncomfortable solitude. At least Debbie has my cut to keep her occupied; all I have to do is, stare at her perky breast moving around under her shirt. Actually, keeping track of Debby's firm young breasts is not at all a bad sideline.

The bell over the door rings with a tinkling sound, diverting both Debbie and I from our tasks.

Her's of healing the sick, and mine of watching her firm young body move around inside of skin-tight clothes. Nole is the bell ringer. Walking in under the ringing bell, Nole's friendly grin precedes him into the room. "Hey, how's the bed, I mean, the head, the head?"

"It has gotten a lot better since Debbie has been working on me."

"Good, good, I thought that might help. Well, as soon as you are bandaged up here, you and Mike come over for supper."

Nole turns to leave, "Oh, by the way, Marty told me to ask, what is an Archie Bunker Super Hoochie?"

"We'll tell you after dinner, nothing in life is free."

Pushing Nole's front door open, we spy a small living room cluttered with fishing boots, jackets and old furniture. Marty and Dawn stroll in from the kitchen; turning, Dawn throws both hands into the air.

"Marty, I want you to go to Shorty's and get a gallon of milk for dinner."

"OK, Mom, want me to take the wagon?"

"Al has the wagon already; he went to the store for me earlier. Maybe the Boys can take you?" Dawn looks at my bandaged head, "Oh, I hate to ask Ben, especially after his accident."

Drawing my eyebrows together in thought, I gape at Dawn. *Accident I can't remember any accident. Oh, that accident. R*eaching up, I touch my forehead where my bandage is. I have just enough class not to touch my other sore spot. I've never been allowed to consider a random act of stupidity an accident. My father was always tough on random acts of stupidity.

"That's OK, Dawn. I don't mind taking Marty to Shorty's, wherever Shorty's is?"

Walking by, Marty grabs my shirtsleeve, "It's not far, I'll show you."

Following Marty from the living room, the three of us head into the cool Oregon evening.

Dawn trots out onto the front porch, "Don't hang around with Shorty all night; I need that milk right away."

We're all slamming car doors in the midst of this plea for responsibility. Dawn begins waving at us, thinking that we didn't hear her. *We're not that responsible, but really. We're just going to get milk, come on?*

Hanging the little Stang into gear, I swing by the porch. "Have no fear Dawn, we'll be right back."

Dropping the Mustang into reverse, I back us down the long driveway, kicking sand up as we go.

We're at the four-way stop, the only one in Pacific City.

Al and Rob, with Scott in the back, pull up to the other stop sign. Marty waves out the window at Albert, and Robby waves back, pulling through the intersection. We stop next to Albert, our windows are within a foot of each other.

"We're going to Shorty's to get milk, want-ta come?"

"Yea, we've got Mom's salad makings here, but she won't need them until dinner time."

Shaking my head, "Yea, she said she can't cook without the milk anyway. You guys might as well come along."

"See you at Shorty's."

By this time two other cars have pulled up to the stop signs. They are just setting there, apparently waiting for us to complete our conversation.

Looking over at Marty riding shotgun, I comment. "You know, man, I love small towns."

"Why?"

"Two cars waiting for us to finish talking, and they don't even honk."

Marty shrugs, "You just don't know small towns, Ben. They were just listening in on our conversation, trying to get some gossip."

"They were still nice enough not to interrupt."

"Well, that's true."

We're driving through Woods, the town that's not a town. Steep coastal mountains rise on our left, heavily forested with tall pine and fir trees to our right is a beautiful rolling meadow. There's a lovely farmhouse, and a big red barn, snuggled down along-side the Nestucca River. The road is a good quality, well maintained, without many ruts or chuck-holes. It's pushing eight o'clock; the sun is slipping below the tree tops.

Marty gestures to our right; doing his bidding, I swing off of the road and end up on a mud and cow flop driveway. "This is Shorty's dairy; it's cool, man. You'll like it."

Passing a small, wood-frame, one-story house, Marty continues his tour guide description. "This is where Shorty lives, a dairy like this might produce two hundred gallons of 'grade A milk', a day. Shorty milks twice in a day, by hand."

We're ploughing on up to the big white barn in ruts of cow flop. The aroma wafting up from the piles of cow paddies is intense. If the demand for cow shit ever out strips the supply, Shorty will be a rich man. Walking out of the barn, Shorty stands at the entrance. A short man of about sixty-five, he's wiry of frame, with large forearms and a bucket in each hand.

Mike, Marty, and I climb out of the Mustang. Standing around in the cow flop, we wait for Albert and Robby, with Scott in the back, to drive in. Shorty waves at us. I don't know if he is a friendly guy, or if he recognizes Marty. Marty raises a peace sign in greeting back. The other guys drive up; they're taking their time getting out of the station wagon. We stand there and wait, waiting for a bell weather to choose a direction.

Marty starts the procession toward Shorty, "Hey Shorty, what's happen-in-man? Mom sent us for milk."

Shorty smiles at Marty, then looks away toward the ground and to the left of us, "Hi Marty, hi Albert, come on in, bring your friends, did you bring a container?"

Marty lifts a one-gallon jar in both hands. "We brought two."

Shorty is dressed in a red and black flannel shirt, old Levis and knee-high rubber boots. His voice is soft and raspy as though from disuse, "Come on in, this way, boys."

Shorty won't meet our eyes when he speaks. Glancing shyly sideways, he smiles after every sentence. The smile is kind of his punctuation.

We troop along behind Shorty, three rows of two boys per row, Shorty is the head of our column.

Clearing my throat, "Ah-hmm, I've never been in a dairy before, this is really... something? You don't see a place like this every day."

"Do you like it, really?"

Like it, is not exactly how I would describe my feelings about the dairy. But I can tell pride of ownership when I hear it, "Yea... like I said, this is not something you would ever see in Concord, California."

Shorty swells with pride. He even swaggers a little, striding through his domain, "This un over here, she is Old Blue, I named her after Babe the blue ox. This un on our right now we call her Martha after my mother. I always stop and pet her. She would get her feelins' hurt if I didn't. And this un is..."

Walking down the barn, Shorty stops and introduces us to every animal in the barn. They're all his family.

Shorty stops to explain. "I won't buy one of those new, fan-dang-gulled milking machines. If-in you buy one of those dam machines, ya got to have more cows to pay for it.

Pretty soon, you're just workin' for money. What's the use of that?"

"I sure can't see why anybody would work for just money" I reply for the group.

So far, everywhere we have been on the dairy; cow flop has been the one ubiquitous substance tying the place together.

Walking into the milk storage room, is like walking into an operating room; so clean, so sterile. You can't even smell cow manure in here. Shorty takes Marty's milk jugs and sets them down by a large stainless-steel vat. The vat is fourteen or fifteen feet in diameter, and four feet high. It's refrigerated to keep the milk fresh.

Shorty opens up the top of the vat; picking up a pristine stainless-steel bucket, he dips out two gallons of ice-cold milk awaiting shipment.

"Now you boys, come on over to the calving barn; Thalma just had her third calf."

A little over an hour and a half after we got to the dairy, we started to crawl back into our cars. Albert spots the big two-story house next door, "Let's go over and see Helen."

Marty shuts the door of the Mustang he's holding, "Let's go."

The next thing we know, Albert and Marty are staggering toward an old ramshackle house. The four of us look at one another, Mike shrugs, and then we follow. All of us join the procession, up for any new adventure.

Climbing up a long set of stairs at the top, Marty knocks on the rickety wooden door. He's looking through the small panes of glass which fills the top half of the door. The glass is so old that much of it has slumped toward the bottom of the small square panes, distorting the interior.

Even with the distortion from the old glass, the figure within is a thing of beauty. Over Marty's shoulder, I can see a young woman walking toward us. She has long, brown, naturally curly hair. Her generous figure is only partially hidden by an old white fisherman sweater. Pulling open the door, this sumptuous vision throws her arms around Marty. Giving Marty, the lucky mug, a full-bodied hug; Marty hugs her back, lingering in her embrace. Envy fills my heart; why Marty?

Turning to Albert she throws her arms around him; first Marty, now Albert? This winsome beauty throws an arm around both of them, herding them into her house. What a couple of lucky dogs. At least, now I know why we came by to see Helen. Helen is beautiful.

Helen looks over her shoulder, "Come on in you guys."

Helen is in her mid-twenties. There's a womanly air about her, she has porcelain skin and the fine features of a classic Greek beauty. Hair, long dark brown hair, frames the eloquent features of her fine-boned face. Filing through the open door we're in awe, this is a real woman's house, cool.

More women come trooping down from upstairs. Hippie chicks, these are hippie chicks, for sure. At least they look like hippie chicks. Lose women? Real cool.

Helen still has an arm around Albert and Marty, "Guys, these are my roommates, Beatrice and Sharon. Guys, these are Marty and Albert's friends."

Beatrice is a heavy-set girl with ponderous breasts and wide hips. Sharon, small in stature with wild, frizzy red hair, has a demeanor to match.

Beatrice breaks ahead of Sharon, jogging down the stairs, "Albert you big hunk, give me a hug; I could juss eat you up."

Beatrice speaks with a slight lisp. She's joking, of course. All this enthusiasm for... Albert? Crushing Al with a big bodied hug, maybe she's not joking? She lays a deep and serious kiss on him for good measure. Nope, she's not kidding.

Al gallantly fights free of her grasp. She coos to him, "Oooo Al, you're so cool." His face burns red with embarrassment.

Spotting Al's embarrassment, Helen joins in on the fun, "No Al, Bea's right, you're gorgeous to look at."

Albert brightens to this complement, flexing his sizable arms, Al turns and strikes a pose.

Sharon joins the feeding frenzy, "OH Al, you're just so cool!"

Mike points to the rest of us, "So what are we, chopped liver?"

The feeding frenzy for Albert's ego is quashed with Mike's comment.

Helen waves a graceful arm around the room, "Well, boys find a seat."

We all find seats on the couch and old chairs scattered around the living room.

Helen offers us herb tea. Being gentlemen, we accept, waiting a time with patience for the water to heat.

I've never drunk herb tea, only real tea, iced. After tea and genteel conversation, with Led-Zeppelin playing in the background at a hundred and twenty decibels, we take leave of our new friends.

Pulling into Nole and Dawn's driveway, we all crawl out of the Mustang. Marty grabs the now warm milk, one jug under each arm.

"I sure hope Mom cooked something while we were gone. I'm hungry."

The house is dark and silent. Somehow, it has kind of a hungry, pissed-off air about it. Feeling that Marty has just voiced a forlorn hope, I, for one, don't feel inclined to follow him inside and try and forage in Dawn's kitchen. Not tonight, I don't.

"Come on, Mike lets go home and re-heat some oatmeal."

***

The next few days pass without much to mark them, one from another. We now have a full array of Archie Bunker Super Hoochies. An Archie Bunker Super Hoochie resides on at least every other hook. They've been saving the day for us. We haven't been skunked since Joe gave us one. Some days, we get eight fish, some days ten, one- day we got twelve. We aren't doing great. We're not getting rich, but we're making expenses now.

This is a day like yesterday or the day before. It could be a day like tomorrow for that matter. It is a nice, flat calm, Oregon ocean with a lump of five or six feet on it. There is a slight breeze of five to ten knots blowing from the northwest. It is just another day until my side starts shaking.

"Mike, take the wheel, I've got a fish on."

Mike is lying up under the bow, catching a catnap. His feet are sticking out over the gear locker, which is just aft of the bow cowling. Mike's face appears between his- sea boots, his eyes still heavy with sleep.

Putting the fish cleaning rack down forward of the fish box, I turn to Mike, "Come on, I've got one on my heavy. Time to go to work."

As the days have passed, our sharing of tasks has worked into a routine. That routine seems to be working just fine. Both Mike and I are eager hands, willing to do more than our share. This makes light work for both of us.

'My side,' is the port side, I put the gear out in the morning on that side, then run the port side gear most of the time. 'Mike's side' is on the starboard, he does the same on he's right-handed, and I'm left.

Mike pulls out one of his levitation tricks to remove himself from our sleeping quarters. Our sleeping quarters are a small hole up under the bow. Sleeping is done a-top some mildewed life jackets. They're almost as old as the boat.

It takes me five minutes to crawl into this hole, and ten minutes to crawl out.

To extricate himself from our foc-sel, Mike levitates to an elevation almost equal to the bow cowling. Then, he lets the boat idle forward while he remains stationary. It is sure a neat trick, but I just can't get the hang of it.

In ten seconds, Mike is standing beside me. "Let me take the wheel. You grab that fish."

"I've got him."

The heavy is coming up at a steady pace. My arm is going around in a circle, straining each fiber of my muscles. Cranking up the thirty pounds of lead, and ten pounds of stainless steel seven-strand wire is something akin to work.

The second spread down has the fish, reaching down I grab the line snap.

Mike prods me, "I've got one on my side. I'm going to get him, while you land that one." Mike's voice is cracking with excitement.

This is the first time we've had two fish on at once.

Sliding the net under the fish I scoop the salmon up into the air. He's high, high over my head, thrashing and fighting. Flipping from the net, the twelve-pound salmon flies into Mike's back; striking him between the shoulder blades, the flopping fish knocks him forward and into the davit. The gurdy handle slips from his hand, the handle spinning round and round. The cannon ball is in free fall toward the ocean bottom.

Mike shoves his body into the spinning handle; the handle strikes him square in the chest with a dull thud. This may seem crazed, but it is the safest way to arrest its speed. If he tried to use his hands to stop that spinning handle, he would draw back a stub. Courage, pushing your chest into a handle rotating at sixty RPMs and gaining speed, just takes courage.

The salmon is flopping all over the deck. I'm chasing him around, trying to hit him in the head with a gaff hook. A cold, wet smack hits me in the center of the back. I find myself staring out through the green mesh of our salmon landing net…somehow, I don't think this is an accident. Looking around at Mike and grinning, I'm kind of proud of him. It takes a lot of skill to hit someone in the back with a ten-pound salmon.

We have two salmon on the deck, flopping, and tangling lines causing bedlam. Mightily, I raise the means of their destruction.

These two beautiful, predatory fish meet their ends in a rain of blows. Our gaff hook sends them to Valhalla for salmon.

Mike pulls the net from my head and shoulders, "I've got another one on the next spread!"

"Go ahead on that one; I'll get these two cleared away!"

We're both shouting, breathless with excitement. Less than five feet apart, yet we're loud enough to be heard back at the Cape. This is the first time we've ever caught more than one fish at a time; we're in-um!

I'm working, straightening up the deck Mike is bringing up another fish, which he lands without a net. I gaff the two fish on deck, stowing them away.

"I've got another one, clear that one away too. As long as I'm catching fish, I'm going to keep pulling-um!"

"Get-um, get them, I'll clear these!" Every fish we bring aboard is a three-to-four-dollar four-dollar-bill, and that's a lot of money, to us.

We're both as high as a kite. Adrenaline flows through our veins like we are athletes, and this little flurry of fish is the Olympics. The deck is clear; Mike throws another fish onto the deck. It's flopping and tangling gear in its death throws.

Adding to the confusion I throw another fish onto Mike's fish. Again and again Mike and I pitch fish onto our deck. We're in-um, we're in-um!

This bite has been going on for about an hour. Every fish is getting us more and more excited. Every second or third spread comes up with a salmon. For us, it is like finding El Dorado. Gold is shining everywhere. Now, this is fishing. We're making a lot of money in no time at all, and we ain't even working.

Having taken the wheel, I'm trying to keep us in the fish by using landmarks. I sighted in on Cape Lookout and lined up two trees at Sand Lake spit. Peering just over Mike's head, he is landing a bottom fish worth about twenty cents.

Bottom fish have very sharp spines about two or three inches long. When caught, they array these spines straight out to do maximum damage. The spines are laden with bacteria and are very painful.

Jerking like mad, Mike is trying to shake the hook free. Nope, no good, he's playing with the dang thing; getting serious, he picks up the fish and runs the gaff under the fish-hook. Pulling the monofilament line taunt along the side of its body. Mike lets the fish drop toward the deck, jerking the gaff-hook up. The light bottom fish flies toward Mike's hand like it has wings. Three or four spines are embedded into this hand.

"You firkin son of a sea cook! You lousy no-good-for-nothing bucket mouthed twenty cent fish!"

Rotating the gaff, Mike beats the whole Whalen-stuffing out of this poor fish. Bending down to one knee, Mike betters his position for beating our offending denizen of the deep. While beating him, slime starts flying from Mike's and the fish's heads at the same time and about the same color. It is kind of a clear, translucent, viscous mixture. The slime is of a kind rarely seen in polite company.

'A dog gone mad would resemble the scene I'm witnessing.'
Standing at the wheel station, I'm watching in horrified

fascination. '*Mad, he has gone mad. Oh my God, what do I do with a mad man on a small boat?*'

"Mike... Mike, are you feeling all right? Do you want to go in? Is there anything I can do for you? We can if-in you want, go in that is?"

Hearing my own voice, I'm tentative, trying to sound calm. I sound like a mother asking her child not to throw a temper-tantrum in the supermarket. Mike turns on me, his face bright red, his eyes red-rimmed and watery, slimy substance dripping onto the deck. He stares at me intently, slowly rising to his full height. He spreads his feet, bracing against the roll of the boat. Shifting the gaff-hook, the sun glints off the six-inch long stainless-steel spike. Blood and slime drip from the gaff to the deck. Drip... Drip... Drip. Slowly, ever so slowly, using his shirt sleeve from elbow to wrist, Mike wipes slime from his dripping face.

Quietly, Mike whispers, "Go in? Why the hell would I want to go in?"

Fear and adrenaline flow through my body; the flight or fight instinct is strong within me. What does one do when face to face with a mad man?

"You just don't look like you feel that well. We can go in if you want. Or maybe I could give you a break?

Do you want to lie back down? Go back up forward. That'd be all right."

"You want to do something for me?" Mike stares at me for a long moment, "So, you want to help, huh, do you? You can do something for me. Get me my... my damn allergy medicine from the console. Give me two of them damn pills."

He gives me a big grin, letting me know that he is still getting even with me.

Reaching the consul, I rummage around in the junk.

"No. No, I can't seem to find any pill bottles."

"That's all right. I'm so busy, I didn't even notice my allergies until you mentioned them."

"Man, you scared the heck out of me. I thought you'd gone off your rocker."

"Yea, I know."

***

It is morning; we had that little bite yesterday. Big Bertha Butts is putt-putting up the beach toward Cape Kiwanda. For once, the cloud of blue smoke is not visible; fog is swirling around us, hiding our smoke. Breaking to a stop just above the high tide line, Bertha's doors crackle open. The wind catches me full in the face, cutting in its chill and force. The beach is shrouded in a black mist. Headlights are gleaming in the fog, but we can't make anything out.

The sound of fishermen preparing for the sea can be heard in the mist. An outboard is being warmed up down south. There is the squeak of a davit up north. An order is given by a gruff voice next to us.

Working on the old Bloody Wog, we're preparing her for sea, too. Nole and Marty appear from the fog, like apparitions, except they clomp in their sea boots. Marty's shoulder-length hair blows in the wind. Nole's beard is dripping from the fog, a twenty-five-cent cigar protruding from the droplet-encrusted beard.

"What are you guys doing... Ben, Mike, where are you going?"

Cinching down one last time on the lashing of the port pole, I straighten to Nole's question. "We're going fishing. What are you doing?"

Nole shakes his head, "Well, I don't think that's a real good idea."

"Why not? You can't catch any fish on the beach."

Nole looks at me and then at Mike, cracking one of his big grins. "Oh, I don't know about that. A lot more fish have been caught on this beach than in fifty fathoms. You see, I don't like to go out if I can't see a hundred yards. Nor, if the wind is blowing fifteen or better."

Turning toward the sound of the breakers, all I can see is fog. "Well, we're almost ready to go. What do you think, Mike?"

Surf breaks on the beach out in the fog somewhere. Cold seeps into our bones, we're waiting for Mike to render his judgment. "I don't know. Nole and Marty know a lot more about this than we do. Let's wait, see what happens."

This sounds like sensible advice to me. "OK, we'll wait and see what happens?"

What happens is, Hogie's son, Benny, pulls up next to our rig. He's about twenty- five. And, fishing here has been his life. His boat is a twenty-two-foot Kelso boat, 'brand new and well built, with a Volvo inboard-outboard unit'. He is a highliner's highliner, and doesn't even talk to toads like us.

Benny pops out of his rig, a newer Jeep pickup. Rich! Man, to be a highliner.

Watching him prepare his boat, we gawk. Benny is at the pinnacle of dory fishing society. Standing over six feet tall, with broad shoulders, his black curly hair is sticking out from under a navy watch cap. Powerfully built, he is quick of movement and efficient. In five minutes, the boat is ready. Not even noticing the weather, he backs toward the ocean.

The sound of squealing breaks. His Kelso dory can be heard rolling off the trailer and then splashing into the sea. She must be A-beam, too, by now.

Pulling out of the fog, driving his rig above the high tide line he parks beside us. Throwing a two-finger salute in our direction, Benny trots into the fog. It is as though he never was here, except there is his empty trailer.,

"What about him? He ain't worried by this weather?"

Marty shakes his head, long hair flopping, slowly rubbing his chin. He's deep in thought.

"That's Benny. Benny can get away with that, he's a highliner."

"Maybe we should be doing what he's doing. Maybe we'd be highliners too?"

Marty wiggles his long hair again. "Naw, it's just not that simple, you can't be a highliner by following a highliner. Follow a highliner all you get is, is... depressed? Benny is a vacuum cleaner. The area behind his boat is devoid of all marine life."

Placing a hand on the gunwale of the Bloody Wog Mike mumbles, "Well, he won't have much competition out there, not today he won't."

Swinging aboard the Wog, Mike puts on his bear jacket. It's big, it's hairy, it's bulky, mostly it's ugly. It lives up under the bow, with the moldy lifejackets.

Nole hunches his shoulders against the cold. "Let's go down to my boat. Get some coffee. We'll wait and see what the morning brings. Generally, when the fog blows off, the wind comes up, you just don't want to be out there when that happens."

Heading up the beach, we grope our way toward the Nole's Ark. The four of us stride along, behind the line of dories, the front of their rigs snuggled up to the sand dunes.

Some of the boats are standing empty; others have a crowd standing around them. Sipping steaming coffee they're telling sea stories. Like us they are waiting for the weather to tell them what to do next.

These men seem to be enjoying the camaraderie of each other. And yet, they spend most of their time alone. When a man spends most of every waking hour alone, there is a comfort in sharing a cold, windy morning with men of the same back ground.

Walking along, voices are coming from the fog, just small snatches of conversations. Little parts of sea stories, bits of these men's lives, bits of which they feel proud enough to share.

A deep husky voice booms forth. "Man, it was rough, it was so rough, I was hanging on with both hands and my dick. If I never see waves that big again, it'll be just fine o..."

The next voice is more languid. Soft with the long vowel sounds used by the younger generation. "Like wow man. She had the best set of knockers I've ever seen. We were dance-in all over that fucking floor. It was really cool man. I'd grab her by the hands and spin her around; just so I could see her tatas jiggling'. She could have popped out one of my eyes with those nipples?"

Emerging from the fog, we spy a young man with long hair holding court. Three other long-haired young men, all up-and-coming dory fishermen, listen in awed silence.

One or two men from each group acknowledge us with a nod or a wave.

Striding past Archie Bunker, he lifts his head in greeting. Not a complete nod, not an invitation to visit, just a neighbor saying hi. But; his eyes say do not stop here, *'no hippies around my friends.'*

Archie returns to his story. He's telling a good one to a group gathered around his boat. Mike and I slow our walk. We want to hear a little of what he's saying.

"This huge smiley, is looking me right in the eye, daring me to try and net him. He has the subber rubber stretched out. He must have been a thirty-dollar fish. God, I needed that fish, so anyway, like I was saying, this was my first-year fishing. All I had was this little old sport fishing net. God, what a net, 'The Maxi Net?' Right under the brand name, it had a sticker. 'Net-em-All, the Big and Small.' Grabbing up my net, I've got all the faith of a true believer. Slipping it under this forty-pound King salmon, about half of the splitter slid into the net, but the bigger half wouldn't fit. Lifting my net with a mighty hoist, and out he flops. The splitter hits the end of the line stretches the subs out. All the way out, I swear! He turned and looked me right in the eye. His expression said, so you think you're tough, watch this. He spit the hook right at my face. The hoochie, flasher, and line would have hit me right in the face if the gurdy hadn't stopped it."

Having lingered long enough we pick up our pace. The next set of voices has just the insight we need. "No shit, there we were..."

Interrupting the story teller, another voice asks, "Do you know the difference between a sea story and fairy-tell?"

"No... Tell me, what's the difference between a sea story and a fairy-tell?"

"A sea story starts with; No shit there we were, and a fairy-tell starts with, Once upon a time..."

Arriving at the Nole's Ark; Bob and Robby are already there, yarning with Albert.

Bob turns to Rob, "We've got some cups in the console, go and get them. We'll share our coffee with these guys." Rob trots off into the fog, to do his father's bidding.

***

It has been about an hour and a half. All of us have exhausted our fish stories. The fog is beginning to lift, and the wind has gone from fifteen to a steady twenty knots.

Standing up from his fish box, where he was setting, Nole stretched.

"I've had enough of this, I'm going back to bed."

Bob unbends from the gear tray, bearing his weight.

"Me too."

Rubbing the soft blond stubble of my chin, "Bed, back to bed? Now that does sound good.

***

It is just after noon and it has turned out to be a beautiful day. Mike and I just finished a warmed-up bowl of mush. We're heading out to work on the Bloody Wog. I have hopes of finding Debbie in the office. I'll rap with her for a while if she's there. No need to tell Mike about my little plan, is there? Naw, why let him in on my good ideas?

At the Wog, we begin work on the projects discussed after our morning nap. Mike is putting a front on our console. He is cutting up a piece of plywood we salvaged. Plywood found in a road side ditch is free game, or should be. This plywood still has a luster to the paint. It's in fine shape. Being that before we salvaged it; it announced to the world what a great store the P. C. Market is. But the sign had come adrift in a winter storm and was lying face down along the road. Doing no one, no good at all where it was, we kind of saved it.

Me, I have plans to clean the plugs on Big Bertha Butts. Maybe, just maybe, she won't pollute the pristine Oregon air, quite so much. Also, she sure could use some extra power, pulling out of the surf. We're just getting a good start at our work. The Fiddler rumbles to a halt in his old beater of a pick-up. Dust settles on the scene as he ambles from his seat.

"Hey boys... how's it a hang-in?" his voice a quite southern drawl.

Lifting my head from under Bertha's hood, "We're hanging in there, good Fiddler. How are you doing?"

"Fine. It's really fine and dandy... just came down here to do a little work on the old Fiddler. You boys want a beer?"

Mike straightens up at that question. "Yea, we'd love a beer."

Being stupidly honest, I shake my head in the negative, "You should know that we're not twenty-one yet?"

"I don't remember asking your age. I asked about your thirst."

It dawns on me. The Fiddler knows we aren't twenty-one. He's just being a nice guy, "If the question is thirst, the answer is parched."

Fiddler reaches into his cab; throwing a beer to Mike. Handing me a beer, he smiles shyly. "Want some bear sausage, made it myself?"

The only kind of meat that Mike and I have eaten in the past three weeks is fish, and clams, and fish, and crab, and fish, and salmon, and fish, and bottom fish, not to mention mussels. Mostly, Mike and I have survived on oatmeal, fish and free meals from Nole's table. All meals from Nole's table are, in essence, fish.

Bear sausage sounds like a feast. Besides, working on your fishing boat, sitting on a beach in Oregon while drinking beer can only be topped off with bear sausage.

Pulling his Buck Knife from its pouch, the Fiddler flips it open with a flick of his wrist. He lays a greasy paper bag on the hood of his rig. Unwrapping the treat within, he is agonizingly slow. The wind blowing around us is puffing about twenty-five miles per hour. But the sun is out now. The sun is a warm cocoon against the cut of the wind.

Fiddler unrolls the greasy paper bag, pulling out a dirty sausage. The sausage is about two inches in diameter, and about half of it is missing. Red meat, thickly marbled with white fat, protrudes from a sheath of bear gut. This is home-made, hand-packed sausage; smoked in an old burnt-out refrigerator. Man, it doesn't get any better than this.

Jumping down from the Bloody Wog, Mike stumbles toward the meat in a catatonic trance. Laying down my Craftsman, half-inch drive ratchet, I join the mesmerized march toward the meat. Meat such a lovely sight.

The Fiddler's Buck Knife slices the sausage into eighth inch thick morsels. The Fiddler keeps cutting sausage until Mike and I have bellied up to the fenders. The bear sausage is salty, with is a strong taste of game, and a greasy aftertaste. It's a taste that mixes very well with warm Blitz beer.

"Well tell me, Fiddler, do you fish here year-round?" I ask around a mouth full of bear sausage.

"Naw", the Fiddler's mouth is likewise employed chewing bear sausage doused in beer. His pink gums flashed in the sunlight. "I, smack smack, tend bar in the winter time; last winter, I was a bouncer for a while. I ain't a gonna do that again. I'd rather crab. And, you can find yourself dead, fishing crab off the Oregon coast."

"Why don't you want to be *a* bouncer again? Especially if working on a crab boat is so dangerous?"

The Fiddler shakes his head. "Man, O man, those bars, they ain't so healthy either... you know?"

Finishing chewing, "Mumm," Mike gulps, "This is good, really good. The beer washes it down just right. Oh, I don't know Fiddler. Bars aren't so dangerous, just a bunch of drunks staggering around. You ought to see Ben and I when we're drunk. Give us a girl a piece and we're a couple of Teddy Bears."

Fiddler pushes his Greek fisherman's cap back on his head, his black oily hair shining in the sunlight. "Well, I can sum it up with one story. It happened last winter and still gives me the shivers thinking about it."

The Fiddler pops one more piece of bear sausage into his mouth, which he chews with gusto. "Oh man oh man, let me tell you about them bars. It was a Friday night, and I just got a job in this bar, I was supposed to be the bouncer. I wanted to make a good impression; it being my first night and all. I was a-wearing my brand-new pair of cowboy boots, a brand-new cowboy shirt, a red kerchief, and of course, my Stetson".

Mike pops his second beer from Fiddler's six-pack. "Fiddler, you aren't that big. No offense but you aren't any bigger than me. You just don't look like a bouncer."

"Well, I'm not; like I was a say-in… This was my first weekend working there. I wanted to impress the new boss. You know how it is? New job, good looking' babes, sitting on my ass and being paid to guzzle booze. It was a real good job for a fisherman.

It was a nice place. Down by the waterfront, all sorts of people came in there, some people after work, some couples out for the evening. All sorts of people, nice people, nice places.

It was around nine o'clock. Seven bikers come in, all liquored up. The boss-man, he told me to watch-um. So, I did exactly that, I sat there on my ass at the end of the bar sipping a beer, scared shitless, just watching. They were no problem, not till about their third round.

Their waitress was a real looker, knockers pointing to heaven, and legs that go all the way to paradise. This little waitress was a heavenly body in her own right.

She was serving a round to the bikers. About five of them cornered her at their table; they wanted her to get on top of the table to dance. Rowdy! Rowdy as hell. Past talking to, way past talking to. Not drunk enough not to know what they were doing. But they were drunk enough to not give a damn.

Two or three of them started putting their hands all over this lovely young thing. It was my job to stop them, but, what could I do against five guys? Five bikers? Seven, really, except a couple of them had wandered off.

My boss, he comes by again. "Hey are you going to stop them or what?"

Being a fellow of some logic, I ask, "How?"

"Kick the shit out of them."

Here my boss has given me a task, and I do want to keep this gig. So, up I jump all the way to the top of the bar. Running down the length of it, about forty feet, and then I jump. I lit right in the middle of their table and all hell breaks loose! The table is wet from spilled beer. My new cowboy boots slipped out from under me, whoosh."

Fiddler raises both hands in an arc starting at his belt and gliding above his head. "My feet fly into the air, coming up about even with my head, I catch two bikers under the chin, one with each cowboy boot. Then I started to fall. As I'm falling back toward the table, I grab out in panic. The only thing to grab hold of is the leather vest of the guy on each side of me. This pulls their heads together as they are breaking my fall. One of their foreheads

149

cracks the other guy in his nose, breaking it. You know... breaking bone can be heard for quite away.

When I saw what I'd done it scared the hell out of me. Me? I'm a peaceable type of feller, myself. You know me? I sure didn't want-um mad so, I let go of um. Well, it was just about this time that my back hit the table.

The Fiddler is into the story; his hands are moving with every detail. Raising a knee, he breaks an imaginary table leg over it, while balancing on one skinny leg.

"All four table legs break. One of the legs snaps off, catching a biker in the lower unit. He-he-he... if-in, you know what I mean? I can tell you, he's out for the count.

So, the table is falling, I'm falling, and beer bottles and booze is flying everywhere. It's chaos. Scared? I'm scarier than a hound dog down a well at sheep dipping time. We're talkin' scared. My hands fly out again, looking for something to grab. I find a crotch, the crotch of the biggest guy there. Hanging on for all I'm worth this time. Me, the tabletop, and their beers are all in free-fall. The biker whose crotch I've got a hold of, he comes on down with me. Although, he did keep trying to pry my fingers lose all the way to the floor. It-was somewhat kind of irksome?

I hit the floor with a thump and raised my head to look around. Lo and behold, bikers are lying all over the floor. I extract myself from my arms and legs. When the two missing bikers start coming at me, from two different directions. Lordy, Lordy, boys, my mind stops working totally. Survival instinct took over.

Jumping into the air coming down in a Karate stance I scream, 'aaa-eee.' They both stop in their tracks.

Looking around once more, I command them, "Get your trash and get out of my bar."

The whole place breaks out in applause. I belly up to the bar and drink two Jack Daniel's, fast just to calm my nerves. Later that night I went in to get my check, the boss wanted to know what was the matter, so I told him I quit.

He said, "You can't quit I'll give you a raise."

I told him, "I don't want a raise I want my check."

He told me, "All right, all right I seen you working tonight, you're good, and I started you low. Too low, I'll double your salary."

Man, I'll tell you, I needed the money... bad, but I told him. "Well, this is the first time I ever bounced anybody; I don't think I'm going to like it."

Mike and I are pounding the top of Fiddler's rig in gales of laughter. The Fiddler is wearing a shy smile. You know; it just might have happened the way Fiddler is telling it?

Marty and Albert pull up to us in a cloud of blue smoke and gravel dust. The dust settles on us, the bear sausage, and our beers. Popping from their launch rig, they join us.

Albert shakes the hair from his eyes. "Hey man, going to be a parr-tee at Helen's house. Tonight. You guys up for it?"

"Yea we're always up for a party."

Albert's hair blows into his eyes again. Using his fingers spread like a comb, he clears it one more time. "It'll start in a couple of hours. Around seven, Dad is cooking a salmon. Be there or be square."

Marty and Albert turn on their heels and head back to their rig, going where we know not? They don't even stick around hoping for a beer from the Fiddler. Strange?

***

The rock music rattles the glass panes as we stand at the door. I've been knocking at the door for a couple of minutes to no effect. The sound of my puny knocks has not summoned the Goddess Helen from her lair. Opening the door, we stride in. Mike and I are pristine in our cleanliness: freshly showered and shaved our hair still wet and slicked back, both of us in clean Levis and flannel shirts. We're dressed in our going to a hippie party finest.

Stepping into Helen's foyer, our hostess spots us, finally. Gliding toward us, she's dressed in a long skirt topped by a muslin blouse. It seems to me that she's not wearing a bra. Her long, slender arms wrap around Mike, giving him a full-bodied hug. Long and lingering, standing by their side with a hangdog look on my, face, I'm hoping for a hug. Helen does not disappoint. Disentangling herself from Mike, with some difficulty, Helen turns to me. Her arms slither around my neck. We hug. What seemed like an eternity of hugging, when seen from afar, is only an instant in time when I'm in the embrace.

Looking deep into my eyes, Helen murmurs. "Welcome to my home."

In that instant, I give her my heart, although I'm just a kid in her eyes.

"I have a big favor to ask of you tonight."

My mind races ahead, *"She needs me to spend the night. Maybe there's a bear getting into her house. Protection from a bear? Or, maybe the heat is off, she needs someone to -warm her bed. Yea that would be better".*

"Whatever you need, just let me know. I'll do anything for you."

"Could you pee on my pot? Our pot plants aren't getting enough Nitrogen. When you pee tonight, use our garden. OK?"

Meandering up, Marty opens a beer. Handing it to me as Helen glides away, trailed by her long and flowing hair.

"God, Marty, she is so beautiful."

"Yea." Marty throws an arm around my shoulder. "Did she ask you to pee on her pot?"

"Un-hun."

"Me too."

On the back porch, Nole's salmon is on the Bar-B-Que. The salmon is wrapped in tinfoil; with the coals a-sizzlin-away. Juices escaping from its tin cocoon set the aroma of baking fish onto the breeze. In a corner of the kitchen, Bob is drinking a beer with his son Robby. Marty and I wonder over to the couch, and flop down. It's too loud for conversation; sitting on the couch our heads are bobbing in time with the music. Slowly sipping our beers, we're just kind of letting the party happen around us.

Stepping in front of us, Nole jerks his head toward the back porch. He wants us out back, where the Bar-B-Que is. Stepping out onto the porch, Nole closes the back door. He shakes his head and clears the music.

"There, that's better. Marty, I want you and Ben to run to the store, grab some things for dinner."

Helen is out here rapping with Nole. Well, that's OK, Nole is an interesting guy, isn't he? I shouldn't be jealous just because Nole and Helen like one another, should I?

Marty sticks his hand out for the keys, "Sure, Dad, give me the keys."

"Here's a list, try to get everything on it, if you can't. Well, then... substitute something that will work."

"Sure, Dad sure, we'll get it all."

"Not like the milk... I want to eat tonight. I want food in you boys if you're going to be drinking."

"Ah Dad."

Heading back through the house, Marty has the keys jangling in his hand. Cornered by Beatrice, Albert sees us. Fainting right, Albert rolls left; making good his escape, he is out the door hot on our trail.

We're walking down the long stairway when Robby pounds down the stairs after us. "Hey, I'm coming."

Marty's head swivels back up the stairs, "Far-out, man."

At the car we pile into it according to our place in line. Marty is under the wheel, with me in the front seat, riding shotgun. Albert and Rob climb in the back. Marty has just gotten the car started when Bea pulls Al's door open, hopping in, she plops onto Albert's lap.

Looking around from the wheel, "We all in?" Marty hangs the wagon into gear and pulls a U-turn on Highway One.

Beatris grins big, "I jusst made it. I didn't know we were going anywhere. Where are we going anyways?"

Albert, fighting a game but losing a battle, is being molested. Beatrice has her mouth clamped on Al's. Her hands roam his: firm, young, weight lifters, physique at will.

Bea is able to control the match at will. If Albert grabs her roving hands to protect himself from her nimble fingers, she presses her kissing attack. When Al uses his hands to hold her head, shoulders, and her large ponderous breasts back, her hands are free to roam at will. Albert has been raised a gentleman, like the rest of us. We all understand that you never use force to get sex.

This situation is confusing. Can you use force on a girl not to have sex? If so, why? Al has chosen the strategy being used by the political powers in Vietnam. Don't fight hard enough to be victorious. Just grapple with your foe and fight hard enough to keep them from winning. This strategy has made for an interesting war, and it is making for an even more interesting ride. Fascinated, we watch this hormone driven Valkyrie trying to seduce the mortal of her choice.

Glancing into Robby's eyes, we both grin in merriment. We are doing our best to suppress our laughter. While driving, Marty's full attention is being paid to the rear-view mirror; he also is mesmerized by this titanic battle being played out in the back seat. Smirking over at me Marty is delighted, smirking back, I feel my face hurting from my happy… happy expression. But, we don't laugh out loud, oh no, we don't dare laugh out loud. Entering Woods, Marty slows for a stop sign.

Rolling to a stop Albert explodes from the car. Jumping into the creek he vaults a barbed wire fence. While Albert is making his vault to safety, Beatrice jumps from the car, she gives voice to her passion.

"Albert! Albert! You puss-sse-whip-son-of-a-bitch. I don't want to FUCK YOU Albert! I just want to be your friend."

"You got to leave me alone; I'm a virgin, for Christ's sake, you can't treat people like this!"

"Albert, come on back, I promise, I won't do anything that you don't want done to you. I promiss, honessst."

Beatris's lisp is strong in her passion and excitement.

***

It is just past midnight and I'm drunk. Lights swirl around the room in a sickening dance. Rock music pounds into my head. Lustful demons are being driven into my soul, I'm upright only because the Goddess Helen is allowing me to rub the small of her back, and her upper posterior. *'I may never wash this hand again; it's so blessed.'*

Nole is wearing a pair of shorts, and his hairy leg is in the way of my drunken caressing. This obstacle is not sufficient to check the lustful wondering of my left hand. "Ben, quit rubbing my leg, what's wrong with you anyway?"

"Wrong, wrong? I was just rubbing Helen's butt, she has such an appealing bottom; there's nothing wrong with, with just touching."

Staggering up Mike sways back and forth while maintaining a ten-degree list to the port during his sway.

"Less-go-Ben, we gotta get up in four hours and fish."

"Fish, we're gonna fish tomorrow. Are you sure?"

I shake my head maybe the world will stop spinning if my head is moving.

Staggering down the steep staircase Mike and I are hanging onto one another and bouncing from handrail to handrail. Helen's giant dog bounds up the staircase; A "Hound-Behemoth", of multitudinous breeds; all of them BIG, all of them Ugly; carries a medium-sized stick in his mouth. We continue our stagger down toward the driveway.

The old hound is looking for a good time; grabbing the stick from the dog, Mike drops it.

Slurring at the big, shaggy mixed breed, "That's no stick for a dog like you, a real hound got-ta-have a real stick."

Old hound Dawg is bouncing around Mike like he is a T-bone steak; but he waits for his stick. Mike is concerned; this mutt is not being challenged in his self-designated task of bringing back every stick cast away by man. Mike drops the stick at his feet; vaulting the handrail of the rickety staircase, Mike disappears into the rain forest. Two minutes of rustling around in the woods ensues. Appearing in the porch light, at the bottom of the stairway, Mike is toting a log about nine feet in length and ten inches in diameter. The mammoth mutt races toward Mike; Mike, the log, and the dog all converge at a point on the steep hillside.

The three of them disappear from view, rolling down the hill and into the ditch near State Route One. Splashing can be heard; staggering into a roadside light somewhat near Big Bertha Butts, Mike and the log are a muddy mess. The beast is excited and happy; finally, he has a stick worthy of his prowess as a retriever.

Mike staggers a little way from the hound so he can get a running start and then launches his 'stick/log' like a participant at a

Highland game in the Caber toss. The mutt follows the caber deep into the woods, the poor hound is not to be seen again that night; his struggles to bring Mike the stick back, are unobserved.

CHAPTER FOUR

"Grubs On"; My mind returns from the Beauteous Helen to the present state of my stomach, which is empty. The Douggers explained his grocery buying technique while we were buying groceries for this trip. On the beach, in a warm store, with a full stomach it makes perfect sense. Now, hunger is gnawing at me twenty hours a day. It's now that I see the one fatal flaw in the Douger's grocery buying theory.

The Douger's theory when buying groceries for a trip is. "There is no need to have excess food aboard. If you buy food you don't need, you'll just eat it up when fishing is slow and get fat."

I don't want to get fat, so this sounds fine to me. It sounds fine while standing in a store aisle surrounded by excess food. Two hundred miles at sea, burning twenty-five hundred calories a day and eating less the two thousand; there seems to be a flaw.

The Douggers is extremely fair in the food portions. He does all the cooking, loading our plates before he calls me in to eat. He is exact in his sharing of food. It's, it's, it's, just that the portions are so small!

The Douggers stands in the Dutch door most of the day. The diesel stove flaming away next to him. Poor little old me, I'm out in the gaff hatch standing in the wind and the cold. Pulling most of the fish, I'm burning calories like we have a fish hole stuffed full of excess food. We don't. I am a teenager, which means I'm hungry all of the time. Teenagers don't eat; they feed, I had an idea once. I suggested we eat one of our fish.

The Douggers patiently explained to me, "If we eat the fish, we can't sell the fish. If a fish comes aboard shark bit and is unsellable, then we can eat it; after all, we don't want to waste five dollars' worth of fish. Not on us, do we?"

His logic is impeccable, we sure wouldn't want to waste money on feeding ourselves.

Hearing the words, "Grubs on." I react with speed and total focus of my goal, GET FOOD!"

Turning in the gaff hatch I propel myself onto the deck, with a thrust of my forearms. The Alley Cat is beating straight into fifty mile per hour winds. She's charging up and down thirty-foot swells. Making it to my feet I'm blown backwards, almost into the drink. Bending forward I begin my passage to the cabin jumping from bin board to bin board. I am jumping over piles of fish in the checkers. The boat rolls hard to port. Landing on a bin board my foot slips, off balance I'm falling toward a checker full of albacore. Throwing myself over the fish, I end-up my trip forward by rolling to the pilothouse door. Standing up at the door I open it and walk in. The Douggers looks up from the table where he is sitting; holding our bowls of mush. He's keeping them from over-turning, or flying off the table.

Stopping at the stove, where the teakettle is whistling away, ah... the stove, the stove is diesel fired, such a warm and friendly presents in the house. Reaching into a cabinet I pull a cup out; Doug's cup is in the sink awaiting my ministrations. Spooning instant coffee into my cup, I do the same for the Dougger's. His cup is in the drain of the extra deep sink. That, is the only place, it can safely sit untended in this weather. Making coffee this morning is a little more work than usual. Seas are harassing my every movement.

I can't set my cup down, or it will fly across the house and break out a quarter inch thick safety glass window. Holding my cup, I unwire the kettle. Pouring hot water into our cups; I wire the kettle back down, one handed. Picking up the Douger's cup I head to the table.

The Douggers has piled soupy mush high in our bowls, spooning powdered milk on top.

It is better when you stir the milk in good. Grinning at me from the table Douggers is proud. He was able to prepare a hot meal in this weather.

"Well, you hungry this morning?"

"Oh, you-bet-cha, this looks great."

The method employed to eat on an albacore boat is the *"brace."* The brace is sitting with legs spread out, jammed into the seat across from you. We brace and flex against each and every rock and roll of the boat.

Still holding both coffee cups firmly in my grip I eye ball Doug. My elbows are planted on the table to further support my position. Doug and I need to exchange a cup of coffee for a bowl of mush. This must be done with timing and finesse. The Douggers and I are about to do a juggling act extraordinary.

The Douggers nods at me, "OK... now."

Releasing his grip on the bowl of mush at the same instant I release my grip on his coffee. Before the sea can throw either item from the table we grab for what we need. The exchange is made with nary a drop spilled.

Grinning at Doug, "We're getting pretty dam good at this."

Doug grins back, "You get good at juggling at sea, or you go hungry."

Nodding in agreement while I slip the bowl of mush into the crook of my right arm. My coffee cup grasped in my right hand for ease of eating. My left hand takes a spoon held out to me by Doug. We are set to begin breakfast.

Eating is done in silence all polite table conversation was exhausted long ago. Although, the silence is comfortable. We're in an exhausted haze, too tired for small talk. Doug and I power down hot mush and powered milk as though it's ambrosia of the Gods.

One of The Douggers food saving strategies is to only have two meals a day. Breakfast is my only break. We take dinner after shutdown, and that's after dark.

Taking advantage of my time off, I push it, by having a second cup of coffee. Coffee helps to fill the hole. Besides, we haven't had a fish for fifteen minutes. The Douggers is in a mellow mood, and I don't want to return to the deck, not just yet. I try a conversational ploy as a delaying action.

"Douggers, I didn't mean to get personal with that question about you losing a boat. I just didn't know. I've never met anyone who sank a boat at sea before? I was just wondering, what was it like?"

"That's OK Ben, it's only natural to ask someone about that kind of thing."

Douggers rears back in his seat. Swinging his legs onto the seat, he settles back, his head resting against the galley window. The weather still requires The Douggers to brace himself, one arm is on the table, one arm is thrown over the settee.

"Well, it was back in sixty-two. The Columbus Day Storm got us. God, I remember it like it was yesterday. All day long... no wind, not a breath, it was flat calm and glassy slick. But a big lump, I mean a BIG lump. My son was with me; he must have been what, thirteen or fourteen years old? Just a kid."

Taking Doug's cup from his hand, I carry our cups to the steaming kettle. "Keep talking, I'm listening."

The ritual of making coffee begins. Nodding and grinning at Doug I encourage his remembrances.

"Like I was saying, big lump. I told my son, if we get any wind on this lump, this ocean will get mean. Real mean, real quick. By wind, I was thinking twenty to forty knots.

When we shut down there was not a breath of air, we had good fishing all day long. At shutdown it was eerie. These big long rolling mountains sliding past us and on down the coast. We couldn't run for port. Why?

I got up around midnight and the wind had arrived. God, had it arrived. It was blowing fifty or better. I got dressed and pulled the flopper stoppers. And then, we ran for Coos Bay. She was a beam sea all the way in. We were rolling our guts out. Almost two hundred miles out, way off-shore. The thirty too forty foot waves were popping and snapping all around us. I owned the Betty Lou then, nice little forty-two-footer, good sea boat.

All the time we were running in, the wind keeps coming up. When I got up the wind was moaning in the rigging, blowing about fifty knots, by three A.M. it was shrieking. A piercing scream that sounded like it could peel paint. By three, it was blowing over a hundred miles per hour, at least that's what the weather report said."

A cup of coffee in each hand I'm ready to stagger back to the galley table. All I'm waiting for is the Alley Cat to begin a charge down the face of a swell so that I can use the motion of the boat to my advantage. There is no need to walk up hill, while the boat is climbing one of these swells. The Alley Cat tops a swell and slides into the trough, straddle legged; I stagger toward the table. Passing Doug, he reaches out for his cup, I hand it off to him as we pass, using my now free hand, I grab the table. The move swings me into my seat. Plopping down, a little coffee spills onto the table. Using my shirtsleeve, I wipe it up.

"Thanks," Doug takes a sip of coffee. "It was about three in the morning. I'd been on the wheel since I got up. It was rough, too rough to be on autopilot.

Every time a big one got a hold of us; I'd round her up into it. Slow her down to control her. It was tough sledding but we were going to make it. The storm was throwing everything it had at us, and the boat was handling it.

Suddenly, I felt a big thump, heard a crash. There was a sound of breaking wood. My son came tearing out of the foc-sel his eyes as big as saucers.

He yelled, 'Dad, Dad, there's a log sticking through the hull. Water is gushing in. Do something, quick!' He screamed, 'I think we're going to drown!'

"He was so scared, awakened from a sound sleep by a log crashing through the hull next to his head. Well, I'll tell you, I bolted down that hatch, scared as hell, hoping my son was wrong, having a dream, maybe just panicked by the weather. He wasn't.

The light was on in the foksle in the shadows I could see the log sticking through the hull. There was about three feet of a pilled processed log sticking into my boat. Probably, it had been lost off a ship during shipping, probably, during this storm, the Columbus Day storm. Grabbing my son's sleeping bag, I stuffed it around the log, to stem the flow of water into the boat. It worked pretty well, I'd just gotten the bag packed around it nice and tight. A big wave caught the boat and dropped it about twenty feet. The log twisted port and ripped a hole in the bow all the way to the stem."

Wiping his eyes, The Dougger's hand trembles with the memory.

"Ho-man, it was ugly, just ugly. The hole was about a foot wide and four feet long; it was two, no more like three feet, below the water line. The log twisted free and a wall of water gushed into the hull. Hit me full in the face. Water... and fear, knocked me backward into the bulkhead and autopilot."

Heaving a deep sigh, Douggers sits up a little straighter. His demeanor changes,

Doug is back in charge; not the story, not the memory. Looking at me out of the corner of his eye, a small grin is playing on Doug's lips.

"Well, we should go back to work, what do you think?"

"Oh, come-on Doug, you can't leave me hanging. How about I do the dishes while you finish your story? You couldn't send me back aft, not without knowing what happened."

Standing I begin gathering up dishes to wash, Doug reaches over, gripping my forearm. "Go ahead and relax, I'll finish my story. Then, you can go do the dishes. Let's see, where was I? Oh yea, the water knocked me backwards and into the autopilot. Water was pouring in, I saw it was no use, no use trying to stop that flow.

We were sinking, no doubt about it. Turning I climbed out of the fok-sel on my hands and knees. The bow was going down fast.

Crawling into the pilothouse, I yelled at my son, "Get our lifejackets... fast we're sinking!"

I took a position with the LORAN; I needed to know where we were. In those days we used World War Two surplus LORANs. It took about five minutes to get a fix. By the time I had my fix, my son was back with our lifejackets. I grabbed the radio mike; those were the days of the big set. There wasn't any such a thing as a VHF. Anyway, I sent three May-Days and two positions.

My boy and I pulled ourselves up to the pilothouse door and out onto the deck. God, that wind was bad, we were blown down as soon as we got the door open. We had to crawl out on deck. The boat was sinking by the bow, the water was already in the house the electrical system was out. We didn't have deck-lights or radios anymore. It was scary as hell. My son and I crawled up to the stern. I grabbed his lifejacket; he grabbed mine. We fell over the stern, and into the sea.

Man, oh man, I never want to experience that again. It was worse than anything I lived through in Europe. Maybe that was because my son was with me, maybe, because there was going to be no rescue? Nobody was going to make it out alive, not from this hell. Maybe... it was some of both?

We'd hang onto each other. A comber would pick us up, and then throw us thirty or forty feet. Hitting down the face of the wave somewhere? Ending up submerged, we'd swim for the surface. It was tough; it was double tough.

About the time that we'd break the surface, the comber would crash onto us all foamy and florescent. Did you know that you can't float in white water? Water filled with foam and air weights less than solid water. So, when we were in the foam, it was like fighting through slime to get a breath. No matter how hard we'd kick and fight we just couldn't get to the surface. I remember being just desperate for a breath of air. I would have given a hundred dollars just for five minutes of breathing without gulping salt water."

Doug realized what a huge amount of money he was willing to pay for a breath of fresh air and reconsidered. "Well, I would have given ten dollars, that's for sure. We'd been in the water about two hours, it seemed like two centuries.

Sometimes... the waves would leave us alone; the swells would just lift us up and let us slide down the back side. Sometimes, they would pound us with an intensity that seemed as though they were evil beings. It seemed they had a special hate, just for us.

My son was weakening. His hands kept losing their grip on my lifejacket every time we were tumbled by a wave. At one point during the night, we were tumbled by one of those evil monsters.

A capping swell picked us up and threw us about thirty feet. When we hit the face of the swell, I lost my grip. My boy, he was just gone. Then, the next capping wave hit us, knocking us further apart. Yelling Will's name, I became frantic. Swimming first in one direction then another; striking the water with my strokes.

Distraught, man... I couldn't stand the thought that my son was going to die. He was going to die alone.

Then another one of the evil monsters picked me up and threw me down the face of the wave. I landed on top of my son. This time I grabbed a hold of him, and I held him. I was never going to let him go.

It was sometime later we topped a swell. I saw a red and green light heading right for us. There was no way that he could see us, even if he had heard our MAYDAY. Even if he were looking for us, he couldn't find us in this maelstrom. It was still another hour till sun was up. The boat was going to cruise right by us. But here he came. Every swell we topped he was closer, and still on course. Heading right for us. You know I don't know if I believe in God or not? That night, I believed, man I believed. I was praying hard not for me... for my Boy."

The Dougger's voice is choking with emotion. Taking a sip of coffee, his hand has a tremor. Doug returns to his story, looking me straight in the eye.

"The boat heading for us was a fifty-footer. She was an old wooden slab, rust staining her sides, the paint peeling off. One of the poles was broken, and the stub was lashed in the rigging all helter skelter. But, she was the most beautiful vessel I've ever seen. It was closing in on five in the morning by then, we were both so tired. Yelling our voices horse, waving at the pilothouse for all we were worth. It did no good, no good at all.

He didn't see us. The boat just held its speed and course trying to make port. I could see that we were lost, lost for good, this was our only hope.

Then one of those evil giants that had been harassing us all night... picks us up. It dropped me and my son on the deck of that old slab as she cruised by. The boat just rolled her windward rail under and we poured aboard. Us, and about a thousand gallons of water. The deck was littered with lines and gear and stuff, just

168

stuff... and now us. I made it to my feet and grabbed my boy. We went forward to the aft door and slid it open.

I told the guy, "You saved us, you saved us, oh thank God, you saved us!"

He was on the wheel trying to control his boat in the weather. Looking around at me, he said, "Saved you hell, we're sinking, get on the pumps, get on the pumps!"

Well... we did just that. I pumped an old whale-gusher iron pump all the way to Coos Bay just to keep us afloat. A third of the Albacore fleet sank that night; the Feds declared it as a natural disaster. I had to start all over. With nothing... at forty-two years of age, that sure wasn't fun."

Getting up I'm awe struck by the story. "I don't know what to say. I didn't know I just didn't know."

Picking up a bowl in each hand I head for the sink. In my mind there was nothing else to do but the dishes. I feel as numb as though it was me in the water. Doug was right, he could remember it, like it was yesterday.

Standing at the sink running a small amount of our precious fresh water supply into the sink, I fall to thinking. It is no wonder that Doug is so tight-fisted with a buck. The Douggers had to start fishing twice; without two dollars to rub together. Twice?

As Kipling wrote in his poem 'If,' on the day his son was born. "...to bet it all on one game of pitch and toss, lose, then begin again at your beginning, and never breathe a word about your loss, then you'll be a man, my son."

Just like Kipling said; The Douggers had to stoop and build up what he had just lost, with worn out tools. That would make King Solomon tight fisted with a dollar.

But, on the other hand, some of the most generous people I know come from poverty, what about Tom-Tom, Unk and even, one fish Bob. *Remember? Tom-Tom invited you to dinner, the first time we met.*

***

The bell over the door at Hogie's rings a greeting as I enter the store. It's about seven in the evening. The place is bustling with fishermen. Marty, standing toward the back of the group, is awaiting Debbie's attention. I join him.

"How'd ya do today, Marty?"

"We got a bakers dozen how about you?"

"Couple of hand fulls, nice size fish though."

"Good, good," Marty lowers his head to my ear whispering. "Do you know Debbie's Dad, Tom-Tom?"

Peering at Marty, I give a little shake of my head. I've heard of Tom-Tom he is a highliner of some renown. I've even heard he runs with Benny, you don't get any higher than that in dory-men society.

The fisherman just ahead of us in line has longish black hair, thick and wavy. He is wearing the mandatory hip boots of a dory fisherman, and a hooded sweatshirt. Like most of us in the room he's burly, strong looking.Marty pokes the fisherman on the shoulder, turning, he smiles at us; his expression is open, one of enjoying the moment.

Marty grins his ain't this cool grin; "Tom-Tom; this is Ben, Ben Neely, he bought our old boat. Ben I want you to meet Tom-Tom, he is a high-liner, and Debbie's dad,,, Tom is cool."

I stick out my hand to shake, we exchange smiles as though we are sharing a secret, "Nice to meet you."

Still gripping hands Tom-Tom says, "Yea, you too, I have heard a lot about you."

Not sure how to respond to the news that he has heard about me, I feel a little uncomfortable pursuing the subject. In my awkwardness, I fall back on a question that any fisherman can ask another,

"So, how did you do today?"

Tom-Tom rubs his bristly jaw, "Oh, forty fish, and five salmon."

Forty fish? Fish in the dory-men's code are silver salmon; salmon are king salmon. Let me see now, that figures out at four dollars a fish for silvers; a hundred and forty dollars of silvers. Fifty dollars' worth of kings, that's a two-hundred-dollar day. *Not bad, not bad at all.*

"Golly, you did good, real good."

Tom-Tom flashes me the big smile of a highliner. "Oh, I did OK, Benny, he did better than me. Where were you fishing today?"

"Up by the Cape, how about you?"

Up by the Cape too, you should have done better. When we're finished in here; lets go see your gear. I want to see what you're fishing."

Man, oh man, we are going to get some advice from a highliner. I've heard of Tom-Tom; he's a bona fide highliner, helping bottom feeders like us? When you're lucky, you can use soup for brains.

***

Standing on the port side of the Bloody Wog, Tom-Tom is fingering one of our Archie Bunker Super hoochie. Peering up at Mike, who is standing beside the steering console he inquires, "What is this thing?"

Sticking his chest out Mike purports.

"That's our best producer we caught thirteen fish on that today."

"Why don't you guys come to my house for dinner tonight? I'll give you some gear to try."

Marty and Albert are standing on the starboard side of the Bloody Wog fingering the same colored hoochie as Tom.

Marty looks over at Tom-Tom, "All of us, you want all of us to come to dinner?" "Of course, all of you, I've only seen you guys travel together, in a heard, like buffalo."

Mike, always concerned for his stomach asks, "What time should we be there?"

"Oh well, make it seven, you-bet-cha seven o'clock that'll be just fine."

Turning on a heel, Tom-Tom strides off toward his rig, a new Jeep pickup.

Swinging toward me Mike ponders, "What did you say to make Tom-Tom want to help us the likes of us?"

"I asked how he did today… that was all, just how he did."

We all shake our heads at the quirks of life, twenty minutes ago, we were low liner slugs, now we're on our way to Tom-Tom's house to get dinner and free gear, from a highliner no less.

***

Big Bertha Butts rolls to a stop nose to nose with Tom-Tom's new Jeep pickup. It's in the driveway of the little fisherman's cottage that houses the beauteous Debbie. All five of us are dressed in our best fisherman's finery; flannel shirts and Levi's. We're all ready to eat short salmon and glean fishing knowledge from a true highliner.

I have a secret hope, maybe this dinner will break down the professional wall of store clerk to customer. This wall is keeping me from asking Debbie out on a moonlight stroll. In my heart of hearts, I know that it is not the mystic of Debbie being a store clerk that keeps me from asking her out. Heck, I couldn't get up the nerve to ask a girl out in high school, even when I had money and a cool car. I sure can't ask out the local beauty queen with no money to spend on her. Can I? Walking to the door, we're a long line of fishermen... All of us making sure not to get caught on the crab grass. We're on our best behavior this night, which isn't saying much. No one has knocked yet. However, the door flies open. A large woman is standing in the light streaming out of the opening.

Calling over our heads in a loud penetrating voice she waves us through. "Come in, come in, come in.

173

You're letting in the mosquitoes, don't just stand there. God, I wish I would have known there were going to be this many of you. Jesus, I hope you're not hungry... You don't like salmon, do you? Call me Ma."

Ma has hit us with so many questions and statements no one can figure out what to reply, or which question to answer.

Tramping into Tom-Tom's abode we gaze around. Tom-Tom sitting a-top his big easy chair, waves toward the couch with his free hand. His other hand is busy clutching a Henry Wineharts beer. "Sit, sit... You got'ta be beat."

The group sits down at his command. We're all here to learn the meaning of life from this wise man as he sits a-top his easy chair. He has the secrets of catching. And we are seekers of that wisdom. Tom-Tom has gleaned his wisdom on the deck of a troller. A troller is the very pentacle of trolling. A Guru with, the secret to the meaning of life, could not be more revered by us, than this middle aged fisherman.

There are small piles of fishing gear on the coffee table; hoochies with different size flashers, spoons with different size hooks. It looks like the back wall at Hogie's, only without price tags.

We're listening to Tom-Tom with rap attention. That is until Debbie glides through the kitchen door. Her hair, pulled back, is in the new hippie chick style, revealing her high cheekbones and cute little ears. I cannot pull my eyes from her as she enters the room. She sways up to the couch and sits. Sitting on the arm of the couch she's right next to me. God life is good. Her deep blue eyes wonder down the line of young fisherman staring at her. All the while, Tom-Tom is expounding on the virtues of reading the contents of a salmon's belly.

"You-bet-cha. Cut open the bellies, look at em. You got'ta know what the salmon

are feeding on. Change your gear; give-um what they got. Or, give-um something different, all depends, you-bet-cha. I keep all kinds of gear ready to go. Don't run all the same kind of gear. Of course; sometimes they'll only bite on one hoochie. Then give it to them. You-bet-cha, that's the way. You never know. It changes every day. It all depends, you-bet-cha."

Debbie raises her hand to her hair, gently, running her fingers through the auburn halo. Her fingers stop at the end curling her hair around and around. It's one of the most seductive movements I have ever witnessed. Ever

"The salmon is done; the salad is ready. French bread should be hot by the time you guys get your plates."

That does it for me. I thought I was in love before. Now I know I'm in love. But, but; to be in love with a beauty queen, I can't ask out a beauty queen. Life is so hard.

Debbie is looking me straight in the eyes. Her warm pretty face glowing in health and vitality, "You better come... and get something to eat."

***

In the car, Mike directs his attention from the road to me, "So what are we doing wrong.""Well, we never say, you-bet-cha."

"That's right, you-bet-cha."

"you-bet-cha, we got to fix that, you-bet-cha."

Glancing at me, Mike grins big, "You-bet-cha."

My boots rolled down: salmon blood, fish slime, and salt water, are slowly drying on my shirt and Levis.

Marty drops down on the log beside me, "What's the happening, Ben? You look down."

"Oh nothing, nothing really, you know, just stuff."

Marty shakes his head, long brown hair brushing his shoulders. "No; I don't know? What? What stuff is bugging you?"

I nod at the setting sun, "Pretty sunset don't you think?"

"Yea it is... is that what's bugging you, the sunset?"

"Oh, I don't know?" Sigh. "I just don't know? I'd like to ask Debbie out. But I don't have much money. Heck, I don't have any money. I can't take her anywhere nice. It's just all too much, just too much."

"I think she wants to go out with you. Just take her for a walk on the beach.

She'd probably go just about anywhere."

Shaking my head to the negative, I stare out at the ocean.

Marty slaps my leg. "I've got five dollars let's go get Helen. Have her buy us a case of beer. We'll all get drunk and it won't seem so bad."

Standing up we brush the sand from our pants, walking slowly, we head up the beach toward Marty's launch rig.

***

The Bloody Wog slides onto the beach coming to a slow stop just above the wet sand. Scanning the beach; I'm looking for interesting girls to gawk at. Over our port bow out a hundred feet is a totally unexpected sight. My Mom.

My Mom is standing next to my dad, who is standing behind a sixteen-millimeter movie camera. The camera is rolling away.

Punching Mike with my elbow, "That's my mom and dad. There's Linda too." "Did you know they were coming up here?"

"No, I haven't called home since we got here. Oh man, we've got empty beer bottles all over our kitchen table from last night. Gee-zus, Mom and Dad will think we're up here becoming a couple of drunks."

Walking toward my mother and father I'm worrying about the beer.

Mike departs in the other direction mumbling, "I like your mom… I'll fix it.

Walking up to my mom, she throws her arms around me and hugs. She hugs me deep and long. In her arms I feel warm like a little boy again, just for a minute. Turning to my father we shake hands. I am pulled into a bear hug and embraced on the beach in front of all of these, tough, hard-core fisherman.

Walking up to our little family group, Mike shakes my dad's hand. "Why don't we stop and get a hamburger after we sell our fish?"

My stomach rumbles forth with a familiar sound, "That sounds good to me."

We're waiting in line to sell our catch. Just behind Benny, who is just behind Tom-Tom. Tom-Tom spots Big Bertha Butts and walks back to see how we did. After all, it's been a couple of days since we received his advice.

Standing in the boat, Mike shoots Tom-Tom with his index finger as he walks up.

Tom-Tom inquires, "So Cap, how-ja do today?"

Flipping open the fish box Mike's lofty response is, "We got fifteen fish and a salmon?"

"Good, good going. You're doin' better, doin-better."

"Hey Cap, how did you do today?"

"I did good, made wages, anyway. Who is that with Ben?"

"The big guy, oh, that's Ben's Dad. His family showed up today. They just blew in to see what we are up to."

"Ben's family, that's cool? Why don't you guys come up to dinner tomorrow night? You-bet-cha. Bring the whole bunch up to dinner at my house. Be there around seven."

Mike pushes the hair out of his eyes, "You-bet-cha."

Harry, my father, and I are on a visitation around the fleet. Passing the Kaiuch I exchange the news of the day with Marty. Standing in the Nole's Ark, Nole waves Harry over. Harry saunters on down the line of waiting boats to have a gam with Nole.

I'm looking in on Marty's twenty fish when Bob walks up to us and asks, "Is that your mom and little sister I saw on the beach."

"Yea they came up to see what we were up to, cool huh?"

"Real cool, why don't you bring them over for dinner tomorrow night? It would be good to see them again."Grinning at Bob I bounce my head up and down, "It's a date."

Bob turns on his heel and strides off toward his boat. The line of unloading boats is on the move again.

Noel shakes hands with Harry, "So you guys made it up here, we weren't expecting you, that's great, just great. Why don't you bring the family over for dinner tomorrow night we'll cook up a salmon?"

"A salmon dinner sounds fine by me; we'll be over around seven."

I'm working on the Bloody Wog; preparing her for tomorrow, we'll be carrying a passenger. I want her at her twenty-year-old finest, with my dad aboard. I'm washing the dried blood off the gear lockers and the fish box. Well, not really washing all the blood off her. Mostly, just smearing it around with some soap and water but, the thought is there.

Todd, one of the boys visiting the area from Concord, runs up to the Wog breathless, "We got the beer bottles picked up."

"You do, wow that's great, how did you know to do that?"

"Mike, he told us too."

"Great, great, thanks a lot. That'll be a big help when my parents see our place."

Todd runs his hand through his long hair smiling big at the shared confidence. "We're having a Bar-B-Q, at the Woods campground; why don't you and Mike come on over?"

"Sure, sounds good."

Todd runs his hand through his hair one more time, turning he starts to scamper off. "Hey Todd, when is the dinner?"

Running backwards Todd makes something up, "Tomorrow night ah, ah, around seven."

Turning, he continues his jog toward the beach. Smiling to myself, I'm thinking about the cornucopia of food that we'll have tomorrow. We're invited to two; count them, two different dinners.

***

It's just past five in the morning. Harry is watching me pull the cowling off our new, used engine. In deep concentration, I wrap the starter rope around and around and around the flywheel. Scowling, Harry is not impressed with our starter. Under this scrutiny, I cringe. Gulping, the only thing to do is give the rope a big yank.

"Where is the pull-crank re-wind mechanism?"

"It broke last week."

The engine has been in a slow deterioration phase since we got it. As things have broken on the motor we have disassembled them. Or, we have jury-rigged some type of Rube Goldberg contraption to continue fishing, always without spending a penny on the equipment.

It's easy to see his disappointment with our maintenance program. We remove all the broken parts, sometimes, we even fix them. In his mind, we're on a shortcut to the ragged edge of disaster. In our minds, we're fishermen; keep the boat going, that's the name of the game.

Wrapping the rope around the flywheel again, I yank. The motor catches once with a cough and a sputter. Harry watches, his eyes showing concern. I feel like a need to explain our maintenance program.

"As you can see we have the motor down to the bare essentials now. All the excess parts and pieces have been stripped away. There is nothing left to break."

Dad mutters under his breath, "Not without leaving you a-drift off a lee shore."

He's worried about our safety. I'll reassure him, "Hey, did you see our new oars, they work really well?"

Harry makes a disgusted shake of his head, again. Thinking fast, I decide not to show him our moldy, twenty-year-old life jackets, fearing another shake of his head, and that disappointed look in his eyes.

***

It's just past six o'clock in the evening. Harry is leading us toward the camper. Opening the door; aromas from my childhood waft out at us. Stepping inside, Harry slides around the table, making room for Mike and me.

Mom has been cooking all afternoon. Delicious smells have been driving our neighbors into a crazed state. There's a large roast beef, done to perfection. An Apple Pie sits atop the cabinet, cooling. Fresh baked bread is beside the apple pie with butter melting on the top. The table is set with real plates, not paper. There is a large bowl of salad in the center of the table. Mom cooked like this was a homecoming. In our usual fashion, we neglected to bring food out on the boat. Except of course our cheese and peanut butter. So, tonight's dinner is the first real food we have seen in twelve hours.

"Mom this looks great. I didn't expect a dinner like this. This is great, this is just great. All this food.... food, food? Uh-oh, I forgot. We were invited over to Bob's for dinner."

Taking up my chorus, Mike spouts. "Wow, look at this spread, this is great, man... look at. Oh man, Tom-Tom invited us over for dinner too."

Shaking my head in sad remembrance I mumble, "I told Todd that we would come by their apartment tonight, to eat dinner."

My father's face falls, "Oh no, I told Nole that we'd be over for dinner too, damn what are we going to do?"

Looking around at all my favorite foods, "Let's eat, then we'll go to dinner, and dinner, and dinner."

Tapping the table twice with his fork Mike opines, "Capital idea, thrice."

Conversation comes to a halt as we all dig in. This is a feast. Time passes, we consume mass quantities of rich food, Mike and I are in utter delight.

***

Noel's door opens at our knock. Standing at the door he is wearing his usual big grin, and a nice shirt. He has, "dressed," for my family's dinner.

We're running a little late for our new and revised dinner schedule. Other than late the new plan is working perfectly. We will make all our dinner engagements staying a short time at each. We'll also make a full explanation to all the parties involved. In other words, we are going to throw ourselves on the tender mercies of our hosts.

After explanations to Nole and Dawn a dinner of short Salmon is placed on the table. My family, to be polite, are nibbling at the dinner. Mike looks at the food; although full, instinct takes over. We came to eat, so he ate. Mike eats a second full dinner. A nice slab of salmon, salad, French bread and homemade ice cream for dessert.

Bolting down our second dinner, we head off to Bob's cabin, where hamburgers are on the grill.

Here at Bob's we explain about the two dinners already eaten and pass on more food. All of us pass on more food except Mike. Mike, has a hamburger with the works.

Throwing in a little potato salad on the side, hey why not some chips, a Coke what would a hamburger be without a Coke? Mike groans a little when he gets up from dinner. After all he has eaten three full meals.

We head off to the Woods campground where spaghetti is waiting. Spaghetti, salad, French bread, and cake is Mike's fourth dinner of the evening. At this point Mike is having a little trouble getting up and down at the dinner tables. But that's OK. I'm here to help him. He decides that a second helping of spaghetti would be nice. Harry begins bragging on Mike. Telling all who will listen what a prodigious eater Mike is.

Cool Hand Luke is new to theaters. Luke, Paul Neuman, eats fifty eggs on a bet.

Joining the fun I'm telling all who will listen, "My partner can eat fifty eggs.

Anyone want to bet on it, fifty eggs, look at him eat."

There are no takers. Well, we have one more dinner to get to. So, we head up the hill into P.C. to the beauteous Debbie's house. Where one last dinner is waiting, it's waiting for Mike. We're traveling in Bertha, she's the only vehicle large enough to hold everyone. I'm sure the gas fumes are not helping Mike's digestion.

At Tom-Tom's we settle down for a longer stay, this being our last dinner stop. We are late but they have been holding food for us. Mike eats. It's salmon again. Bar-B-Q-ed over oak and fir coals, salad and French bread covered with melted cheese and garlic. Iced tea is provided as a beverage.

Mike eats another full dinner. It is his fifth dinner of the night. Not counting the two seconds he ate.

Sitting around, we're enjoying the warm Oregon evening. Ma begins broadcasting at her usual decibel rate, "There is watermelon for those who are still hungry."

Debbie, her two sisters, along with Mike, Linda and me are all outside on the porch. Hearing that he'll be required to eat more, Mike crawls up into the rafters of the porch and groans. Laying a-top a rafter, he resembles a leopard, after gorging himself at a kill.

Ma comes out with a watermelon, slicing it she booms up at Mike, "I guess you won't be needing any watermelon, will you Mike?"

Mike groans from the rafters, "You better give me some... for my digestion."

"Well all right then, but don't blame me for how you feel tomorrow."

Taking Debbie by the hand we walk off of the porch, into the darkness. This is a good time to make my play for Debbie. Mike is incapacitated.

***

It's the last day of my parent's vacation. They'll head home this morning. Knocking lightly on the camper door, I wait. It opens a crack. My father, Harry, is standing behind and to one side of the door, his head sticking out into the cold Oregon morning.

"What time is it?"

Harry is dressed in skives and a tee shirt. He's rubbing his hand over his Marine Corps regulation crew cut.

"It's four thirty, I just came by to say so-long and drive careful."

Rubbing his head one more time he yawns. "I'm glad you stopped by, you on your way out?"

"Oh, you-bet-cha, we're headed to the beach."

Harry raises his head, and sniffs the air. Fog swirls into the camper, forcing a chill up his spine. "Are you sure that you're going out? It's kind of foggy."

"Oh it'll be all right. You can't get lost on the north coast. Land is always east."

"That's the problem. You know you're a lot safer a thousand miles off shore than ten." "Yea, I know, but don't tell these dory fisher folk, you'd freak-um out."

"Well, you be careful!"

"You know me, Dad, careful is my middle name."

185

He gives me that disappointed look again. It's like he knows I'm running on the ragged edge of disaster. Me, I've got too much to live for to take chances.

***

The swells have a steep, powerful feel to them. The old Bloody Wog struggles up and over each and every swell. We launched over two hours ago. Following Benny out from the beach we lost sight of him, along with everything else. Except fog, fog and the swell we're on is all that we can see. Fourteen fish are in the box. Our lines are shaking with intensity and regularity. We have no idea where we are, except in-em. Wherever that is? Our new radio blares from behind the wooden flap that serves as the door to our console.

"Bloody Wog, Bloody Wog, Bloody Wog, are you on this channel? Do you hear me son? Can you hear me Ben?"

Mike and I are both surprised by the radio hailing us. We just installed it yesterday at the behest of my folks. When my Mom found out that we had no radio com she wanted that deficiency corrected; today, right now, and on the double.

My Dad bought us a radio so that we could call for help when we needed. Not if, but when we needed it.

I unhook the leather thong that holds the beach-salvaged, wooden door in place. Dropping the lid on the console, it lays there on its leather hinges just as designed. I smile at Mike because he created this masterpiece. This is just one of his thrifty solutions.

Reaching into the console, I pull the mike from its perch, "Bloody Wog back to the call, who is it?", like I didn't know.-

The radio bleats out, "Yes, Bloody Wog, Bloody Wog we read you five by five. I repeat, we read you five by five."

Glancing over my shoulder at Mike, "That's the way they talked in tanks during World War Two, you know. They had even cheaper radios than we do."

Mike gestures at our new radio with his chin. "It's coming in pretty good don't you think?"

A big comber takes this moment to slop over the side, pouring forty gallons of water into the boat, trying to kill our brand-new radio. It drenches Mike and me in the process. We throw our bodies in front of the steering console to save this brand new hundred-dollar piece of electronics bolted there.

Between the combers that keep popping over the gunwales. And the four or five constant leaks we have. It's time to pump the bilge. The floorboards are floating off the ribs again. Floating floorboards is our only bilge alarm.

Turning my back to the wind I am protecting the mike from salt spray. Using the unconcerned tone of a highliner when the weather is up, "Bloody Wog back to the call. "Good to hear your voice, you guys must be getting ready to leave?"

"Yes, we are. We're going after we've had breakfast. Isn't it rough, why don't you guys come on in and have breakfast?"

Mike and I both shake our heads simultaneously in the negative. We're not leaving this bite.

The radio speaker crackles again, "Bloody Wog, come back, come back Bloody Wog. It's kind of rough why don't you guys come on in? We'll buy you Breakfast."

Looking at Mike, I roll my eyes We can't leave this bite. Remaining in my highliner cool mode, I lie.

"Well, we just finished a fine breakfast out here ourselves. We had stake, eggs, hash-browns, the works. We couldn't eat another bite, really, but thanks anyway."

Silence is all that can be heard from the radio speaker. After all, what do you say to such a whopping lie. We couldn't make breakfast in these seas if we were on a fifty-foot troller.

"OK if you're not hungry we won't buy you breakfast, just come on in and say good-bye."

Mike throws a fish over his shoulder onto the floating floorboards. Unsnapping the line he cranks up another. That one flops aboard also. My side is shaking; hanging up the radio mike, where it belongs, I calmly return to work. We hope this conversation is over, but it isn't.

Mike is busy pumping the boat. I'm working on my side. Silver salmon are coming off almost every hook. The radio speaker breaks into our work again.

"Blood Wog Blood Wog, Tom-Tom to the Bloody Wog. You on this side, boys?"It's busy right now; I'm cranking salmon up with one hand, and steering with the other. And, I'm holding the mike in my steering hand. The mike cord keeps tangling up with the wheel, every two or three turns. Stopping everything I'm doing, I unwind the mike cord for awhile, another comber pops over the bow, spilling fifty gallons of water into the bilge. My highliner cool is being tested by the weather and repeated interruptions.

"Yea this is the Wog, we're back to you, what, what do you want now?"

I consider for a moment how that will sound. It will sound harassed and worried; too late now. I'll just have to sound even cooler the next time I press the mike button.

Tom-Tom's voice friendly and jolly; blares from the speaker. "Yea Ben, good to hear you, how is it going out there? What's the weather like?"

"Good Tom-Tom good, you might want to head on out. There are a couple of fish around."

Tom's voice betrays interest "There are? How many do you have aboard this morning?" Throwing my head back in pride, "About a quarter of a hump."

"That's good fishin... you-bet-cha, where are you at?"

Peering around, all I can see is fog. We can't even see the swells charging at us. At the bottom of a swell the top of the wave is obscured, at the top the bottom is. Where we are is in a large swirling gray ball. Into which an occasional fifty gallons of seawater is poured.

Keying the mike, "We're south of the rock about a twenty-minute run. Big lump running, blowing about twenty, just a few sheep around." For my Mom I add, "But, nice."

I'm quite proud of this use of the fisherman's vernacular, while on the radio. I am especially happy about referring to white caps as sheep. That makes me sound like a real highliner in my own mind. Tom-

Tom's voice crackles through the speaker once more. His enthusiasm is gone.

"Well, you better come in anyway the weather may come up even more."

Mike and I know pressure is being applied to Tom-Tom. His actions are outside of the fisherman's code of ethics. Advice is never given to another captain unless asked for. However, I know that my mom and dad are standing next to his boat, telling him to call us in. Making him break the fisherman's code of; "Live with your decisions." Most of the fleet is sitting on the beach, watching the weather. Everyone is probably listening to this conversation. They're trying to figure out what they should do.

Harry must have that disappointed gleam in his eyes, shaking his head yet again. He is certain in the knowledge that we are running on the ragged edge of disaster. Putting the break on the gurdy, I turn and face this ordeal straight on.

Shoulders back, looking into the wind. My long hair is plastered to my head. Chest and shoulders wet from the repeated soakings we've been enduring. Pressing the mike button, I calmly report.

"Ah yea Tom-Tom... we're watching the weather real close, real close. If it comes up any more... we'll pull our gear and head for the beach. Don't worry about us the boat is handling the weather real fine, real fine.

Mike is putting the pump away. Our bilge pristine and dry, or as dry as it gets in the Bloody Wog. "That should put an end to all this calling and bother."

"I don't think so. You don't know my mom like I do. Once she has decided on something, that something happens, and, she wants us in."

Running his fingers through his hair Mike squeezes water off the ends, well the longer we're out here the more fish we'll have at the end of the day."

I agree with him in my heart. The days that we catch are few and far in-between.

"You know you're right, and that doesn't happen all that often."

Mike looks at me funny, like I just insulted him. "I don't mean about you being right, I mean about the longer we're here, the more fish we'll have. We'll operate a delaying action for as long as we can."

Bobbing his wet head Mike is certain we're doing the right thing. Afterall, staying on a large lumpy ocean with the wind coming up is the only sensible thing to do... When you're in fish. Right?

Another large white cap pops over the port quarter replacing a portion of the water that Mike just removed. Mike returns to cranking up his tip line. I go back to work on my heavy, getting a ten-minute reprieve from the radio, we land five more fish. Then the speaker begins squawking again.

"Bloody Wog Bloody Wog Bloody Wog, do you pick me up?

Mike and I both sigh at the same time, and then look at one another. Slinging my head shaking salt spray and fog droplets from my face, "You answer it this time I tired of telling people that we aren't coming in."

Screwing up his face at me, Mike picks up the mike. "Bloody Wog back to the call, Nole come-on back."

"Mike where are you at now? Are you heading in? The weather is predicted to come up even more."

Mike grins at me, his eyebrows arching in an evil fashion. "Yea Nole... we're working on the gear right now, grinding it up. We just put five more fish aboard."

"Mike... I'm glad you're doing so well. But, are you pumping the gear, or are you bringing it in?"

Mike keys the button, defeated, "Pumping."

The speaker is silent once again. We know that the inevitable will occur. And then it does, our fate is sealed.

"Mike you and Ben get your ASS on this beach. Right now!"

My father's voice holds no humor in it and we know that we are sunk, so to speak.

Keying the radio one last time, Mike's shoulders slump; his chin drops to his chest. "We're on our way in... Bloody Wog out."

Nole's voice comes back over the speaker, "Nole's Ark out."

***

We've been running for twenty minutes. Fog! The fog is thick enough to cut with a knife. I've always liked the fog, up until now that is. We still can't see past the next swell. But things have changed. We're charging along in a beam sea at twenty miles per hour. We no longer have feelers down twenty fathoms telling us where the bottom is. Somehow, this situation seems a little more ominous.

Mike goes to the bow getting out two of our twenty-year-old, moldy, lifejackets.

Clipping one on his belt loop he grins and then clips a life jacket to me. "I read once that a lifejacket is generally not available when they are most needed."

Mike hangs them on a davit in close proximity, we may need them. We haven't gone as far as wearing lifejackets, an unacceptable act in fisherman's society. Wearing a life jacket shows a lack of trust in your boat and ability. This is the first time I have ever seen Mike give any consideration to safety, so he must be more than a little concerned.

Taking the wheel Mike grunts, "Foggy."

I grunt back, "Windy too."

My hands are bloody from cleaning the fish; bending over the side I wash them off in the spray. Tearing through the ocean; the Bloody Wog is slapping the wave tops, as she pounds through the combers.

Standing again, a ball of fear begins to tighten in the pit of my stomach. Gripping the davit hard, we drive into each wave. Wondering... How in the heck are we going to find the rock? What if we miss the rock completely? What if we run onto an unprotected lee shore in these huge swells? What if, what if, what if...?

What would happen? Running the likely scenario through in my mind; *The Wog will be running along, everything hunky-dory. We'll be on the backside of a swell, a little taller and a little steeper than the swells we've been riding. Topping this swell the other side will be white with foam. Not just the puny foam of a comber but truly white everywhere. Mike will see that we're heading to our doom. He'll turn the wheel. Momentum will carry the boat closer to shore during the turn. The swell becoming foam, our prop won't have the bite it needs. The Wog will be three quarters of the way through her turn. Then the comber will overwhelm us. The bow will rise until it is into the crest of the comber. The Wog will over-turn on top of us. Throwing us back and down swell. The old Bloody Wog will flop over onto us. Poles, davits, and cannon balls spreading out everywhere. Lines and cables and fishing gear ready to ensnare us. It's going to be ugly.*

We'll be swimming; we're both young and tough, divers and surfers. We'll survive, but we'll lose everything we own. I feel the water tugging at my legs, and arms; the swells tossing us like a piece of kelp. To survive, we'll need to kick off our sea boots, they will drop off after a long struggle. If they don't, we'll drown

Musing on how we'll be told by everyone on the beach, "I told you so." We'll be wet, cold; they'll look at us like, dunder pates. They'll never think; but they also caught 32 fish and 5 salmon with only two hours on the water. We were on the way too our first hundred fish day. Our biggest day so far.

Glancing to the starboard, the swell that just ran under us crashed onto a beach with a loud roar. I can't see it as much as feel it.

Shouting in Mike's ear, "Breakers, breakers to starboard!"

I stick my arm straight out under his nose; a finger pointing toward the sound of our doom. The swell charging at us is changing shape. It's growing, picking its self-up. Becoming taller and steeper, there's no room for it to run. The top begins to cap.

Mike cuts the speed letting the rolling comber slide by, just in front of us.

Cranking the wheel hard to port he gives the old Bloody Wog full throttle, the stern swinging with the thrust. The bow is pointing into the next twenty-foot comber roaring at us like a freight train. Mike cuts her back to less than half speed. The Wog climbs for her very life, and the wave caps. Mike hits full tilt boggy when the white water hits us.

The white water is all around us, old Wog, she don't float as well in it as she should.

White-Water pops over the sides and bow slopping around the deck. Cleaving through the breaker we're down the glassy backside. In twenty seconds we've gone from the jaws of death to glassy smooth water. All is safe. Riding this ragged edge of disaster is sure exciting.

We're running just outside of the breaking waves, following them up the beach all the way to the Cape.

At the Cape, the fog clears up just enough to get a bearing on where we are on this old globe.

Turning right, Mike runs us toward the beach. The Bloody Wog slides to a halt.

Dad turns his back on us and walks away. Walking toward his camper he leaves with Mom, with Linda in tow. We don't even get breakfast out of coming in. Oh well?

Following them up to the camper I stop. I'd just as soon not look into those disappointed eyes and see that shake of my Dad's head. Not again, not today.

***

It is about four in the afternoon. I'm showered and shaved. In front of the mirror, I am running a comb through my hair. The sun-beached ends are in tangles. The comb stops its descent about two thirds through my hair, pulling hard I force the comb past the obstruction. Teeth are filling with sun bleached strands. Mike steps up behind me, his face appearing in the mirror of the public shower and bathroom that are part of the facilities available to us.

Mike's face is quizzical. "Did we get a dinner invitation I don't know about?"

"Ah... no, WE, didn't get a dinner invite anywhere. Debbie and I are going on *a* picnic this afternoon."

Mike shakes his head up and down. "Good, good, I just happen to be free this afternoon where are we going on our picnic?"

WE; ain't going anywhere, Debbie and I, are going blackberry picking up the coast.

Mike grins his mischievous grin. "Is Debbie bringing enough pails for us all or should I get my own?"

Beaming into the mirror, "You'd better bring your own pail. Cause you ain't going to be within ten miles of us."

"What, you think that Debbie is going to give you a little?"

"I know she won't. Not if you're there eating all our picnic and picking all our berries."

Mike throws his bathing accouterments onto the sink next to me. "I'll go out and pick some berries here in case, you forget to pick any."

Shaking my head at my reflection in the mirror, "Nothing's going to happen. You know that and I know that. I just want to be alone with Debbie. So, something could happen if we wanted it to."

Giving me a sideways leer, Mike retorts, "Yea sure Ben, sure."

***

Debbie is dressed in skintight Levis and some type of stretch top that adheres to her body everywhere, and I mean everywhere. Just now she is bending over in front of me. She spreads a blanket out for our picnicking enjoyment. The scenery is exquisite. I lose my breath, just watching her. Our picnic basket is in one hand, and the obligatory AM- FM radio is in the other.

Turning Debbie reaches out, "Here give me the radio for a corner of our blanket."

She places the radio in the far corner. Her movements are so feminine, so fluid, it hurts my heart. She straightens up from her hands and knees. A position she had assumed for positioning the radio at its designated corner. Debbie kneels facing me, her auburn hair long and flowing in the afternoon breeze, trusting blue eyes hold my gaze. A hand reaches out to me; I grab it. Grabbing it like a drowning man I pull her to me. We kiss, falling caddie corner on the blanket. Debbie, in my arms; is kissing me back, her soft curves pressing against me. Debbie's breath is quickening, to match my own.

Breaking our embrace, Debbie's pure blue eyes look deeply into my own. "I only wanted the picnic basket. We need to hold down the other corner of the blanket."

OOPS. We're in a pasture about a quarter of a mile off a back road; screened from view by pine trees. Our blanket over-looks a stream that meanders through the field. It's a lovely place, just a lovely place. Sitting up from where we have fallen Debbie unpacks our picnic dinner. Fried chicken, roast-beef sandwiches, and two different kinds of salads are between us. Eyeing the basket I spy a black-berry pie, packed away, but not hidden from my prying eyes.

There is not a piece of fish in the whole basket. God, what an understanding woman, a real fish-less meal, man life is good. I want to kiss her again, this time not out of passion, this time, out of gratitude. Gazing lovingly at her, I reach for a sandwich.

***

Leaning back on my elbows I tilt my eyes toward the heavens, a raven caws in the background. A light breeze flutters Debbie's hair. It's a balmy, balmy evening.

I'm in with love with; being in love, girls, food, and fishing. While stuffing my gut, I estimate just how much Debbie is going to let me get away with. This is truly an enjoyable little adventure; in the meantime, Marty and Mike are saving a whole family from certain death. Oh well, we all have our little battles.

***

Mike and Marty are hanging out together, fantasizing about what Debbie and I are up too. They're walking along the beach near Kwanda head.

Marty punches Mike in the arm with his elbow. "Look, look at that puker boat over there, it's plugged with pukers."

The boat Marty is speaking of is a sport fishing boat. They're called puker boats by commercial fisherman because people puke while aboard. We think it's funny.

The boat is filled with; Mom, and Dad who is also the captain. Three little girls two little boys, and another middle-aged man. He's an uncle kind of guy. They're all excited, up for their grand adventure of going around the rock.

Dad and the Uncle back the boat into the Pacific Ocean, making a decent job of it. The boat heads out to sea. A lot of progeny are sticking their little heads above her gunwales. The sea has been coming up all afternoon. They aren't going out very far. So, there can't be any danger. Right?

While at sea, everyday can be your last. It only takes one miss-step, one slip at the wrong time, and you're running along the unholy, ragged edge of disaster. Run over that ragged edge and disaster strikes. From that point on, your fondest wish is for a breath of air, just one breath of air without salt water being a major portion of it. I find that when life is coming at you fast, when the situation is demanding the most of you, that's when time slows down. If time slows down for you, you have time; time to think, time to react, time to begin to formulate a plan. That plan is the difference between being overwhelmed and survival. I've been told, that for some people; time doesn't slow. I feel sorry for those poor souls, you see, they miss all the fun of the adventure they're having.

Mike and Marty are moseying on up the beach, watching the last of the fishing fleet arrive with their catches. The sport boat with the family has rounded the rock. She is running back toward the beach.

About halfway back the boat swerves to the port drunkenly; she broaches. At the bottom of a swell, she digs the starboard gunwale into the trough. The boat comes to a sudden stop throwing bodies into the sea.

Women, children, Dads, Uncles, bodies of all kinds and sizes fly from the hull, like being flung by a madden sea monster. The boat finishes up its mad gyrations by slowly turning turtle; the bottom becoming just visible at the top of each swell.

Standing side by side Mike and Marty are struck by the seriousness of the situation. If someone doesn't do something right now... This is a tragedy in the making. A whole family is going to drown in sight of land.

Mike catches a movement out of the corner of his eye and glances to the right. Marty is slipping off his sweatshirt. He looks down to begin his own strip-tease act to see that he has already removed his shoes. Even before speaking, both Marty and Mike begin getting ready to crawl into that fifty-two-degree water. Crawling into the cold, cold ocean to save a group of people, of whom only moments ago they referred to as pukers.

In fleeting seconds, Mike and Marty are in their underwear and tee shirts. They run toward the water and throw themselves into the ocean. They're swimming at a steady stroke toward the boat. She is raising and falling with every swell. When both the boat and the rescuers are on top of a swell the swimmers get a look at their target.

Ten minutes of hard swimming brings them near the boat.

Little heads begin to appear in the swells. Sobbing and crying can be heard in every direction. Marty yells, "Mike!" He points in one direction and begins swimming in the other.

Mike raises a hand to Marty's indication. Marty will go one direction and Mike another, they'll try and collect up swimmers. Finding one little kid around seven, Mike grabs him by his lifejacket. Undertaking the chore of towing him to the boat, Mike is kicking and stroking with one arm, towing the kid by the lifejacket. Mike, is not the most patient person with kids and this one is sniffling and wanting to wine.

"I want my Mommy, I'm c-c-cold."

"Hey kid, you think your old-lady can save your ass then I'll leave you here for her."

"N-Noo please don't leave me, I don't want my mom that much."

Mike's teeth are rattling in his head from the cold, but he forces out. "Well then, kid, act like a man." Without a chatter.

Mike is the type of person who gives of himself carefully, but once you are his friend or have been taken under his wing, he will kill or die for you.

While Mike is towing this little kid back to the dory Marty is busy with two other children. Marty is a sensitive creature; a kind and gentle soul who really cares, he cares about how a person feels. An upbeat guy, who sees the best side of every situation and everyone. Marty is the kind of guy that would have led the band on the Titanic, as she sank.

Marty swims up to one little blond headed girl. "How are we doing good hun?"

Her blue eyes sparkle with fear. "Ca-ca-cold, I'm cold what happened I don't know what happened?"

"It's OK I'm here now. We'll g-g-get you back to the dory and get some help."

Marty sees another little guy flopping around as the swells lifts him up simultaneously. Dragging his little charge over to the other head bobbing on the wave tops he smiles his reassurances.

"Hey, want to join us?"

Marty is shepherding the children along. "Come on now kick I can't drag both of you. You've got to help."

Marty's voice is soothing, coaching his charges back to the boat.

Marty arrives at the dory. The bottom of the boat is at a slant but still above water. The engine is weighing down the stern, almost sinking. There's just enough air entrapped in the bow to keep her afloat. Mike has handed his charge over to the kid's mother, thankfully.

Mike is busy with the uncle who is in the mist of having a heart attack. Everyone in the water is wearing a life jacket except the dad, the uncle, and, of course, Mike and Marty.

The dad is paralyzed with; guilt, and fear, and the cold, he is holding onto the bow-line and is quietly sobbing. Marty swims up to the dad still towing the two children and gasps out between chattering teeth.

"Is-s-s-s th-th-this everyone, is there anyone else we need to sa-sa-search for?"

Mike looks over at Marty and chatters at him, "H-He is useless, I-I-I asked him the same question before you showed up with those two you have in tow. He told me that this is all there is, there is no one else to look for."

Marty gasps, "What a moron!" Then he looks at the dad, "Sorry sir, I didn't mean that in a mean way."

Marty needs to crawl up onto the bow of the dory and attract some attention from shore, or the last of the incoming fleet. The bottom is very slick and laying at a forty-five-degree angle from the weight of the motor. He looks around for a means of getting to the top of the bow he knows he can't climb the wet, rolling, slick, surface.

Marty looks at the dad and smiles his most winning grin. "Could I use your bow line for a while?"

"What for, I need it to hold myself up?"

Marty continues his voice calm. "Well sir, we need it so that I can climb on top of the boat, and get some help from shore or a passing boat."

"I need it to hold myself up. I keep sinking without it, I need it, I need it, you can't have it!"

Mike is less patient with cowardliness than he is with children. Looking over from where he's supporting the uncle's head above the water. In a very quiet voice that only Mike and the dad can hear he says.

"If you don't let Marty have that rope I'm going to take it away from you. Tie a knot in it. Then beat you to death with it. Do you understand me?"

Dad flings the rope at Marty. "Here, you want it, you have it."

Smiling his appreciation, "Thank you, sir. See Mike, how w-we're a-a-all working together here, this is good, a real good thing."

Grinning at the dad, Mike responds, "Yea, that's good… you done real good."

Marty throws the rope over the backside of the boat so that it lays down the centerline of the dory. Placing his feet on the bottom he climbs up the dory like a mountain climber. Reaching the top

Marty stands with his feet spread, his knees flex to account for the roll.

Marty shouts to the shore, "HELP, we need HELP!"

All he can see are busy fisherman trying to get home and to bed. Way too busy to look toward the setting sun. Too busy to see that a life and death struggle is taking place a half a mile from them.

Looking seaward Marty sees the Fiddler rounding Cape Kawanda. He's pounding toward the beach

coming in from a late bite. The Fiddler sees Marty waving at him from the bow. Old Fiddler waves back in a relaxed way. This heightens Marty's concern; will the Fiddler stop; does he understand what is going on here?

The Fiddler continues on toward the beach in his unconcerned way, passing them by. Marty's face falls, he considers yelling; only Marty knows that he can't be heard.

Fiddler rounds down swell approaching the boat from that direction, at the last minute he swings his stern to the group and kills his motor.

"Well, well, well folks, you got yourself quite a-little pickle here; how many is there of you anyway? Marty, why are you swimmin' around in your underwear? Does your Mother know that you're out here?"

Marty pushes the hair out of his eyes. "How many can you take?"

"Oh well now, I don't rightly know, we'll just keep loading-um on until the ocean over-tops the engine well... then we'll throw one back."

With that The Fiddler takes the heart attack uncle by the hand, dragging him over the stern. Picking kids out of the water next, by the time all the family is aboard water is lapping over the motor well.

The Fiddler shakes his head at Mike and Marty. "Looks like you two are swimmin, oh just a minute."

Fiddler digs into an ice chest, turning he pitches a beer to Marty then one to Mike.

"See you on the beach boys."

Marty and Mike grin at one another, tilting their beers they take a swig. It is just like The Fiddler, leave you to your own devices but throw you beer when that's the last thing you need.

Marty grins down at Mike, "You know Mike, The Fiddler is the only guy around who would send people to hell matches."

***

'Walking slowly out of the ocean, Mike and Marty retrieve their clothes. The last of the spectators are leaving the beach. All the ambulances have just left the scene. No one

is interested in the two shivering figures emerging from the Pacific Ocean in the fading glow of dusk. The Fiddler is down at the bar; everyone is buying him drinks. He's such a hero; he saved a whole family from certain death, you know.

It turns out that the boat had lost a steering cable shive. When the shive-axial let go, the boat turned hard on the wave and broached. A more experienced seaman might have been able to cut the throttle and save the boat, or maybe not. It's all a matter of conjecture?

***

It's dark and my shirt is being used as a pillow for Debbie's lovely head as we lay on the blanket. Pulling back from an intense kiss, I can no longer see her features. We are both peaked with sexual excitement even though we've been tentative in this first encounter. I've barely been able to summon up enough courage to brush her breast with my hand, touching lightly as though by accident.

A buzzing, faint but insistence; what is that? An inching on my back, ouch, that stings. Mosquitoes, and lots of them!

Pulling away from Debbie, "We better go."

"But why, we don't..." Debbie halts in mid-sentence. Brushing away mosquitoes, "Let's go, I'm being eaten alive."

Grabbing stuff, we're packing; packing while a swarm of mosquitoes descends on us in a cloud. It's hard to see through them. They're sending out a message to friends and family alike. "Dinner is served."

Giving up on packing we grab parts and pieces from our picnic, and run. The stream has a well-worn path with stepping-stones across the creek. In the dark, surrounded by voracious blood sucking mosquitoes, we take no notice of the stones. We run like the mosquito ravished cowards that we are.

Splashing across the stream I swing the blanket over our heads like a Viking Berserker swinging his war ax. The mosquitoes follow us, their feeding frenzy increases with every step. Clear of the trees we sprint toward the car, the buzz of mosquitoes loud in our ears. Being deeply in lust with Debbie I unlock her door first. Making sure she is safely ensconced inside; I sprint to the driver's side. The door is locked. Some fiddling ensues, during which mosquitoes extract another pint of blood.

Finally getting in Debbie hands me my shirt. "You've got blood all over your chest. You'd better dress before someone asks questions we don't want to answer."

***

It's the afternoon of the day after Debbie and my first picnic; Robby is leaning up against the gunwale of the Bloody Wog. He's wearing a serious expression for once in his life, his face is generally a smirk, as he makes a sly remark, or a full smile as he contemplates how fun life is. Or, he is engaged in a deep hearty belly laugh. To Rob Life is fun, the more jokes the better.

He'll laugh readily at: you, me, or himself all with the same abandon. This summer Rob received the nickname Dumbship from his dad. He finds the name as great a joke as anyone else.

At present his consternation is caused by a complicated life altering decision. He lifts a hand to his watch cap and pushes it back.

"Well, you see I've met this guy, he owns a nice boat and launch rig. He'll lease it to me but he wants someone older, more experienced aboard. In case something should happen. Helen's boyfriend, he wants to partner up with me, but I just don't, I just don't know?"

Robby's consternation is a serious matter. Helen's boyfriend showed up last week. No one bothered to explain his recent absence, since his return he has been strutting around like some type of returning hero. It probably doesn't help that he treats all of us young Californians, with an indifference boarding on disdain.

Gee, I wonder if the fact that all of us would trade the rest of our years here on earth, for one night with Helen has any impact on his feelings toward us. Maybe? I still haven't bothered to learn Helen's boyfriend's name.

"Robby, what's this guy's name?"

Robby shakes his head. "Bill, Bill something he's a contractor in Portland."

"No, he's not. He's a hippie."

Robby looks confused. "You know the guy I'm leasing the boat from?"

Now I feel like Rob looks. "No, I know Helen's boyfriend, he's a hippie."

Robby laughs a deep, happy laugh, "Of course Helen's boyfriend is a hippie. If I thought it would do me any good with Helen, I'd become a hippie too."

Robby slaps the gunwale of the Wog. "That's it, I'm going to talk to Gus. We'll lease that boat and go for it. Thanks a lot for the advice, it really helped.

Robby spins on his heel, striding away toward his truck. Gus? Gus must be Helen's boyfriend. Walking down the line of boats Robby meets Debbie turning the corner, coming toward us.

Swaying past him with a nod and a smile, turning watching her walk, he shakes his hand in a loose motion. He's letting me know that he thinks she looks hot.

Debbie sways on up to the Bloody Wog a smile caressing her pretty face.

"Hi," she greets, "Hogie sent me out here with a couple of Cokes. He gave Mike one. They're in the store, Hogie's telling fish stories."

In greeting I reach a hand out to Debbie. I'm not sure if I'm going to take a Coke or help her aboard. Grasping my hand she gracefully swings a leg over the gunwale. Mounting the boat like a girl raised on the coast of Oregon, which of course she is, she pecks me on the lips. It's a signal that we're a couple. In a small town if only one person sees the kiss everyone in town will know of it tomorrow.

"What were you and Robby talking about you looked serious?"

Popping the top of the Coke bottle with a church key I take a swig. "Robby has a chance to fish a boat, but he needs a partner, an older partner. Do you know Helen's boyfriend? What's his name? Gus? Gus I think?"

Debbie nods in agreement. "Yes, I know him, he's been around the store a lot lately, looking for work on a boat. I don't know, I think he is creepy, you know what I mean?"

"Kind-of, he's not real friendly, but... then we're a click, and he is not a part."

Debbie's blue eyes sparkle with feeling, "It's not just that I don't think he is honest for some reason. I heard that he just got out of jail for running drugs... marijuana, up from Mexico.""I haven't heard anything like that. I don't know where he has been but nobody mentioned Mexico."

Debbie nods her head to indicate how serious she is, "It's not just that he isn't trustworthy, he feels wrong. I feel it more than know it, know what I mean? Well, you tell Robby not to get involved with that hippie. Either that, or you and Mike watch out over him, make sure that Gus doesn't take advantage of Robby."

Nodding in understanding, not in agreement with her proposal, but I understand. Now I know why men talk things over with their wives, you get a whole different perspective from a woman.

***

Pulling the Bloody Wog alongside of the gas pump; I'm here for the nightly fill-up. As the door on old-Bertha opens the hinge crackles and pops at me once again. Feeling guilty about my neglect I walk forward. At the front of the car, I raise the hood. Pulling out the dipstick, oil is dripping in my path as I return to the door. Holding the dipstick over the hinge, oil dripping; plop, plop, plop. The oil plops while I work the door back and forth. My hope is that the cracking sound will subside. It doesn't. Standing there, dipstick in hand, waving the door in the breeze I am daydreaming. A gruff voice interrupts my daydream, which is a shame. In my daydream, Debbie is walking toward me bared to the waist."Hey, did ya see the fight today?"

Looking up from Bertha's hinge, "Fight, what fight?"

Archie Bunker, "Joe," grins at me as if to say, 'Get the joke.'

"Why I go to the fights every Saturday afternoon, don't you know about them?"

I'm still working the door, but losing interest in the job. What in the heck is Joe talking about? "No; we don't know about any fights, what fights, where?"

Joe rubs his crew cut and smiles. This is the first time I've ever seen him smile. "Yep, Saturday afternoon at the fights. It's the Wilson boys; they been fishing and fighting together every year,

210

for five years. Jim he must be twenty now, and Steve he is about seventeen."

Looking at Joe in wonder, I'm confused? This is the first time that he has been friendly to me. I've always been concerned that he hates us.

"Where do you go to the fights? Mike and I like a good fight."

"It's the Wilson boys fight. They're brothers, and there just ain't any love lost between them. Their Mother is religious so they rest on Sunday, but by Saturday, they're tired from the week and Jimmy, he'll be hung over. The combination makes for a fight for-sure. Saturday that's fight day.

This afternoon, I was fishin' by them, trolling south and they were trolling north. They get a fish on. Steven he is the youngster, he was the boat. Little old Stevie, he is the most ambitious of the pair. Our hero Steve, is cranking up a side. They were in fish; cause... when he landed the fish, he raced forward and shook his brother. Jim, he was under the bow sleeping and Steven couldn't get him awake. After a few shakes, Steve gives up returning to his fishing. Another salmon is on the surface; he's working him. Suddenly he's jumped from behind.

Coming from his lair, Jimmy grabs his brother by the hair of the head, pounding his face a few times for good measure. Then Jimmy turns and heads back to his lair under the bow. He figured that was that.

Well, old Steve he wipes the blood from his face and lands the fish. Now, like I was saying, old Steven, he is ambitious. He gets the gear back out and fishing. By this time, I have turned the boat and am following them back up the line. Mind you, just to watch the fun. When Steven has the gear back out, he quietly creeps forward. He positions himself near the bow where Jimmy is sleeping and waits. When he is sure that Jim is asleep he pounces. All I can see are arms flailing above the gunwale. He's pounding on poor old Jim under the bow. The pounding is going along pretty good, when he goes flying over the fish box. Ya see; Jimmy got his boot on his chest and kicked him off.

Steven just picks himself up and goes back to work, like attacking your brother under the bow is just part of the job. Back at work, Steve is cranking up another fish and he's attacked from behind, again. It's like that's just the way they catch fish. Fight fish, fish fight? Funny. I'll tell you I thought I was going to die laughing.

They square off, fighting... punching and swinging at one another. Old Steven slips on some blood, hits the deck on all fours. Jimmy grabs his head and stuffs it into the motor well, down by the prop. Jimmy, he's soaking little old Steven's head really good. About every twenty seconds he lets Steve up for a breath. Then, back in the water. Fish shaking on the lines, the boat going round and round, and Steven's head being soaked by his big brother; all in all, twas the best fight I've seen all summer. A real rip-snorter. You guys should come and watch."

By this time Joe is laughing so hard that there are tears in his eyes. He wipes the tears away and slaps the steering console. Joe is enjoying his story more than I am.

***

It must have been a week, maybe less, since Archie told me about the fight. One day blends into the next. There are no weekends in the fishing business.

Robby is standing next to his newly leased boat. He is as proud as if he had hatched it himself. Standing in the boat at the steering station, Gus is turning the wheel back and forth, looking out over the parking lot like he is navigating the Colombia River bar. Gus sees himself as the indomitable Captain, even though his experience at sea is zero days. Why would you need any sea time to be a sea captain? It's all in having the right hat you know.

Rob and Gus have made a deal with the Portland contractor. A sixty-forty split. A sixty-forty split is the percentage that each party will receive. The contractor will get forty percent of the gross earnings. Rob and Gus will split Sixty percent after expenses. Those expenses of operating a boat can't be much, just little things such as gas, bait, repairs, gear, leads, new lines, and sunders. After-all how much can it cost to outfit a new boat.

Marty and I are standing at Hogie's counter, more leaning against it, like a bar. We're awaiting our drinks. Debbie pulls a couple of Cokes from the refrigerator. Returning, her walk is a study in feminine sway. Debbie hands Marty his Coke and then places the other one in my hand caressing my work roughen hand with the motion.

A toss of Debbie's head sends auburn hair into a swirl about her shoulders. "I hope you told Robby what I said about that Gus. He's going to wind up with both ends of the rope. Did you warn him?"

Dropping my head in shame, "No, no I didn't. He wanted that boat so much I, I just couldn't throw ice water all over it."

Debbie rubs my hand and fore arm. Her touch is soft and caressing, her tone softens. "He's just getting short term pleasure for long term pain. You mark my words."

Hogie walks in from the packing shed, "Hey boys what's happening."

Taking a pull from his Coke, Marty wipes his lips with the back of his shirt sleeve, "Just looking at Robby's new boat, quite a rig, quite a rig."

Hogie looks out of the window. "That's one shaky operation."

Marty turns and looks at Hogie, confusion in his eyes, "looks like a great operation to me. Brand new boat, new four-wheel drive pickup to launch with, what else do you need?"

Hogie grins back at Marty, "An owner who knows what it takes to catch a fish."

This statement is quite an insult in a society where knowledge of just this subject defines your worth. Hogie has judged this man as unworthy; he is unfit for fisherman society. I'm not sure why? Maybe he's a blowhard, or... maybe he insulted Marline? Could it be that he's rich? I don't think so. But, I don't understand why Hogie doesn't like the guy. It must be something.

Hogie continues his thoughts on the subject of the rich Portland contractor. "He takes Robby on, good choice... That Robby, he's a good little fisherman. Then he has a drink or two with that hippie and saddles Rob with him for seasoning. Now, I ain't saying that Robby couldn't use some seasoning. I don't think he needs to be seasoned with marijuana."

Hogie looks at Gus through the window; disgust on his face. "I'm not putting my money on him. He's a bob-tailed nag if I ever saw one. Another thing, that guy couldn't find the beach on a clear day if he were at the Cape. And me, I'm supposed to outfit the boat with gear not on that hippie's name I'm not."

Standing there feeling the cold Coke in my hand I'm stunned. A shiver runs down my spine. I didn't think Hogie with-held credit from anyone. Robby and his new partner Gus are walking toward the fish company door. In less than one minute they'll enter here and Hogie will tell them what he has just told us. Their dream will fly straight out the window.

The bell rings as Robby walks under it, the bell's friendly little tinkle announcing the end of Robby's dream. Rob bellies up to the counter laughing a happy go lucky chuckle.

"Hey Deb, can I get a Coke too, might as well give my new partner one also.

Well, Hogie, we're going to need some new gear for our new boat."

Silence follows this happy go lucky statement of the obvious. "We're going to put all this gear on the Mox-Nix tag."

I'm stunned once again. Robby is going to charge on his dad's account. The thought had just never entered my head, buy stuff and let your father pay. God, it is brilliant.

Hogie scratches his beard, "Your Dad knows about this?"

Robby grins into Hogie's eyes, "Yep."

Hogie pulls a book from behind the counter. "What do you need?"

***

It is just past eight in the evening Mike and I are spit shined and polished. Once again, we are entering Tom-Tom's house for free food.

Standing beside the screen door Ma is waving us through. "Get in here before the food is all gone, I thought you boys liked to eat. Showing up at my table at eight o'clock, you boys should be horse whipped. Come on in, come on in, before I throw your share to the hogs."

We had gotten off the Pacific Ocean only an hour ago, sold our fish, cleaned our boat, fueled her, taken a shower, shared our one safety razor and shaved, then put on clean wrinkled clothes. But, if Ma ain't yelling at you she don't like you.

Atop his easy chair, Tom-Tom's beer hand motions us into the house. "Come on in boys, well how-ja-do today?"

The question is as much a greeting as inquiry. Mike reaches up to touch the mustache he started a couple of weeks ago, "We got a bakers dozen, and one nice smiley."

Tom-Tom gestures at his couch with his beer bottle. "Sit, sit. Girls! Get something for the boys to drink, would you?"

Debbie walks through the kitchen door her face flushed and radiant from cooking. "Ben, Mike, what would you like?"

A beer is what we would like, but it's not what we should drink with Tom-Tom watching. Speaking up for both of us, "A glass of ice tea would be nice."

"Coming right up," Tom-Tom settles back in his chair, reaching out with his unoccupied hand and turning the Citizen Band radio up. The static is deafening. Somehow, in the static, a voice can be heard.

"BUZZZZ, click... Yea.. well, find-deal we're going to run until midnight. Then shut down for a little shuteye. We should be in the area about then. We'll see the lights for sure, for sure, good buddy. Wherrrr... Buzzzz click."

"Yea well, partner, I'm twenty mics behind and five mics outside. I'll get there around two or three in the morning. How many did they get today?"

The first voice returns an engine roaring in the background of the static, "Sounds like most of the boats got a couple of humps, some less some more, but there are fish around."

"Right now, that sounds mighty good to me, I got a bent bank account... buzz click-buzz. The Old Lady says I can't come home and see the kids, until it's unbent. Fifteen or twenty days of a couple a hump would make me all better. All better for sure, good buddy for sure."

The first speaker crackles through the static again. "BUZZZ...Ah well. It is still early in the season. We have till Thanksgiving to iron that little old bank account out. No telling how long this little bite will last. Might be a one-day show, could go on for a month? Ten years ago, I fished a month twenty miles off the Cape, getting between two and five hump a day."

Tom-Tom picks up the radio mike, "Tom-Tom base to the boat that was just talking. Tom-Tom base to the albacore boats, do you pick me up?"The radio just sets there and hisses at us the static loud and unnatural in the living room.

Tom turns to us, "Albacore, just thirty to forty miles out. I'm thinking of running out after a few of em. I'll take a look at fishing tomorrow. When albacore are this close the salmon go off the bite. You guys might want to head out, take a look at albacore fishin it's a kick."

Debbie returns with our tea. Handing Mike a glass, she sits on the arm of the couch next to me. Her soft, lovely bottom pressed against my shoulder, fingers stroking my hair. Tom-Tom glances from her caressing hand to my face. He's looking me straight in the eye, until I drop my gaze. I know what Tom is thinking, and he's right. I'm trying to bed his daughter. I just can't help myself.

To lighten the mood I ask, "So, Tom-Tom have you ever fished albacore?"

Tom takes a slug of beer, tilting his head back, his eyes close. "I was raised on an albacore troller. Not my whole life but from twelve on. I grew up fishing."

Jerking my head in surprise, "Grew up on a troller what was that like?"

"Oh it wasn't bad, wasn't bad at all, after I got over losing mom that is. I was orphaned at twelve; my mother died in a car crash. I've got no other family that I know of, we were living in Point Arena at the time. Being a normal kid, I spent all my free time at the docks. The fish buyer he let us kids hang out down there... Fish, net crab, whatever. After Mom was killed, I just moved in with Tom. That's when people started calling me Tom's-Tom. Tom bought fish at Arena from April until November I fished on one troller or another. Not a bad life but I didn't finish eight grade that is a bit of a hindrance if you want a shore job."

Mike, is moved by this bit of personal history his eyes are moist, "Man, it must have been hard. Very hard to leave your home, and become a deckhand at twelve. What about your father, wasn't he anywhere around? An aunt, an uncle, no-one was there for you?"

Tom-Tom looks from one of us to the other, "You know... when a person hears about what someone else has endured; he thinks, I could never do that, but if it were you, you'd do just fine, just fine.During Tom's monologue, my hand has wondered over into Debbie's lap and is resting on her inter thigh. Looking down I see where my hand is. Jerking it into the air I almost smack her nose.

Tom throws his head back and laughs at my antics, still breaking up, he sputters at me, "Come on, lets go feed you guys so Ben and Debbie can go out berry picking. Maybe... they'll even find some berries this time."

***

The albacore has been off Cape Kiwanda for two days now. The last two evenings have been spent getting ready to strike for them. We have scraped together four rusty five-gallon gas cans. We bought twelve albacore jigs and a skein of albacore line. From Nole, we borrowed some heavy monofilament leader and some micro-presses. The last two evenings, after a full day of salmon fishing, have been filled with exciting stories by old timers who have fished albacore. Scrounging for gas cans has become a full-time evening occupation for me. It has to be, this town has been stripped of all gas containers.

Every forging trip to scrounge parts and pieces is an evening full of fish tails. It seems that all dory fishermen have made thousands of dollars, in a matter of hours fishing albacore.

It's the El Dorado of dory fishing; easy money just pours onto your decks in an ecstasy of flowing adrenaline. Albacore fishing is the Olympic sport of the dory fleet. The concept is; this is the most fun you can have with your clothes on.

To catch albacore, you drive straight off shore two, three, or four hours. The ocean turns from green to a deep, deep blue, warming up in the process. Bringing your boat to a stop; you can look down into the depths of the ocean, forever. Sunlight slants through the waves in shafts, each shaft lighting a moving section of ocean. Swells pick up a light shaft, then drop it. The light shaft penetrates through the waves and down, down, down, until it defuses into a blue haze.

Albacore gear is nothing like salmon gear, it glides along the surface, skipping and jumping. The hooks are double and barbless. Brightly colored feathers cover the hooks; tied to a lead head with crystal red eyes. The albacore line is almost an eight inch in diameter. Pulling them in, is hand over hand, when you're in-um, you're in-um. They're all over the place, like cow pies at Shorty's Dairy. Fish flying over the stern time and again; it's fun, easy money, exciting, dangerous, and rewarding. Mike and I are pumped up. We're ready; let's go get some albacore.

***

It's Saturday morning. Last might Nole decided, the fleet, our fleet is going offshore. We're looking for Bug Eye, Long Fin, Tuna, Albacore. YES, we're heading out; twenty, thirty, forty miles offshore! The old Bloody Wog has an extra twenty gallons of gas stacked on top of our old rusty gas tank. Our whole fleet is gassed to the gills and we're headed off-shore to get rich.Old Bertha is following the old Kisutch up the beach. The dawn is lagging our launch by an hour.

The ocean pounds off to our left the sky lit by stars and a setting three quarter moon. The beach is congested this morning. The usual morning quite is repeatedly broken with the ring-a-ding-

ding-ding of outboards warming up. Every time an outboard is killed the throatier sound of big V-8 engines echoing up and down the beach fills the morning air. Scanning the beach, expensive four-wheel drive pick-ups, hooked to expensive sport boats is all that can be seen.

It must be some kind of holiday in the working world. Everyone who owns a dory is launching this morning. Fisherman only use a calendar to know when a season begins or ends. We never know what day of the week it is.

Today, the beach looks like some kind of Roman Holiday. Sport boats are backing into the ocean, empty trailers are pulling out, sand flying up from their wheels as they speed to a parking place. Fishermen are running for their boats, trucks whizzing by. Lights are gleaming on the salty sand, reflecting off the running fishermen. It's a zoo.

Bertha rolls to a stop just above the surf line. Mike and I exit her recently oiled doors; nary a sound of cracking hinges can be heard over the pounding surf. We have parked a far-piece from the head this morning due to all the activity. Soon, the poles are out and the engine is warm. All is in readiness. Marty and Albert, a little to our north, are making a run toward the ocean. They drop their boat into the ocean like the pros they are. Nole and Bob are outside the surf line, they're waiting, and we're all going to run out together. Running out together will accomplish two things. If there's a problem, we'll be together. Two, we can string out in a line for a larger search pattern. The Dumbship pulls alongside of Mox-Nix, Bob's boat. Everyone is out waiting on us to join them.

Under the wheel of Bertha, I'm driving slowly toward the head; looking for a hole. There ain't any, the ocean is full; at least the beach is. A Jeep speeds past me on the left, cutting right, almost pulling his trailer into Bertha. This jerk stops right in front of us. Jumping from his rig he's going to ready his boat. It's a sport boat. Backing up a bit we go around him, I'm still looking for a spot, any spot, to dump the old Wog into the ocean. Driving slowly north a big high stepping Ford with an empty trailer pulls in front of me, cutting me off. This guy jumps from his rig and runs for his boat all excited, and happy go fishing.Opening Bertha's door, I yell my voice breaking in anger. "You asshole!" Again, I back down and drive around the parked rig.

I feel an urgent need to get the boat in the water. I NEED I mean NEED to get her in the ocean. Our fleet will head out without us. Arcing Bertha toward the cliffs I start to back toward the ocean. Some guy in a Datsun angles past my stern taking the spot I was going to launch. Hitting the brakes and spinning my head from side to side, I'm looking for another spot. The whole surf-line is littered with boats laying broad-side too. I don't know; I just don't know where to go. This is disgusting. What's wrong with me? This just ain't happening.

Pulling around two more rigs I position myself for another run at the ocean. Then, jerk number two races for our spot. I don't know; I just don't know. Our whole fleet is waiting on me. They're waiting on me to get the Bloody Wog in the water, and I'm screwing around. Opting for an act of desperation I swing old Bertha south.

Heading to a section of beach where the Cape offers little or no shelter. Wet sand is flying from our tires; we're speeding toward the last boat in line. Swinging around I back toward the ocean at full tilt buggy. Feeling the first big wave hit the stern I hit the brakes. The Wog slides off the trailer and into the ocean. Speeding away I leave Mike tending to the Wog.

Parking is altogether another problem. The beach is lined with trucks and trailers, God, what holiday is this anyway? Driving up the beach I'm looking for any spot that I can find to stick ol Bertha. There is just no place, turning around I head back down south. There is always a place down the beach. Nope. Trucks and trailers line the cliffs. Side by side, there is just no place to stick Bertha. At last; I find a spot by the Dory King, and I park in the big parking lot that is for everyone. Leaving the keys in Bertha, just in case someone needs to move her, I run for Mike and the Bloody Wog.

The golden glow of the morning sun strikes the mountains to our east. Thuds of my running feet hitting the pavement fill my ears. On the beach again, the sounds of hoarse yells can be heard above the pounding surf.

Thumping along as fast as my heavy sea boots will allow; things have changed. In the time it has taken me to park, Mike and the Bloody Wog have drifted further south. She's a good hundred yards south of the Head. The old Wogs' not getting any protection from the Cape, ocean swells are busting her in the bow. A strong southerly current is sweeping her even further away from safety.

Splashing into the surf, "Mike, Mike? We're not getting any protection. Maybe we should pull the boat? Try up by the Cape again?"

"Naw, it's a zoo up there. We'd only run into the same thing. Better to try our luck here, or the fleet will leave us."

Mike's excited face is alight, his eyes glowing with this new adventure. He's grinning from ear to ear. We're happy in the knowledge, in two minutes, we're on our way to getting rich fishing long fin.

Rolling aboard the Wog, Mike's boots spray me with water. It's part of our morning ritual. As I push us out, Mike drops the engine into the down position. Pulling on the starter rope, he gets a whirr out of the engine. But there's no sound of a catch. Uh-oh, it's at least thirty minutes since we had her warm. This may take a few pulls to get her going again. Mike wraps the starter rope around and around the flywheel. He yanks. A wave breaks over the bow sending twenty gallons of spray into the old Wog. Now the engine is cold, and wet. Mike shakes his head, his face not so full of happy excitement. Re-wrapping the starter rope he gives a mighty yank, falling to the deck with this attempt. Another twenty gallons of brine pours over the bow, Mike, and the uncovered engine.I have a sinking feeling that we're sunk. Mike slips on the wet deck, hitting on all fours, beginning to rise, another large wave breaks over the bow. Water is over the floorboards. Not an unusual event on the Bloody Wog, it just has never happened this early before.

Leaping up and then forward, Mike unties our ores. As he works with the lashing I push us out. The water is at the top of my boots. Even at the shallow of the breaker. So I hold until Mike has the ores in the locks. He's pulling for all he is worth, joining him I push out over my boots. Cold ocean is running down my sea boots, and swirling around my crotch.

"Man, this water's COLD!"

Leaning into the ores, Mike bellows over his shoulder. "Push Ben push, we're going to make her we got her now!"

Water is up to my waist but I can see Mike may be right. We're going to make her? The bow rises to an oncoming wave she struggles up, but the wave curls above the bow, crashing into the Bloody Wog. Two hundred gallons of brine sweeps aft, pouring over the fish box; it takes Mike off his feet. Laying in the swirling salt water for just a second, Mad-Man-Mike is up, pulling for all he is worth; Mike's temper is up. He's attacking the ocean with the same ferocity that he attacked the ore lock guards, on our first day of work together. The ten foot sweep ores are bending under his energy. Mike is focused on making it past the surf line.

Except now we are carrying an extra three to four hundred gallons of water. The sea water is our doom. The bow rises to the next wave, four hundred gallons of water rush to the stern, weighing it down. Adding my weight to the mix, sea water flows over the motor well and into the boat. At the same time, the bow is under the curl of the oncoming breaker. Sea water pours aboard in abundance. If we had an engine this would not be a problem. Two, maybe three breakers, and we'd be out past the surf. But, rowing, our progress is painfully slow. Breaker after breaker takes its swipe at us. The breaking surf is sounding the death knell on our big adventure.

The water is up to my armpits, and I'm pushing for all I'm worth every time that my feet hit the bottom. Mike is pushing on the sweep ores so hard they're flexing to the breaking point. Nole just outside of the breaker line has Buzz in the stern, a tow line ready to cast to us. If we can get just a little closer, just to the breaker line. We'll be on our way to albacore fishing.

The sea is up to my arm-pits. My crotch high sea boots are filled with water, making swimming impossible. I'm not sure that I can get aboard. Every time I struggle to get a breath, Mike is intent on the next swell.

He's digging with the ores; a wave sweeps aboard and through the boat. We are sunk. The ocean is even with the top of the motor well. The boat can't hold any more water. As a wave crashes aboard, the same volume of water flows out the stern.

Sputtering out a mouth full of salt water the taste as bitter as the defeat that has just overwhelmed us, "Mike, Mike!"

"What?"

"We're sunk, the motor-well is under."

Mike looks over his shoulder at me, "We can make it, push Ben push!"

"Mike, the boat is sunk, we're going to sink the motor. We can't get any deeper, I have to hold the stern up all the time now."

Looking down at the motor well, the brutal truth strikes him. The light of adventure fading from his eyes. "OK, Ben, we're sunk, lets' pull her back in."

Pulling her backwards, in two breakers the old Wog is back on the beach. It was just that easy to give up. It's always easy to give up; once on the beach I fall back on the sand, sucking great gulps of air, trying to catch my breath. After an encounter with the Pacific Ocean, it's always nice to just enjoy breathing for a while.

Mike flops down next to me. He's soaked to the bone also, "Huff huff huffi-Well, well... we gave her one hell of a go."

"You-bet-cha Mike, one hell of a go."

Sauntering up, rubber boots kicking sand on us; Hogie's warm and dry jacket is zipped snugly up. "I heard someone was in trouble down here, I didn't expect it to be you guys.

My head shakes in disgust, "The sport boats took over the beach. We had to launch at the south end. The current got a hold on us. And, and... that was it."

Hogie hands me an end of a line that he is holding. "Tie this to your bow-eye we'll jerk her out of there and we'll get your engine running again."

***

It's around eight-thirty in the evening. Out west, where the albacore are; the sun is sinking into a golden ocean. Running between the Rock and the Cape, we're headed in; after we sank the boat this morning, we got her bailed out and loaded up. Mike and I took a shower, bought a hot breakfast at the Dory King, and got the motor running. Around noon we leisurely ran north to the head and dropped our salmon gear. We didn't want to feel bad at being left behind. The fish climbed on board. It was as though they were dying to be aboard the Bloody Wog; which they were. It's our best day of the season. Now we're running toward the beach with thirty-five fish in the box.

Setting on the beach ahead of us is the Kisutch; Marty and Albert are loading her on the trailer.

"Wonder how they did?"

Mike is cleaning fish, so both of his hands are bloody. There's a smear of blood on his glasses and nose. "They killed-um, I'll bet they got a deck load."

In sage agreement I shove the throttle to full tilt boogie aiming right at the old Kisutch, sliding up the beach, gently gliding to a stop; we jump from the Wog. We're going to see our first albacore. We're leaning on their gunwale craning our necks, there's nothing to see but empty deck.

Swiveling his head from side-to-side Mike requests.

"Lift the fish box lid we want to see one."

Brushing his long blond hair out of his eyes Al's face is grim. "You're not going to see one on this boat; or any other boat in the fleet today, we all got skunk."

Mike shakes his head sadly, "Gee Al, not one not even one albacore. Tough luck."

"Yea, we used forty gallons of gas, plus all this new gear we have to pay for. You and Ben are lucky you couldn't get off the beach this morning it saved you about ten dollars in gas. All day, and not one stinking fish."Mike responds, deep irony in his voice, "Yep, we were pretty lucky this morning." Pushing off the gunwale with our forearms, we amble to the Wog.

Marty yells at us as we walk away. "Mike, did you get any today or were you just on a test run?"

"Got thirty-five fish, and five Salmond."

With that comment we begin striding toward old Bertha, but Mike reflects. "You know Ben, I still wish we would have gotten off the beach this morning, God I love an adventure."

"Me too, Mike, me too."

***

Mike, Marty, Albert and I are setting at the table the in our little trailer. We are deeply involved in a rap session. The discussion is ranging all over the map; like the poem of old; "We shall speak of many things, of shoes and ships, of sealing wax, of cabbages and Kings."

Albert and Marty came here originally to let us know that we should come to their house for dinner. That was over an hour ago, and the rap session is still going strong.

The mood in the trailer alters suddenly; turning from a relaxed camaraderie, too a tight tension. The trailer is silent and still; except for Jimmy Buffett singing 'Margaritaville.'

"What, what did you say, Al?" My mind running furiously over the multitude of answers that I can give.

"You heard what I said. Have you and Debbie had sex yet? Done the dirty deed, made the beast with two backs? Ben; have you coupled with her yet?"

Wiping my hands on my salty, blood encrusted pants, I'm drying my sweaty palms. In turmoil, I'm trying to decide, what to say. What to say? Stick to the truth? No, we haven't. Let it slip out just how beautiful she looks with her top off. Laying down on the forest floor and let them use their imagination. I could be a gentleman. Just tell them that what we do in the privacy of our own meadow, on our own blanket is none of their affair. But, we're teenagers. These guys are my best friends. So, by any code known to man, I am honor bound to brag about any sexual exploit that I've had. Even if they are only daydreams.

The door swings open with the force of an angry hurricane. Dumbship Robby stomps into our trailer. "That's it I've had it… no more, just no more!"

A fisherman is always known by his boat's name linked to his first name. Hence Robby Dumbship. Mike is known as Bloody Wog Mike. This linkage is coast wide. In this way commercial fishermen need not be bothered remembering last names. For some of us, it's a full-time job, knowing our first name and where we work.

Marty's eyes tighten with concern, "What's wrong Rob? What happened?"

"Oh Marty, that jerk Gus, he can't run a boat, he can't fish, he can't even get up in the mornings. He's the guy that can go to the bar with Bill the contractor. So, he's the idiot in charge. I ask you does that make sense, well does it?"

Robby shifts his gaze to me, "Well do you think it's fair?"

My mind is busy shifting gears. No longer do I have to figure out how much and what I should say about my sex life. Now, I have to figure out if something is fair or not, turning over the options in my mind, I opt to remain silent.

If I were an old guy, say twenty-five or twenty-six, I could go the bar, then... it would be imminently fair. On the other hand, if I were a junior in high school. One who has two years of fishing experience, it would be imminently unfair.

This is a tough question, Robby seems to have the best point, besides Gus is a jerk, even if he is the beauteous Helen's boyfriend.

Before I can formulate my answer Rob turns to Mike. "What do you think Mike?"

Laying his head back against the front window of our trailer, Mike thinks. Jimmy Buffett has changed songs; he's belting out Son of a Son of a Sailor, with feeling. The smell in the trailer is a combination of salt, drying fish, and gas, with a liberal dash of motor oil thrown in. However, the smell of unwashed, young, hard-working, male bodies, overpowers all those other odors. The interior, lit by one 40-watt bulb, cast our faces in shadow. Dirty dishes fill the sink..

Mike thoughtfully muses, "What's he been up to? We may have to pay him a little visitation tonight. If this jerk has been out of line that is?"

Rob splays his legs for better balance, when you're fresh off the boat any confined space has a tendency to rock and roll, the closer the walls, the more they move.

"Most of the day he doesn't do anything. As soon as he shows up at the boat he gets stoned. I launch the boat, get the gear in the water, then fish it. Gus, he sleeps up under the bow. Around eleven he might get up and do another joint. Then he might fish for awhile or eat all of our lunch. But, by two or three he gets bored with that. He'll do another joint and he's out for the day. It's really not that bad, I fish the boat and give him half the money.

Today, today he wants to play captain. I don't know why? We ran north this morning. You guys heard the weather report, twenty to thirty in the afternoon. We all ran north so that we could run home with the weather."

Marty pulls off his jacket bumping me with his elbow. "Yea, that was the thing to do all right, fish north and run home south. Nobody wants to beat back home, not if you can help it. It turned mean out there this afternoon. Albert and I were running down swell today and I heard this freight-train behind me. Looking around, a comber was coming at us, it was a popping and snapping like a crazed sea-serpent trying to jump into the boat. Hitting full-tilt-boogie, I barely creeped out from under it before we ended up swamped.

Robby pushes wet hair out of his eyes. "Man, I know. Gus and I just ran up from the river, beating into it every inch of the way."

Albert lifts his head in surprise. "But you were up north with us, we fished around you all morning long."

231

"Captain Gus," Robby says with deep irony in his voice, "took over at about two this afternoon. He decided to pull the gear and run south. I thought we were just going to

The Rock, but we blew by there like it was a big lump of stone." Robby smiles at his own humor, "And ran to the river."

I interject the most important question that one fisherman can ask another. "Did you get any?"

Robby shakes his head, salt water spraying in every direction. "Nary a smell. We put the gear out because Captain Gus said so. Then we pulled it because it was so dang rough. Captain Gus makes the decision we should go in. God, he is brilliant."

"When you are as smart as he is," Mike snarls out, his voice dripping with sarcasm, "you don't need to know anything about what you're doing."

We have all taken Rob's side. He's one of our own. Gus is a dope smoking hippie; mob rule is about to break out. All we need right now is a leader, and old Gus would be lynched from the nearest pine tree, and Oregon is thick with them.

Robby shakes his head in disgust, "God, you should have seen him at the wheel of that boat today. It was full throttle, then neutral and back to full throttle."

Throwing in my two cents worth, "Wow, that's really bad for the engine."

"It's really bad for the whole boat. Captain Gus couldn't figure out when to gun it and when to back off the throttle. He'd fly us off the top of a wave, then pull back on the throttle at the bottom when we need it to power up the face. We slammed into every wave between the rock and the river. There were nails working out of the hull we were hitting so hard."

"What are you going to do Rob?" Marty's expression of concern deeply lining his young face. "This guy could get you drowned." Robby shrugs, "Quit."

The trailer is silent except for Jimmy Buffett singing, <u>God's Own Drunk</u>, my mind reels with the consequences. No boat, no more big days on the ocean, no more Robby Dumbship in our fleet. It's a lot to comprehend and the information was conveyed in just one word.

***

A few days later, Robby is kicking around the fish company, when he meets Yerdal the Turtle. It's a very providential meeting indeed. Yerdal is fifty-two, he is real old, I mean real old. But, he's cool. Yerdal live in an old milk delivery truck painted a camouflage green. It's his home on wheels. Yerdal is a thin, emaciated, skeletal figure of a man. When viewed from profile, his Adam's apple is his dominant feature. Laughing at the beginning of every sentence, Yerdal is just cool.

Leaning at the counter of the fish company, Robby is drinking hot chocolate. Hogie sitting in his chair, is leaning back, hands clasped a-top of his head. Hogie's low mellow voice rumbles fourth from his corner.

"Hey Rob, you gave it a shot. You can't make a silk purse from a sow's ear, and you can't make a true hippie work. A hippie is always going to knock a home run out of the park. He is never going to trade a day's labor for a day's wages. When I was in the Highway Patrol, I saw derelicts like Gus all the time. They ain't going to change; big talk, done everything, seen everything, been everywhere... And, they're always on their way to jail."

"I don't know why Bill, the contractor wouldn't let me run the boat. I was running the boat anyway."

"Bill's a drinker; a real good drinker, if you can't drink with Bill you can't do business with Bill."

"I don't see why he couldn't just trust me?"

"People are how they are, don't go around trying to change them, most people have learned all they are going to learn by the time they are twenty-two. Hell, they know it all by then anyway, if you don't believe me; just ask any twenty-two-year-old."

The bell over the door tinkles, announcing the entrance of a small skinny man with: a wrinkled face, sparkling happy eyes, and a protruding nose.

"Ha-haha-ha, hey do any of you fellers know anything about these here boats? I just saw one a-hit on the beach. He were-a-going thirty miles an hour. Ha-ha, damm-dest thing I ever-did seed."

Dropping his hands from his head, Hogie leans forward to the arms of his chair.

"That is the way we land these boats. They're called dories, they're designed to launch through the surf and then, at the end of the day, land through the surf."

"Ha ha ha well I never? Gee so everybody just goes out a fishin' in these here boats? What do you catch, haha… hahaha?"

Hogie grins at the skinny man, liking his open honest manner. And, his childlike enthusiasm, "Would you like a cup of coffee?"

"Ha-yup ha-yup, why a-shore."

Hogie drains the last of the morning's coffee into two Styrofoam cups. "You see, most of the boats here fish commercially, going out early, coming in late, and selling their fish right here. The price is fifty cents a pound for silver salmon. A buck for king salmon. We just bumped up the price. All the trollers went off shore chasing albacore."

"Ha-ha-ha...yup are you a telling me, that a feller can a-take one of these here boats, and make money with a-one?"

"Nope."

"Ha-haha I sure do a-like these here boats, that is a crying shame, only certain fellers can a-sell you fish, huh?"

"No. It is like this; fishing is a trade that takes time to learn. The first year of learning to fish is fraught with minor disaster. Lost gear, being one day late and one foot out of step all the time. The first year is a dead loss in the fishing game. The second or third year, if you're smart... and lucky you might break even. From the forth or fifth year on it's a crap shoot. Good seasons make a few bucks, bad season you'll go broke with everyone else."

Yerdal's voice raises and falls during every sentence. It has kind of a down south back up the holler, Goofy quality. It makes you want to spit out your coffee laughing.

"Ha-ha-yup well it sure sounds good to me where can I buy one of these here boats?" Hogie turns to Rob, "Robby, take... What was your name again?"

Ha-ha-ha. hup why everyone just calls me Yerdal the turtle; a-cause I travel in my house that's a why... I painted it camouflage a kind a-like-a turtle."

Hogie drops a hand of Rob's shoulder. "Robby, I've got an almost new Kelso boat out in the lot. It's the blue and white with a sixty-five Merc on her, show her to Yerdal for me, would you?"

Robby and Yerdal walk out into the Oregon sunshine, a slight breeze blowing off the ocean is bringing in the smell of salt water and low tide.

"Ha-ha-ha-hup, so does you know much about this here salmon fishing business? Cause I sure don't."

Rob grins his big easy going grin ,"I've been around fishing for a while now. My

Dad started me years ago."

"Oh my oh my, years of fishing, you sure are one lucky feller, cause I taint never been out in the Pacific Ocean. Not once.

Robby looks over at the old milk truck, then at how Yerdal is dressed. Deciding that Yerdal doesn't have two dimes to rub together. But Robby, like Hogie, likes Yerdal. Showing him the Kelso boat, a top of the line dory, with an almost new fifteen hundred dollar engine on her couldn't hurt anyone.

"Here is the Kelso boat." Rob lays a hand on the gunwale of an almost new dory, the paint still sparkling, gear boxes clean and neat, everything orderly. Everything about the boat said I'm a fish producing fool. Buy me.

"Gosh... ha-ha-yup ha-ha... this is really some-thing'. Well, what do you a think Mr. Hogie would want for a little beauty like this-a-one"

Rubbing his chin deep in thought Robby reflects, "Well I don't know for sure...

Maybe five maybe six grand?"

"Ha-ha-ha-ha-yup even I can afford five grand, do you think you could a go out in the ocean and teach me to do this here fishing… if-in I was to buy this here boat?"

Rob laughs his deep happy belly laugh sounding just like Yerdal, "Why a shore, switching to Tom-Tom speak, "You-bet-cha. It'll a cost you forty percent off the top."

"Ha-ha ha-hup... that sounds fair to me, you make more money selling what you know, than what you do."

The old wrinkled man stretches out his hand toward Robby; Robby reaches toward the outstretched hand, with the handshake, a new partnership is formed.

Yerdal, and the Turtle, Yerdal's new boat, become the newest member of our fleet. Yerdal goes inside to Hogie, pulling an old worn checkbook from the pocket of his old worn pants, he writes out a check for the boat, on the spot. You know, you can't always tell a book by its cover. Even a checkbook.

CHAPTER FIVE

The weather is down today it is actually nice. The swells are still rocking and rolling the boat, but the wind is almost gone. The sun is up high enough that it no longer blinds me when I look out on the horizon in its direction.

The Douggers calls me to breakfast… what is this, I glance at my Timex it is only O-nine hundred hours? Doug has breakfast ready a whole hour early and it smells great. Once again, I thrust down with my forearms and propel myself onto the deck going to get one of the two meals a day that we eat.

Walking through the Dutch Doors the place smells great, I look at my plate already on the table in this calm weather day with a cup of coffee alongside, what a breakfast? I sit down, my stomach a grumbling and my mouth a watering. There for the first time ever are eggs on my plate, setting next to the eggs are two count em two pieces of toast, and some potatoes. What a breakfast!

"Man, O man Douggers, this looks great, just great. I sit at my place and dig in. Doug watches me eat with gusto for a while then he also digs in. We eat in silence until I have wiped up the last of my egg yolk with my last bite of bread, "Would you like another cup of coffee to wash down that breakfast?"

Nodding with a contented gleam in my eye, "That would be very nice."

Doug stands and carries our cups to the sink, he administers the rites of an instant coffee connoisseur, preparing us an additional serving of coffee.

As I take my first sip Doug drops his bomb, "Did you like your breakfast, did you get enough to eat?"

The actual fact is I am in such a calorie deficit that I could eat another breakfast just like that one, only this time with a pound of bacon, but beggars can't be choosers.

"It was great, Douggers, best breakfast I've had aboard."

"Good Ben, good. I've got a little bad news I am worried about the fish, I think some of them are not freezing the way we need them to, so I need you to go down into the fish hold today and take all the fish on the bottom of the bins and put them on the top, and all the fish on the top will have to go to the bottom of the bins. Do you understand?"

I gulp down the coffee in my mouth and gaze into his eyes, "We have about twenty tons aboard, you want me to move forty tons of fish?"

Douggers shrugs his shoulders and smiles his ain't this the shits smile, "Basically, yes."

So, I shrug back and grin my ain't this the shits grin.

Half an hour later finds me in rubber boots and rain gear, standing in four hundred gallons of sixteen-degree bloody brine water. Taking all the fish from one bin, I place them into another bin. I now have an empty bin, going to a third bin, I then put the top fish at the bottom of the bin I just emptied.

All the time the four hundred gallons of bloody brine water is washing around my boot tops, it sucks.

Every once in a while, the Douggers looks into the hatch and gives me his ain't this the shits smile, I always give him one right back. I considered this a crumby job; it is hard work, I am sweating in a sixteen-degree hole, with water dripping from the pipes that carries the brine water over head. Doug is right, it is a shitty job.

Then about two hours in, Doug pops his head into the hatch, "Ben I've got some more bad news, I think we need to get the refer system going again. Having it off all day is not a good thing."

"OK Doug, whatever you think." I didn't understand what that meant, but I was about to find out.

About five minutes later the first trickles of brine water begin to spout from the holes in the overhead piping system. Within a minute, the full volume of water is flowing, brine water is hitting the ceiling and running everywhere. It is raining bloody salted seawater all over me; I throw my hood up.

For the rest of the day, I work throwing fish in a shower of bloody brine. It is miserable. Eight hours later I crawl from the hole soaked in sweat and bloody brine, the Douggers uses the deck wash hose and hoses me off as I stand there on the deck nude.

Lesson learned from this experience; you do whatever you have to do to keep fishing.

***

Back up in Pacific City just last year; it's another beautiful day out on the Pacific Ocean, flat calm and glassy slick, a ten-foot lump, long and low; rolls under the boat, every two minutes or so. The lazy lump lumbers towards us in an unrelenting line of swells for as far as the eye can see. It truly is, another beautiful day on the

Pacific Ocean, days like this are why I want to be a fisherman. That is if I ever grow up.

The motor has been purring along since five this morning. It's now two in the afternoon. Trolling is inherently hard on outboards. Running at full throttle requires a mix of oil in the gas high enough to lubricate the engine. That oil mix at low speeds can foul out the spark plugs and does most days. To cure the fouling problem, we put the engine in neutral and rev it up, this blows out the excess oil.

The Bloody Wog climbs to the top of a large lump, she begins her descent into the next trough. The poles are making a squeaking sound by rubbing against the leather in the pole rests. The motor changing from the purr of two cylinders working in sweet harmony to an unholy cacophony of noise and vibration. I'm at the wheel; slipping the boat into neutral, I throttle her up to full speed for ten seconds. That should clear the plugs. It doesn't, confused, I wait for about thirty seconds, then try it again. This time the engine revs up and dies. Mike is pumping the bilge out, he's sitting on the motor well next to our engine, pumping into the well.

Taking a deep breath of fresh salty air filling my lungs with the smell and feel of the ocean, letting out the breath in a sigh, I reach for the hand crank gurdy. We have to pull the tip-line. Before she tangles with the other tip-line. Mike groans, straightening up, walking forward, he begins to pull in gear. With no speed on; the gear will quickly tangle, causing hours of work. It is possible to pull the cowling from the engine, wrap the starter rope around the flywheel and pull it enough times to start it before the gear tangles. It is just possible. But, if she won't start, then she won't start. It's a real mess.

It plays out like this. The gear is tangled. You need to get it in, with the boat drifting toward a lee shore. Of course, the motor

241

won't start, like I said, a real mess. We've been told that when an engine dies the gear first. Then work on the engine.

The gear on my side is in. A sprawled legged stroll brings me back to the engine. The cowling comes off first. Then the engine's restart process begins.

My father, when he was here in Oregon, nicknamed Mike and me. I was nicknamed Zasa Gabor and Mike got the moniker of Eva. These names were hung on us because of our lack of mechanical ability, according to my father. Neither of us took shop in high-school. Mike knows he's going to college, I've been handing tools to my father since I was two. I should have taken shop, as my dad says hind-sight is 20-20.

Harry could tare down a Model T engine and rebuild it, on the side of the road in the Arizona sun, with nothing but bailing wire and a pocket knife. At the tender age of fifteen, in fact, he did just that. Mike and I can't. We know that air and gas, and fire, must all arrive at the same place, at the same time, in a confined space for an internal combustion engine to work.

We just don't understand all the mechanisms and how they interact to accomplish this feat, this our first season, we've been fighting a steep learning curve, concerning the internal combustion engine.

Handing the cowling to Mike, he hands me the starter rope in exchange.

Spreading my legs to account for the roll of the boat, I wrap the rope around the flywheel, six wraps, I'm ready to pull, bracing I wrap the end of the rope around my hand.

Yanking with all of my might, the engine spins round and round with nary a cough or wheeze.

Repeating this same procedure over and over again, until I sag onto the engine both of my hands on top of the flywheel. Spent.

"Mike, it's... huff huff huff, it's a good thing we pulled our gear before we started this ordeal."

"Yep, you-bet-cha." He's leaning against the console one hip thrust into the steering wheel, "You done?"

Pushing off the flywheel with both hands, I straighten my body, "Huff... huff, huff, yep."

Mike takes the starter rope from me, "Maybe, we ought to pull the plugs... see what they look like?"

"Good, huff huff, I'll get the tools."

"That's OK you're whipped, I'll get the tools."

Now, the tools live up under the bow, with the moldy life jackets and Mike's old bear coat. They reside in a gunny sack borrowed from Hogie; our tool collection is not extensive, it consists of; a couple of pliers, a Crescent wrench, and a rusty ratchet that won't spin. The rusty ratchet has a spark-plug socket rusted onto the ratchet.

We also have a couple of screwdrivers for emergencies. Oh, and a hammer, where would a boat be without a hammer? This has been enough to keep us afloat and running for two and a half months now.

To find the tools, Mike steps over the fish box, bending over the gear locker he's sticking his head deep into our sleeping quarters. The bear coat flies from the bow, followed by three moldy life jackets and an old hunk of slimy, moldy cheese. Next, our sack of tools appears from the moldy, dark, damp hidy-hole we sleep in. The tools don't land on the deck or fish box like the rest of the junk. They're handed to me.

Mike returns the moldy life jackets to their appointed place under the bow as bedding and then places his bear coat back where it belongs.

Placing the tools between my feet I shuffle through the bag. Finding the ratchet I begin pulling plugs. Pulling plugs is easy. All I do is set on the stern of the Bloody Wog hanging my butt over the ocean. Leaning out and around the engine where I can get a look at the plugs. As a safety measure, I jam my feet into the steering cables to keep from flipping over backwards into that cold cold ocean.

Mike flops down on the other side of the engine to lend a hand. Handing me a slice of cheese across the open water. My hands are oily with smears of grease on them. This cheese, is the first food I've seen in eight hours. Popping it in my mouth I'm chewing with gusto.

"Mum, good."

"Is it good, really?"

"Oh yea, taste grate… it really does."

"Good... I was a little concerned."

Mike pops a chunk of cheese into his own mouth, also chewing with gusto.

Smiling at me around the globs of cheese.

Two hours have passed; Mike's face has grease and oil smeared across his nose and forehead. We've pulled and reinstalled the plugs three times now. Pulling on the starter rope until we're sagging with exhaustion. There is more wrong with the engine than what ails her. More wrong than we can figure out, for sure for sure good buddy.

It's Mike's turn, he's pulling on the starter rope, as he has been doing for fifteen minutes. "Huff... huff, huff, I... huff, huff, I don't think it's plugs."

"Nope?"

"Nope."

"What do you think it maybe?"

"Huff huff huff, It may be a Marty problem."

"Wow, that serious?"

"Well; what else could it be?"

"Yep, if its not plugs we may need Marty. Marty knows. He knows how to make an engine want to run, you are right, I wonder... where they're fishing?"

Mike smiles at me, still chewing on his glob of cheese, "It don't matter... Marty will come."

Walking forward to the steering console Mike pulls the leather thong from the beach salvage door. Dropping it on the leather hinges he pulls out the mike.

"Kisutch Kisutch Kisutch, Bloody Wog to the Kisutch."

The radio hisses at Mike in reply, "Kisutch Kisutch Kisutch, Bloody Wog, to the Kisutch."

***

It's another thirty minutes of drifting toward a lee shore, watching the beach drift closer and closer. Standing up, I can see a

245

blue and white dory running down the coast, the bow raised high, the front third of her bottom clear of the ocean. Every time she slaps down on a wavelet spray shoots out in front of the bow in a white arc thirty to forty feet.

Shading my eyes, "It's the Kisutch."

Mike mumbles; "Good... wonder how we're going to get Marty aboard?"

"Good question."

Mike wipes grease from his hands, "Albert is a good boat handler... he'll, he will... just drop him off."

The radio crackles and hisses at us again, "Wog. Bloody Wog, pick me up there Ben, Mike? Come on back."

Reaching for the mike I withdraw it, stretching the coils almost straight. "Wog back to Kisutch... Albert, like what's the haps man?"

"Mechanic delivery. Are you accepting deliveries between now and sundown?"

Keying the mike, "We're always open for business here. We've been thinking about how to do this. Michael and I have been talking, we think..." I release the mike to think for a second, "Back your stern toward our stern and get her close. Marty can jump aboard. What do you think?"

"A well thought out plan, well thought out."

My chest expands with pride at the compliment.

Marty is standing next to Al, a large tool box in one hand. The arm holding the tool box is hanging down much closer to the deck than his free hand. Marty grins and Albert raises his free hand, giving us a peace sign. Al pulls the throttle back; old Kisutch drops from up-on-step into displacing her full weight. Her speed changing precipitously with the movement of Al's hand on the throttle; Marty's momentum throws him from his feet. Falling onto the fish-box Marty catches himself, Al has the wheel to brace against. Albert, he just looks cool while Marty picks himself up. Albert swings the Kisutch past our stern throwing her into reverse. The prop jumps from the water beating the surface into a white froth having very little effect.

My plan had not taken into account that all dory men remove the reverse hold down mechanism. That way, the hold down won't engage and rip the motor well off, during a beach landing. Albert's prop is whipping the water uncontrollably; the reverse gear brings the prop to the surface where she gets no bite. The Kisutch is wiggling her stern as she slowly inches her way toward us.

Marty laughs at the problem then, Marty, being Marty, takes action to correct it. Carrying his tool box to the stern, throwing one leg over the motor he squats on top of it. His tool box sitting on his lap. Albert gains some control over his boat, and she lurches toward us at an increased speed. The Kisutch's stern plows through the water barging a large wake behind her. The old Bloody Wog begins to slide down the face of a wave toward the Kisutch. Our sterns are closing fast. Marty's eyes grow in diameter as our distance diminishes. Watching the on-coming disaster we're all hoping that some act of the Gods will avert it. Albert slides the gear shift from reverse to forward gunning the motor.

Kisutch stops in her tracks, settling right down. The boats are laying about five feet apart now. It's apparent; this is going to be more difficult than we thought. A ten foot lump makes for a sizable swell during docking procedures. None of us have ever docked one of these boats. Our harbor is a beach. We approach it at full speed and never slack off on our approach. Docking our boats is done; by sliding onto the beach at full tilt boogie. Slow speed control is something we know nothing about. It takes practice to bring a boat to a stop where and when you want it. Watching Albert maneuvering around in these large swells, it's becoming obvious that Marty is not just going to hop aboard.

Albert throws the Kisutch into reverse and starts up the swell at us. The boats collide, splintering wood like we're making kenneling, then they bounce apart again. Marty is thrown aft by the collision. Catching himself, by slamming the back of his hands between the heavy toolbox and the stern of the Kisutch.

Marty's expression turns from surprise to pain with the encounter, straggling back up to a sitting position he grimaces in our direction, running on the ragged edge of disaster can be painful.

Albert's face takes on a determined look; watching over his shoulder he hits reverse and revs her up. The Kisutch responds by jumping at us again, this time we're on the downward slide of the swell, the Kisuch chasing us toward the trough. At the bottom of the swell, we crash again, the Bloody Wog, bouncing off the Kisutch leaving another trail of splinters.

The Kisutch pulls away from us. She is getting ready for another run. Marty gets up from his squatting position on top of the outboard, he and Albert spend a minute talking, Marty making hand motions in the air. One hand slides past the other hand in a smooth motion, then shooting off into the air again. Marty points to the port pole and then at us.

Turning to Mike, a quizzical look on my face, "What do you think the plan is?"

"Something to do with hands sliding past one another in one smooth motion, I think."

"I think, you think right."

"You think?"

I'm relieved; we're giving up on the stern shattering idea that I came up with. Pursuing ideas like that, you can wind-up swimming in the Pacific Ocean, without a wetsuit.

The radio crackles Marty's easy going tones burst forth from the speaker. "Ah, yea... Mike, Ben? We've been thinking. This stern method of docking is a little hard on the boats. I was thinking... If you pull your starboard pole and we pull our port pole, Albert can just drive by, dropping me off. What do you think, huh?"

Michael reaches into the console pulling out the radio mike. "Marty, why that is a capital idea just a capital idea. Come on over we just happen to have a chunk of age cheese available, if you're hungry?"

Glancing down to the fish box I realize where the piece of cheese I ate earlier came from. The old, moldy, slimy cheese has been trimmed down to reveal a shriveled inter section. It was good though.

Marty's languid voice continues from our speaker. "We'll make two passes. I'll hand off my toolbox the first time.

One of you guys grab it, the second pass I'll jump aboard. We'll get you running again, OK?"

Michael keys the mic, "Ben is working on the pole right now we'll be ready in two minutes."

The Kisutch is spinning donuts just down swell from us as Marty works on their port pole. He swings it to the forward pole rest. Swinging our starboard pole into its forward rest, I lash her down for good measure.

The Kisutch is ready. Making her charge at us doing about eight knots, one pole in and one pole out. She looks like a one arm knight. Her lance pointed just high enough so that she may not skewer us. Unless, of course, we happen to be up swell from her on her approach. There couldn't be more than a fifty-fifty chance of that happening, could there?

The Kisutch charges by, less than one foot from our starboard side. Albert, with intense concentration in his whole being, is on top of the job at hand. Marty is holding his forty-pound toolbox over the side his face contorting at the effort. Reaching out, Mike snags the box as it goes by. The box is doing eight knots. The momentum swings it into the boat and onto the fish box. It lands on the age cheese we had promised to Marty. Cheese parts and pieces squish out from under the tool box. A mortal man would be sicken by the sight. Not Mike.

Inspecting the ooze, Mike pronounces, "It's kind of pretty, don't you think?"

"No, pretty ain't the word that comes to mind. Hazardous, that's the word that calls out to me."

The Kisutch, up swell, is running in a large circle, coming back around at us. Setting on the fish box, Marty is slipping off his sea boots. Sea boots off; Marty bends down, finding his tennis shoes.

The Kisutch is down swell from us again she is making her second run. The pole jutting over the bow looks even more like a knight's lance. Albert is a little unsteady in his approach this time, the jutting pole bobs and sways menacingly.

Marty is standing on top of the fish box. One hand is lightly holding onto the console behind him, one foot on the gunwale. Marty's body tenses for the jump his legs flexing with each wave.

"Mike, watch the pole… this time Albert seems a little wild."

"Not wild so much, just confident." Mike glances over his shoulder at the onrushing Kisutch,

"DUCK!"

We both hit the deck as the port pole of the Kisutch rakes us from stern to stem the Kisutch skipping along our side. Mike being faster than double geared lighting got to the deck long before me.

He hits first, and I throw myself on top of him. While lying there, I congratulate myself. For once, I got a better position. Here Mike thinks he's so smart, being faster than me. I'm the one on top this time...

"Uff-da," Marty lands right in the middle on my back. Mike still winds up on top, even being underneath.

Landing on my back throws Marty off his stride. He trips on my shoulder blade stumbling toward the port side. Barely stopping his head long run before plunging into the sea. Marty performs this miracle stop by grabbing onto the handrail. His head, chest, and waist hanging over that cold cold Pacific Ocean.

"What are you guys doing on the deck? I almost went over the side stepping on you like that."

Mike flexes his arms doing a push up, removing himself from the deck lifting me with him.

"Sorry Marty, it just seemed like a good idea to get down as that pole came over.

"Yea it did look a little exciting over here for a second or two."

Flopping down on the fish box, I smile up at Marty, "Welcome aboard, would you like some aged cheese?"

Scooping up some crumbs of cheese in one hand from under the toolbox I raise them toward Marty. Marty has a mother, she packs him lunch every night, Marty goes home to a hot meal every evening. Food is abundant in their cabinets it fills his home in every shape and form. Moldy squished cheese ooze holds no interest for Marty.

Marty's face takes on a disgusted slightly greenish tinted scowl, "No, no thanks Ben, I just had lunch."

shrugging my shoulders, "Moss-v-ka," I grunt and begin picking out yellowish cheese from the mess in my hand.

***

Half an hour has passed since Marty landed on my back. He's deciphered the motor enough to know that she doesn't have fire. An essential element, of the elements: air, fire and gas. That must meet at the same time, within that tiny, confined space, as required by an internal combustion engine. He is well on his way to fixing the problem. His shiny chrome tools are flashing in the Oregon sunlight.

Albert is down south about half a mile, fishing again.

Marty is sitting on the port side of the engine. I'm on the starboard lending a hand. Leaning over for a ratchet from his toolbox, Marty asks.

"What's that?"

"What?"

"That, that water."

Water is pouring into the Wog from a gap between the motor-well athwart-ship member and a stringer running fore and aft. The gap is about an eighth of an inch wide and three inches long, and right between Marty's legs. The amount of water pouring into the boat is the same as from a tea kettle. However, this stream never stops.

"Oh, that, it's a leak. Didn't the old Bloody Wog leak when you owned her?"

"Oh, sure, she leaked, but but, you couldn't see her leaking, that's different."

Mike is squaring away the deck. Our Handy Billy bilge pump is beside him; picking it up from the hand rail, Mike brags.

"We got us three bilge pumps, this one and two, count, um, two of the best bilge pumps in the world."

Eyes wandering around the deck, Marty disagrees. "I don't see any other bilge pumps?"

Eyes sparkling, Mike grins wide, "You just don't know what the best bilge pump in the world is."

"What is the best bilge pump in the world?"

"A real scared man with a five-gallon bucket." The fact that we don't own a five-gallon bucket escapes all of our attention.

***

It's nine in the evening on a Friday night. Mike and I pushed through the doors of the nicest restaurant on the Cape, as the Dory King, deigned not to admit us, as we smelled of fish.

It has been three days of good fishing since our last breakdown, or we are learning the trade. We are opening the door of the best restaurant at Cape Kiwanda. This is our first time in here, tonight; we hunger, a good day fishing, makes you feel rich, and it's late, we don't have anything to cook. Except for short salmon, poverty food.

The best restaurant in Cape Kiwanda doesn't mean the same thing as the best restaurant in say, New York, or San Francisco. It is a family dining place. Sea food is prominently displayed on the menu. The Kiwanda Inn caters to tourist, not to eighteen-year-old fishermen.

Mike and I are a little nervous. Pushing through the double doors we go in anyway. There is no need to be. Setting at the biggest table in the place is Hogie, Marline, their two girls and, my beautiful Debbie.

Hogie waves at us as we enter. "Come on over boys. Have a seat."

The leading citizen of Cape Kiwanda just beckoned us to his table. Mike and I strut on over; our chests puffed out in pride. Getting up, Debbie finds us a couple of chairs. We sit like invited guests.

Hogie's mellow voice rumbles forth from the corner he has claimed. "Have a seat… join us, we haven't ordered yet, so you're just in time. We had us a long day today. I thought I'd take the crew out to dinner."

"Yea, we had a long day too. We didn't get into the fish until four o'clock. We had to stay."

"You boys did all right today. Staying out late like that. The fish went on the bite, you got your share. It's like I always told Benny, stick and stay and make it pay."

Arriving at our table, the waitress distributes goblets of water. Popping chewing gum, she inquires, "What'll-it-be?"

She poses, her pin hanging over her tag book, like the sword of Damocles. Hogie, dips his finger into a goblet, he begins lightly circling the top. His moist finger going around and round. Smiling at the young lady, his face a work of innocence. A high-pitched squeaking sound pierces the restaurant.

The restaurant has great acoustics. Sound travels to the far end, bouncing back undiminished in volume or intensity. People at other tables begin looking up into the air and around the restaurant.

Hogie's finger keeps up its' lazy circling, his eyes glancing around, searching the restaurant for the sound. Our waitress stops writing, she too is searching the air for the screech. The din stops as suddenly as it began. The restaurant is now totally silent, all conversation has stopped when the squeal started. Other patrons, like us, are all looking for the irritating racket. Then the ringing ceases, gone, just completely gone? Ah, blessed silence. The restaurant returns to normal, conversations once again filtering through the building.

Our waitress starts taking our orders again; Hogie's finger finds its-self reinserted into the glass of water, wiggling around. Then, as though of its own volition, the finger begins circling,

255

innocently circling, the top of the crystal goblet. The piercing sound fills Cape Kiwanda Inn once again. People stop talking, they're searching as though the source will jump from the ceiling and shout, "Here, I'm here."

It doesn't. Everyone is swiveling around, looking for that damn sound. Soon, Hogie's finger is dry, and it stops.

Once again, Hogie's index finger finds it's-self swimming in the Crystal goblet. Just nonchalantly swirling. The finger climbs from the water. Finding the lip of the goblet. Circle circle circle, squeak squeak squeak.

The manager of the restaurant burst forth from the kitchen. His eyes, joining the rest of us, we are all searching the ceiling; searching for that God awful sound. We all join the manager in his deep rooted desire to find the offending noise, even Hogie.

The manager is a twenty-year-odd young fellow. He seems duly impressed with his position and power; looking at our waitress, he demands, "When did this start? what did you do?"

Our waitress shrugs her shoulders and pops her chewing gum at him. "Gee Harvey, I don't know it just started."

Hogie points toward an overhead fan near our table. "It sounds like it maybe coming from there."

The manager walks to our table peering up toward the fan. "It could be from there?"

Hogie points at the fan with the finger that is not busy circling the Crystal goblet.

"It sounds like it's coming from that fan to me, don't you hear it?"

"Of course, I hear it. Why do you think I'm out here? But it sounds just as loud over there."

The young restaurateur points back toward the kitchen.

Hogie grins at Mike and me, then winks. "Turn the fan off. Maybe the sound will stop?"

The manager leaves for about five minutes. By the time he returns three fans in our area are beginning to slow down. The fans slow, as does the squeaking. But, somehow Hogie's finger slows down also. All three: fans, squeaking, and finger come to rest at the same time.

The prissy manager returns to our table, "Well I guess I was right. It was this fan." He turns on his heel, returning to the kitchen.

Hogie grins at us once again. "I think it's time to turn some lights off."

Hogie inserts his finger into the goblet. He begins circling the rim of his glass. A piercing sound fills the restaurant again. Our hero, the manager, explodes from the kitchen. He's looking for the offending sound, and boy, is that sound in trouble.

Hogie being helpful offers, "Maybe it's the lights; sometimes those ballast devices give out with a hum or a squeak."

The noise comes to an abrupt stop, the restaurant falls into a deep silence. Everyone gives a big sigh of relief. Hogie's finger is dry, the dry finger lifts its-self from the goblet, Hogie inspects it; in full view of our feisty manager.

Showing that he is in charge, the manager lets us know, "It's not the damn light it's another one of the fans."

Our young hero is not going to truck any advice from some sloppily dressed patron. Even if he is the richest man in Cape Kiwanda. With a flourish, Hogie reinserts his finger into the goblet, swishing it around into the water. Looking the manager right in the eye he begins the innocent circling of his glass. Wonder of wonders the fan, I mean light now, starts making the squeaking noise, again. That awful high-pitched clatter that comes and goes.

The manager spins in place looking; looking for the offending device spittle flies from his mouth. Shrilly the man of the moment gives his orders; "I can't believe it. We cannot have this. I will not allow it. Will not allow it!"

The manager's voice is as shrill as the squeaking sound that is offending the entire restaurant.

Smiling amiably Hogie says, "I don't think it's the fan this time. I really do believe you need to turn the lights off; or I'm sure, that dam sound will just keep squeaking.

Hogie's two daughters keep whispering and giggling at something. Mike's face is alight in pleasure. Marline bends over and whispers something to the girls. They settle down, looking straight ahead again. They look neither left nor right, avoiding each other's eyes with a force of will. All of this body language has finally penetrated my thick skull. It's Hogie. Hogie is making the squeaking by rubbing the top of the glass.

The manager looks at this mottley crew, dismissing Hogie and the rest of us out of hand. After all, what could a scruffy old man know about fans, or neon lights, or squeaking, for that matter?

By the end of our very nice meal most of the lights and all of the fans are off. This really is a much nicer restaurant without all those bright lights and whirling fans intruding on your dining experience.

Walking from the restaurant, Hogie has to push hard against the double doors. A breeze of twenty knots hits us full in the face. She's a blowing from the north, the doors had to be pushed open into the wind. No mean feat; once outside, I take Debbie's hand, we're standing in the cool wind. Looking deep into Debbie's eyes I ask. "If it's too rough to fish tomorrow... can we go to our field?"

Debbie squeezes my hand, "Yes, that would be nice."

CHAPTER SIX

Boink. My head bounces off the door jam. The Alley Cat must have taken a wave wrong again. What has it been, three days of bad weather now? Three, maybe four days. It's so hard to keep track of time at sea. One day blends into another; there's no way to tell them apart. It hasn't blown less than forty knots since we left Moss Landing. Will it ever be calm again?

Standing in the doorway, I'm leaning my forearms onto the Dutch door. The wave that just hit us, bringing me back to reality, has the back deck awash. Douggers is forward listening to the radios, looking for fish. I'm in here because we aren't in the fish. We haven't had a hit in two hours.

The four radios blaring in the pilothouse are truly annoying. Each radio has a distinctive personality. There's the VHF, with its clear easy to understand reception. That's my favorite. The Single Side Band makes everyone sound like Donald Duck. It reaches, man does it reach. But who cares how the tuna boats are doing off Chile? Then there is the Mickey Mouse, "Citizen Band radio," with its skip, static, whirrs, and squeals. The C.B. is my least favorite radio. When I get my own albacore boat, I won't even have a C.B. aboard. The big set, "A.M. radio" is static all the time. All the time a background of noise, the static is left over electro-magnetic waves from the big bang. The Douggers loves the big set… even the static from it.

The den from the pilot area really is annoying. Each radio squeaking and squawking louder than the others. Finding fish is a lot of work. I want to be a tuna boat captain, but man? I don't know if I can take all the noise that goes with the job? A flash in the sun catches my attention. The port hotline just hit.

Turning in the door, I croak out, "Douggers, HOTLINE!"

Opening the door, I begin my run toward the gaff hatch. The port longline hits. Now we have two fish on. I've got to get those fish. Letting them hang would piss off the Douggers. Jumping the first bin board, I redouble my efforts. Mounting the next board, changing my pace to avoid a pile of albacore. Aiming to hit the top of the next bin board, I'll drop into the gaff hatch, while grabbing the hotline.

The gracefully planned maneuver goes awry. I'm a little short in my step. Instead of landing on the bin board, my toe catches the top. My body arching forward, I'm falling... Opps! Shooting out my leg to catch my fall, I overshoot the gaff hatch. The last chance to stop my momentum is now.

How? How am I going to stop this topple into the Pacific Ocean?

Out of the corner of my right eye I see the top of the davit flying by. My right arm shoots out, reaching for it, my fingers closing around the two-inch pipe. Swaying right my left leg steps into thin air, then onto the Pacific Ocean. The Pacific Ocean doesn't hold any of my weight. In fact, I can feel it sucking at my left leg, trying to pull me in. As the wave rises at the stern, my boot fills. Wetting my pants to the knee, this is kind of scary.

Time? Einstein's theory says, time is a variable, he's right, you know. From the instant my toe hit the bin board, time has slowed to a crawl. In my time frame this fall is taking about five minutes. I realized as the davit drifted by that I should grab it. I thought about my other options and ran over the consequence of each. I knew just knew that the Douggers was watching me fall overboard. I also knew that if I hit the water he would spin the boat on the spot and pick me up. Even before I got wet, so to speak.

My mind asked, "But why get wet?"

"Well," I answered myself, "it'll make one heck of a story to tell my P.C. buddies over beers. Lost overboard, a hundred miles at sea, sounds exciting."

"If you make the Douggers lose this little school of fish he'll be irritated with you. The Douggers only gets irritated over money. You're his employee twenty-four hours a day."

"So... I'll grab for the davit", and I do.

Right now, I'm hanging here on a two-point purchase. My right hand has a tentative hold of the davit, and my right toe is caught under the cap rail. The cap rail is a one-inch diameter pipe welded to the top of the gunwale. I need to turn around to get my good left hand onto the davit, but my toe?

My toe is just barely holding on to its purchase. If I try to spin where I'm at... both feet will end up in the Pacific Ocean. Both feet in the Pacific is not a good thing, not good at all. I'll wait, Doug'll come and get me.

Now time is dragging again, this time not in strength I pull. Pull with all my might. A good way. Looking behind me toward the bow, I don't see any Doug? Well, it's up to me, my toe is dug into the cap rail if I move it I'll slip. My right arm is fully extended my left waving in the air. Using my full strength my body raises toward the safety of the deck, slowly, very slowly. Kicking my left leg in the struggle. My boot fills with water… again, the Pacific Ocean sucks at me, calling me into the depths.

The reality of the situation dawns on me. If I screw this up I'm going overboard. Doug didn't hear me when I yelled FISH ON. There will be no rescue. If I slip, the Alley Cat will just keep on trucken at five knots. I'll watch the stern disappear over the horizon… I pull up.

This time I'm serious, my left arm reaches around, grasping the davit. PULL! Oh, my foot? My foot is slipping, dig it into the gunwale. You've only got three points of contact with the boat; don't lose any of them. Just a little more. Pull!

Now, I'm standing just aft of the gaff hatch. Safe? Stepping back, I drop into the hatch. Pulling the hotline in-board, I begin pulling our fish. We have five fish hanging on the gear. Life is good, life is very good. I'm alive. We're the in fish. I'm not sure which the Douggers will be happier about.

Pulling fish steadily for twenty minutes or so we have twenty-five more fish on the deck. The lines are clear. Jumping from the gaff hatch I begin my journey forward. I'll tell Doug about the fish and the near fall over the side. Walking into the pilothouse I'm blasted once again with the volume of the radios. No wonder Doug didn't hear me or the fish beating the deck. Arriving at the wheel station I find the Douggers sound asleep.

Deciding not to wake him, I disengage the pilot. Turning the boat 180 degrees, we begin a chargeback through the fish. Again, the fish climb on the lines for twenty minutes or so. Once we're through the fish, I go forward to turn the boat. This time, Doug wakes up.

Yawn, "What's happening, why are you up here?"

"We got into some fish. I'm turning on them again."

"Fish? We're in fish? Why didn't you wake me?"

"Well you see..."

"See? I see you didn't wake me. Whenever we find fish you always, I mean always wake me!"

This last sentence is whispered with a deep intensity. The Douggers is madder at me than ever before. All I've been doing is catching fish, what did I do wrong?

I've been told, so now I know. When we're in the fish, wake the Douggers. Shrugging off Doug's complaints I head back on deck. Got to do my job, I'll do better next time. Once in the gaff hatch, I fall to thinking. I had better not tell him that I almost fell overboard. That might make him even madder.

To mask my misery at being such a lousy deckhand, I dream of Debbie. Beautiful Debbie; It was after that nice dinner at the fancy restaurant that we made love for the first time, or was it...?

***

Debbie and I are walking across a green field. The grass clutching at our knees as we stroll through the undulating surface, the off shore wind of twenty-five knots is just a breeze in this sheltered meadow. The grass is rustling. There's a gentle swishing sound as we walk. Ah, the sweet smell of pine is carried by the breeze, this is our field. The one where mosquitoes eat you alive if you don't leave by dark. We learned that lesson, we'll leave, O we'll leave! It's only ten in the morning. No picnic this time, we're here for love. Debbie holds a blanket to her lovely chest as she sways through the grass. Finding a spot to her liking, she spreads out the blanket. Lowering herself to the blanket, she lays back. Smiling a come-hither invitation, she places one hand under her head.

Oh man oh man, maybe it's the time, this time? We know why we're here and I'm armed with a condom. The cool morning, the blanket, the girl. It is 1972, the sexual revolution is in full swing. How can any woman hold out against such odds.

The sun, is high overhead, it's well past noon, Debbie is in my arms, our clothes lay in a heap at the end of the blanket. I gaze into her deep blue eyes, they are the blue of the ocean out on the albacore grounds. The blue of the sole of a saint. I look into their depths and drown. Drown in the feeling of being in love. We're so in love we must have one another. The time is now the place is here. She loves me, I love her, it is only right that we make love.

Debbie, in her passion whispers to me, "Honey, I just want you to know that the man who takes me for the first time. That man… will be the man I marry."

Fear clutches at my chest. Marry! I can't get married, no not yet, I have to go up the Amazon and hunt for diamonds. To the north slope and drill for oil. I have to sail around the world in a small yacht. Married men never get to do what I want to do.

Rolling away from Debbie. "We've got to go?"

"But, but why?" Her voice hurt, on the verge of tears...

"I got to help Mike. On the boat. I've got work to do."

Debbie reaches for me, "What's wrong what did I do? It's all right Honey, we don't have to go."

Dressing. "I've got to go. Mike needs help. The weather might be down. We'd better go fishing. I really got to go. Let's just go before something happens that we don't mean."

Opening the trailer house door I brush past Marty sitting at the settee. Mike is on the other side of the settee, his feet stretched out.

265

Rob is leaning against the stove, his hands in his pocket. Whatever conversation they'd been having, comes to a complete and abrupt halt. Silence fills the room, shoving past Rob, I throw myself onto my bunk.

Marty looks around Robby's body at my profile; which is staring at the ceiling. "Ben, like what's the matter man? You look like the Vietcong just took Lincoln City."

"It's worst than that Marty." There's a morose lilt in my reply.

Mike knows me best of all. Asks the question that hits home. "What happen Ben, Debbie dump you for her Air Force guy?"

"No, it's worse than that, she offered me sex."

Silence nothing but silence. Finally, Robby asks the question on everyone's mind. "And?"

"And nothing, I turned her down."

Mike gapes at me in disgust and horror.

"You... You turned her down? Are you nuts? Sex. Sex with Debbie is all you have wanted since you met her. That's the reason all the rest of us have backed off. And everyone else in the dory fleet."

"I know I know!"

Marty gently probes, "What happened Ben?"

"Marty... she wants to give herself to her future husband. I don't want to be a husband, not now. When I'm old, maybe when I'm twenty-six or twenty-seven. I sure don't want to lie to her, and I don't want to be married in a year or two. I haven't even gotten to go up the Amazon and hunt for diamonds yet."

Mike pokes his head around Rob's body this time. "When are we going to the Amazon Ben?"

"I don't know. I've always wanted to go there. For three, maybe four years. We'll have to have enough money to launch an expedition."

"How do you know there are diamonds there?"

"Oh! A story in National Geographic. It was about this guy who had this business buying diamonds off the tribes in the upper Amazon. Then he disappeared. They think he was eaten."

Mike's eyes are aglow, his voice a whisper, "Cool!"

Marty, with his soft heart, brings us back to the moment at hand. "So, Ben, what are you and Debbie going to do?"

"I don't know Marty. I dropped her off at her house we kissed good by just like a regular date. I think we're OK?"

"That's good that's real good."

***

The next two weeks: brings flat calm weather, fish, and eighteen-hour days. From dawn until dark we fish. Each morning, we rise at four A.M., Pushing the Bloody Wog through the surf before sunrise. The fish aren't hot and heavy. Just a steady one or two all day long. From the first gear getting wet to the last cannon ball being set on the deck, we are busy.

The whole fleet is in a work mode. This is the last run before the end of the season. For those of us who have not broken even yet, it is a do or die effort. For those fishermen who depend on salmon for a livelihood, this is where the tenor for the whole winter is set.

It is a wonderful and stressful time; we don't know if the weather will turn bad tomorrow so we fish today. We don't know if the fish will disappear tomorrow, so we fish today. Each fish filled day leaves us wanting one more and wondering if tomorrow is the end. But still, dreading the next day filled with eighteen hours of back breaking work.

At the end of the day, we fall into bed exhausted. Debbie and I only see one another during unloading and fueling. Poor tender petite little Debbie is working twelve-hour days. Mike and I are putting in eighteen-hour days because we are finally seeing hundred-dollar days. We're in em! As is the rest of the fleet.

Nole has a standing policy; if we are hungry, we eat at his house. Whenever Bob sees us on the beach he offers to feed us. As does Tom-Tom. Mike and I were too exhausted to cook. We depend on the kindness of fishermen to eat.

Then one day our motor died. Died dead. It is so dead that Jerry the magnificent mechanic couldn't even fix it. We're out of the fishing business just when we had figured out how to make money.

In my last phone call home, my dad mentioned that he had just bought an older new used engine. It's a thirty-five-horse outboard just like we have but older. We can have it if we need it. After about five minutes of consultation Mike and I agree to go get that older, new used engine, from California. Motors in California must be cheap, dirt cheap, dad only paid thirty-five dollars for this old new engine.

We stuff my Mustang full of leaky gas cans. These were the cans we had collected for albacore fishing. They've been stored on top of our trailer all this time. We fill up at Hogie's and start off at home. It's eight in the evening and we've been working all day.

Mike and I drive all night. It's eight in the morning when we drive into his driveway. Mike opens the door of my Mustang dragging his coat out with him.

"Mike get some breakfast, I'll be back in two hours with our NEW motor."

Michael turns and sticks his head into the open window, "Two hours, then we'll head right back up."

We didn't count on our mothers. Mothers who have not seen their boys all summer do not feed them breakfast and then send them back to Oregon. Not without a fight they don't. It's another two days before I get back to Mike's.

At Mike's, four hefty muscular teenagers meet me. The Driveway is filled with boys, and bags, and surfboards. What's going on here?

The new, old old old motor sticks its prop from the trunk of that little old Stang. Motor and the gas can fill the trunk to capacity. Mike stands a little apart from the group, he nods his head in a come here motion, I saunter his way.

"Like what's happening Mike?"

"Cosmos, Wayne and Caesar want to come along with us. Is that OK?"

"Sure, it is. They can't be much trouble."

Two surfboards, three bags, five athletic teenage boys, and one new, old old old motor, and gas can, fill my little sixty-five Mustang to the brim. To the lippen full, see how many guys fit in a phone booth, gut busting brim. Yep, they couldn't be much trouble, could they?

The details of the torturous ride to Oregon are too painful to relate. Just let it be known that I laid-to, for seven days in the worst hurricane to hit Australia in twenty years. We were laying-to in a thirty-six foot sail boat. Winds broke the wind meter at a hundred miles an hour. The waves were forty-foot combers. Getting dressed was not possible so we slept fully clothed. Wet to the bone for seven days, no hot food; the thought of being driven onto the Great Barrier Reef a constant companion. And that experience, that experience, was nothing compared to what those guys did in the back of that Mustang.

Pulling into the parking spot in front of our little sixteen-foot trailer; a cloud of rock dust swirls around the red Mustang, welcoming us home. Climbing stiffly from the driver's seat I glance over the top of the Mustang at Mike. I see the same pained expression on his face that I feel on mine. It's been a long twelve-hour drive. Folding the seat forward Cosmos climbs out. Once out, Cosmo remains bent. His walk reminds me of one of man's early predecessors, not a very graceful predecessor either. Caesar follows Cosmo out of my side of the car. Caesar is able to shuffle in an upright manner. Be it; a very stiff shuffle.

Wayne climbs out on Mike's side, I can't see him over the top of the car, he is bent, too bent to see.

Cosmo, Mike's little brother is a girl magnet, Cos is so good looking that he has a fan club. Most of the girls in Cos's fan club don't even go to our high school. The fan club gave him a dinner where he received a "HUNK" award.

Wayne is a Christian. That's it. He's a Christian; he don't smoke, cuss, or drink. He's saving himself until marriage. Right in the middle of the sexual revolution he refuses to bring his weapon out. I sure don't understand it. It's all right, though, that leaves more targets of opportunity for Mike, Caesar, Cosmo, and me.

Caesar is another story. He is the movie's ideal leading man. Caesar has shoulder length hair and a beard. A beard at eighteen, for God's sakes. It ain't right; it just ain't right. The girls at school loved Caesar. Caesar loves the girls at school. Everyone is happy except the rest of us guys. I'm a little nervous that Debbie will drop me when she gets a look at these two hunks I just brought into town.

It's ten thirty P.M. and we're all bushed from the twelve hour drive. All five of us troop into our sixteen foot trailer. Where are we going to sleep? Looking around, I opine.

"None of us are going to sleep with the other."

"There's a picnic table in front of Archie Bunker's trailer. Cosmo can sleep there."

Cosmo blinks at Mike sleepily. "Where? Where can I sleep?"

"On the picnic table it will be all right. By the way, Archie don't like us, you better get up and move before he wakes up in the morning."

"Oh, OK. What time does Archie wake up?"

"Around four? Maybe, earlier we've never seen him leave his trailer. He always gets up too early."

Cos rubs a hand sleepily through his hair, "How will I know when four is?" Shaking his head sadly at his little brother, Mike mutters; "If, you miss four this morning and don't get up, you won't have to worry about tomorrow."

Cos's eyes open wide, "Oh?"

Turning to Caesar Mike inclines his head toward our home. "You can sleep on the trailer floor, just throw a bag down."

Wayne looks down cast, "Where can I sleep?"

Mike and I chorus, "In Big Bertha Butts."

Yep, our guests are no trouble at all; no trouble at all.

***

Our guests have been here for six days. We have become a group of hunter-gatherers. Fishing's been steady, until yesterday. Wayne and Cosmos have been picking berries, gathering mustard greens and clams. We have been contributing short salmon and bottom fish to the mix. We eat like kings, sea kings, but kings just the same. There are plenty of hands to cook with plenty of time, now that we have a beach crew. The beach crew has a lot of time for surfing, exploring, and coming up with gourmet meals.

This morning, the wind, is a blowing. She's a howler all right, so, the whole fleet stayed off the ocean. No fishing today. We've given ourselves a day off.

Glancing up from his cup of hot chocolate as the bell over Hogie's door announces my entrance, Marty grins. He's leaning against the counter, blowing on his cup. Debbie is writing up Marty's purchase of a dozen hoochies. Heading straight to the big coffee urn, I pour a packet of chocolate into a Styrofoam cup. Filling the cup with coffee smiling my biggest smile at Debbie. Man, she is beautiful today.

Marty clears his throat, "Ben, I'd like you to meet David. David this is Ben." Reaching toward one another, we shake. David is tall and reed thin, around twenty. Hair falling to his shoulders in waves, he's sporting a goatee. David smiles at me, showing perfect teeth.

Through his smile David says, "Nice to meet you."

I smile back, "Good to meet you too."

Sipping his chocolate Marty wipes his mouth with the sleeve of his shirt. "David is one of my Dad's students. Dad invited him up to visit us, see what a fishing community is like. David is going to be a writer."

Marty is impressed with David's future profession. Heck I am too, having never met a writer before I don't know what to say.

Not wanting to be quoted sounding like some unrefined fisherman, I say nothing. However, an unrefined fisherman is exactly what I am, standing there I just gawk.

Finding myself in this uncomfortable quandary, I grin, like a jackass. I'd like to get to know someone as cool as David. But, but, he'll think I'm a country goober, one who just fell off the fish box.

Marty leans back on the counter resting both elbows. "So, what are you guys up too, on our day off?"

"Mike and I are taking the Bloody Wog out to the Rock. We're going after bottom fish. We have five hungry mouths to feed."

"You got bottom fishing gear?"

"Naw... we're going to spearfish, no cost, no ware or tare, all profit, or food."

David interjects, "May I come along with you this may make for a good story."

My head bounces up and down feeling a smile cress my lips. Maybe he'll write something about me.

"Yea no problem, we wanted Marty along to run the boat while we're both down."

Marty smiles his happy go lucky grin, "Of course we'll go."

"Fine fine, this is working out just fine." Turning to Debbie I reach toward her with my empty hand. "Debbie, would you like to have dinner with us later? Say around four this afternoon."

Debbie reaches toward me our hands meeting in the center of the counter. "Of course I'll come to dinner with you. Maybe we can go out somewhere after dinner, just the two of us?"

"Sure, we'll go to the beach." I quickly unclench Debbie's fingers, hoping that David won't think I'm a woose because I'm nice to my girlfriend.

***

It's around ten in the morning. The Bloody Wog rises to the on-coming comber the bow plowing through the white water. I throttle up on the back side of the wave. The Wog accelerates down the glassy back side. At the bottom I pull her back a little to give the bow a chance to rise into the next breaker.

David standing behind Marty, is grasping the davit, his knuckles a bright white, his face the same color. Marty also has a hand on the davit. His knuckles are a relaxed pink, as is his face. Mike and Caesar's demeanor are also one of nonchalant unconcern.

David is the only point of tension in the boat. That's to be expected. It isn't every day that one rides a twenty foot slab of plywood through the Oregon surf. And, onto an ocean that no one else will venture out on. David is showing true grit just being with us. Mike, Caesar, and I are in our diving gear, mostly. If something were to happen we could just swim ashore. Marty, he has been doing this kind of thing since he was old enough to reach a davit. This is the first time David has even seen a dory. He's taking it on faith that we will be able to get him back ashore. What a concept, this crew responsible?

The plan is for the three of us dressed in black neoprene to do some spear-fishing. What we don't need to feed our clan we'll sell. David is along to get material, and for the ride, he is going to be a writer you know?

"Marty, we'll get to the lee of the rock. Then one of us will set your anchor and we'll all get wet."

"Sounds good," Marty nods at the plan. "In the lee we'll be just fine. Sea Gull targets, but just fine all the same."

Out on the wind swept ocean, spray flies over the starboard side. The wind whipping through the rigging alternately howls and whistles at us. The sound changing as we rise to the top of a swell or drop into a trough, while quartering our way down to the rock. The swells picking up our port stem quarter and then sliding under us. In five minutes the Rock is off our port side. I spin the wheel and run her in behind the massive granite structure. Haystack Rock blocks the wind, diminishing it to an occasional gusty breeze. The ocean is flat behind it, just a gentle low swell.

Marty moves forward pulling the anchor from under the bow. Then he pitches it into the Pacific Ocean. Line feeding out through his hand as the anchor tumbles toward the bottom. The loops of line are uncoiling, jumping up and down in a frantic rush to get overboard. The anchor hits the bottom, halting the mad rush of line. The anchor catches, swinging the bow into the light gusty wind.

The rock is a massive granite up-cropping rising two hundred and fifty feet above the ocean floor. It looks like a giant sore thump, the walls thrust vertically through the ocean swells. Haystack Rock rounds near the top, then becomes pointy. The top of the rock is covered in sea gull guano. Giving the effect of a thump swathed in a giant white Band-Aid.

Haystack Rock is infested with birds whose greatest pleasure is derived from a direct hit on an innocent fisherman. If, there is any such a thing as an innocent fisherman?

Mike, Caesar, and I finish-up dressing in our dive gear; by donning hoods, flippers, and face masks. Strapping on our weight belts like gun fighters, pulling our spear guns from the fish box adds to the gunfighter like machismo. Caesar pulls the double rubbers on his gun back, hooking them into place. Mike, he owns a Hawaiian sling, which is basically a pointy stick and surgical tubing. It's a cheap device, but extremely effective in his hands. I have a birthday present, a nice birthday present at that. It's a pneumatic gun; shoving the spear into place compresses air in a chamber. Pulling the trigger sends the spear on its way, with a resounding whoosh. The gun looks twenty first century cool, you got to love it.

Mike rolls off the gunwale backwards, sea water, splashing Marty and David. Pulling his face mask into place, Caesar follows Mike over the side… me, I'm still shaking spit out of my mask. However, in less time than it takes for a salmon to hit a hoochie I roll over backward.

Bubbles exploding around me; my world is white. In seconds the bubbles have risen to the surface. Expanding their existence trying to push the surface apart. As the bubbles are bursting on the surface, icy water dribbles into my wet suit. Cold, icy fingers run over my torso, and up my legs. Reminding me that it is a cold cold business that we're involved in here.

Looking toward a shelf on the rock I see Mike and Caesar breaking up sea urchins. The water is turning a purple haze as they beat the sea urchins with the butts of their spear guns. Breaking the urchins up will attract fish. Lots of fish.

Little fish will come to eat the sea urchin row. Bigger fish will come to eat the little fish. Still bigger fish will come to eat the bigger fish. And, we shall take the fish that come to eat the still even bigger fish. Then, we will eat the still even bigger fish we take. It's a jungle, sort of thing.

All we have to do is wait. Swimming to the ledge I join in on the whole sale destruction of the sea urchin population. I have a small twang of guilt about the total annihilation of every sea urchin on this ledge. Life just isn't fair, is it? The feeling of guilt disappears; the first little fish is feeding off the urchin row. The progression of predator and prey has begun.

Returning to the Bloody Wog we hang out, letting our chum ledge work. Marty and David are deep in the mist of a rap session, hanging onto the side of the boat the conversation happening above us can be overheard.

David's languid, educated sounding voice can be heard as he expounds on this experience. "This is so natural. Man gathering his own food from the sea. It's the way we are supposed to live, you know. Man is measuring himself against the elements. The hunting game with the most basic weapons. Taking only what he needs, this story writes itself."

Marty's mellow tones expound his own world view. "I've been raised knowing where our food comes from. Death is part of life, it's a cycle. In some ways the whole world is like a reef. New life is built on the death of our predecessors."

David's voice excited by this new concept he is playing with. "Man is a predator, a natural part of his environment. Taking food is almost a creative art form, like writing. I compare all life's experiences to writing, one of the truly creative art forms. I feel that what I do is so important.... Because I can communicate to everyone what it is like to be here, and do this. Do you know what I mean?"

It is time. The fish are gathering for the slaughter.

Mike is already heading down to the schooling fish below. Bending at the waist I kick my feet straight over my head and power toward the ledge. A four pound snapper presents his broadside to me. Lining up his gill plate I squeeze the trigger. Whoosh, the spear flies. The fish, pulling and tugging on the line, the fish flopping out his death throws it is time to return to the Wog.

At the Wog I poke my spear over the gunwale, Marty, using a gaff hook pulls the fish from the spear. The fish hits the deck. Marty spins the gaff around to where the hook is pointing skyward. Raising the gaff high over his head, then he brings it down with a resounding smack. Again and again, he repeats this maneuver until the fish just lays there and quivers.

Spinning the gaff around so the six-inch curved hook is pointing downward. Marty crashes the hook through the cod's gill plate and into the deck. Glassy dead eyes look into David's soul as the fish is thrown into the fish box. It's about this time Mike pokes another fish over the gunwale. Marty repeats the procedure.

The fish are coming to the sea urchin chum like it's a Swedish Smorgasbord. A steady stream of fish are coming over the side. Marty's capable gaff hook dispatches each and every one. Marty is happily carrying on a conversation with David. As each fish is pushed over the gunwale, Marty, rips it from the spear, beats the whole whalen snot out of it, and pitches it into the fish box.

While he is executing God's creatures, Marty is discussing the beauty found in nature. He expounds on the Zen-like quality that can be reached while commercial fishing. Marty is moving on to one of his favorite topics, Karma.

"Karma is so right, a person receives the treatment back that he puts out, it's also biblical, reap what you sow a beautiful thing."

About this time Marty notices that David is not participating in the conversation anymore. Marty looks up from the latest victim of the deadly gaff hook, "You alright... you aren't getting seasick, are you?"

David's eyes are filled with disgust, misreading this new light Marty comes up with the answer. If David is not seasick, then maybe he wants a turn at the gaff?

"David, do you want to take a whack?"

David's eyes grow in diameter, "A whack? No I don't want a whack." David crosses his forearms in front of his face.

Marty straightens up; he and David are eyeball to eyeball. "Go ahead, take a whack. Don't you want to see what it feels like."

No! I don't want to see what it feels like. Have you gone crazy? I know what it feels like. It hurts.

Marty smiles his big, friendly grin. "No, it don't, not after the first whack, you stun them, then... no more pain."

David stands from where he is sitting on the fish box. Stepping back he hops onto the box. Then down into the open section just in front of it. "Don't you hit me! You could brain me."

Marty throws the gaff in the air watching it flip end for end. He catches it with the gaff end toward himself. The six inch: stainless steel, blood encrusted hook pointing skyward.

"What? You're kidding, right? I don't mean taking a whack, I mean you give a few whacks."

Marty is holding the gripping end toward David, thrusting it at him in a friendly manner. Now the disgust is plain on David's face. It was one thing when Marty was offering to hit David in the head so he could experience what the fish were going through. But, but, the very thought of executing one of these innocent fish, like a common fisherman is more that David's psyche will allow. He turns from Marty in disgust.

"How could anyone think that a writer, a WRITER for God's sakes, could whack a fish to death just for a story."

The fun being had by the guys on the surface is over; over for now. Marty and David spend the rest of the outing, saying nothing. Not a word, not a sound, David sits quietly, while Marty takes care of the fish. Pulling and whacking and throwing fish into the box; Marty can't quite keep his grin to himself. David watches, wincing with every blow Marty delivers.

Marty feels bad that David doesn't like him, but it's OK. It will make one hell of a story to tell us guys.

***

The night sky is filled with stars, the wind of the afternoon has diminished to a slight breeze. The ocean is calm and it's late. Too late to be out and about, I've got to go fishing tomorrow.

My fatigue is invasive; my body is heavy. Weighted down, it's like I'm wearing a suit of iron, I'm filled with tired, each and every muscle is slow following the commands of my brain. I crave sleep like a thirsty man craves water. In two words, I'm spent.

Tires crunch the gravel as I roll to a stop. I never thought that seeing our little red and white trailer would look so good. My head lights are off; I don't want to wake any of my tribe. Opening the door I stumble from the car. Pulling myself up by the door frame, quietly closing the door; I set out for my bed. Aaah BED.

I can smell the ocean and the pines, far off and pleasant; it's a link to reality. Debbie's smell also lingers. Like awaking from a dream, it's present but not within grasp anymore.

Once inside the trailer I quietly sidestep Caesar, trying not to wake him. Creaking down on the bed, I slip off my shoes. Laying my head back on the bed I listen to Mike and Caesar breathe. Mike's voice comes to me in a whisper.

"Where the hell have you been? What'd you do... break down?"

Too tired to lie, I just respond, "No, no we didn't break down."

"Ben, where have you been?"

"With Debbie. Why?"

"You've been gone since eleven this morning. We just been wondering what in the world you could be doing for all this time."

"I been been getten getten... well you know."

"No Ben, I don't know, getten what?"

Rubbing my eyes with a closed fist, I hesitate, should I admit where we've been, and what we've been doing. Ah well, why not? "We got laid."

"Yea we figured that." Shifting position in his bed Mike faces me. Pulling his pillow from under his head he bunches it up. Mike's head is propped up in his rapping position. I'm doomed; it's time to tell all.

Mike's voice in its' normal modulation. "Go ahead?"

Caesar moves into a better posture for rapping. "Yea Ben, let's hear what happened? Did you use any protection?"

Sighing resignedly with the realization that there will be no rest for me this night. Having made a conquest, it is incumbent on me to speak to the tribe. I must tell my story. The tribe will have to be told, like a brave coming back from a big hunt or a raid on a neighboring village. The conquest was mine; the story must be told.

Mike, who knows all, asks about the white elephant setting in the room. "What about Debbie wanting to give herself only to the man she's going to marry?"

Running a hand over my face, "I don't understand about that. She didn't say one word about marriage.

I told her that I had a condom, maybe that was what persuaded her."

Caesar shakes his head to the negative. "It wasn't the condom Ben. She loves you; she wanted to give herself to you."

"To me? Why me?"

Mike sits up in his bed, "Because you big galoot, you couldn't take your eyes off her from the first day you met her. Girls like that."

Smirking into the dark, "Yea I know," I agreed.

Mike says, "It's good that you used protection. We don't want you a dad. Not yet anyway."

"Well I used protection the first three times. Then, we kind of ran out. The last two time we did it bald headed, so to speak."

We all sit *in* silence. The story is told; the tribe knows. Now all we have to do is go over the detail's, ad-nauseam, or until dawn.

***

The salmon season is grinding down. The fish are getting more and more scattered. It's scratch fishing on the good days, and a desert on the bad ones. Debbie is planning to drive down to California and spend a week with her grandmother. Tom-Tom is making calls. The albacore are off the coast almost within striking distance for a dory. After an evening of dinner and planning, we have a plan. Tom-Tom and his running partner are heading down the coast looking for better fishing. They will drive down the coast looking for fish. Mike and Caesar are going along to get a feel of the other ports, other fishing spots. Me, I'm staying here. Debbie and I will drive down to her grandmother's house next week. Then we'll all meet in Concord at my family's house.

To kill time, I'm taking the Wog out fishing. The rest of our fleet has gone home Nole and Bob are back at school. Many of the boats are heading north where the salmon are schooling off the Colombia River.

283

It's Yerdal the Turtle and me, we're the only ones left here. It's been really scratchy, but today we found a few. Trolling north Yerdal passes me going south, pole tip to pole tip. He's standing at his wheel watching me work. I crank up a spread and take off a salmon. Yerdal waves. Cranking again I pull another fish Yerdal waves again. The port side in the starboard side out the Wog is going in a large circle. Grinding around and around on the fish. Every time I pass Yerdal I'm pulling a fish. Every time I pull a fish Yerdal waves at me.

Late afternoon, fishing's done for the day, I'm walking toward the fish company. At the counter Yerdal the Turtle is buying hoochies, Archie Bunker super hoochies. Dinging of the bell diverts everyone's attention to me. Across the counter from Yerdal, Debbie gives me one of her smiles. Hogie, kicked back in his chair, is resting his hands a-top of his head. His head is resting against the back wall.

Auburn hair, soft and lovely frames Debbie's beautiful face. Debbie's perky little body looking a little more rounded and more mature. She has been changing daily since that first time. I'm about to speak to Debbie; see if we can get together again tonight. When, Yerdal's laugh interrupts my unspoken thoughts.

"Ha-up, ha-up, oh-boy there he is. Ha-up Ha-up why, you should-a seen this here feller a pullin fish. I never seed such a sight. His big old arms just a-going round and around. When he comes to a stop, a-fish pops out of that thar ocean. He don't never stop."

Leaning forward in his big old office chair Hogie's grin is infectious as ever. "Yep old Bloody Wog Ben is turning into a good little fisherman."

Pride explodes from the pit of my stomach up through my chest, bringing a flush of red to my face. For Hogie, who never gives a compliment lightly, to say I am becoming a good fisherman is high praise. High praise indeed. Puffed up with pride I'm too puffed up to remember why I'm here. I was here to ask Debbie over to my lonely little trailer house this evening. Grinning like a mule eating bramble bushes, I stride back home, alone.

***

The end of the season is here. I know, because our old old thirty-five horse Evinrude, is hugged to my chest. Me and the engine are precariously balanced on the gunwale of the Wog. Looking down at the five-foot drop, I'm trying to figure out how to get me and the engine to the ground, without breaking me, or it. After thinking about it for awhile I hug the engine tighter and jump. We hit the ground with a, "metal clanking, woolff", coming from the both of us. Limping and dragging I pull the old old outboard to Hogie's storage area.

Tomorrow, at O-dark thirty, Debbie and I head for California. We'll be taking her car. Debbie wants to show Grandma what she bought with her summer wages. We'll overnight at Grandmother's house, then on down to Concord for a week of R and R together.

It's just me and her for however long it can take us to drive to Woodland, California. My plan is to take a long time to drive to Woodland. I wonder? Maybe a little stop at our favorite spot? This is going to be a real vacation. Yep, a real vacation.

***

Debbie's car is at the stoplight of Kirker Pass and Clayton Roads, two of the main roads in Concord. The light is just about to

285

turn green. A white Ford station wagon pulls up next to Debbie's 69 Chevell. The station wagon's horn sounds off in an obnoxious blare. Debbie's steering wheel is under my left hand. Her shoulder is under my right. Debbie is laid up next to me like a sick cat to a hot brick, as my grandfather would have said. Lazily looking over the top of Debbie's head, I'm trying to see the goof-ball honking at us. The goof-ball is Marty. Waving and grinning at us, Marty has some hot looking chick cuddled up next to him. They also look like a sick cat and a hot brick. Marty points at the shoulder of the roadway; I high sign him back. In less than five minutes we're on the shoulder. I haven't seen Marty in three weeks. God, I missed him. Reaching out I give Marty a big hug. He hugs me back. The doe eyed brunet beauty with Marty, is just standing there while Marty is hugging Debbie. I figure what the heck and throw my arms around her and get a hug too.

Stepping back and looking at Marty I spy his teeth. White, straight, strong teeth, with no metal to be seen. Marty has a newfound confidence. He's a new Marty. The brown haired, doe eyed, beauty, looks up at him adoringly. It's a wonder what the removal of an ounce of metal from one's mouth can do for a young man's senior year. It's plain for all to see; Marty is as happy as can be. This is going to be a very good year for Marty.

"Marty, we're going sailing tomorrow. Mike, Patty, Debbie and I are going to take out the Skinny Linnie, you want to come? Bring your new lady friend if you'd like."

"Sure, we'll come. It'll be fun."

Standing on the shoulder, we work the details out.

The next three days with Debbie are the best I've ever had. It's a love fest, interrupted by gourmet meals, days of sailing, and parties with friends. It's wonderful, just wonderful, our five-day vacation. But, all good things must come to an end.

***

The twin stacks from the Moss Landing power plant jut from the rolling hills, billowing steam into the sky. Highway One turns to a more southerly direction, passing a small harbor on our right. The road dips toward Whiskey Slough and the bridge that crosses it. Crossing the bridge, Moss Landing Harbor comes into view. The poles of the trollers and seiners look like a denuded forest, huge draggers sit next to many of the docks, it is big harbor. Not just a bunch of docks in a large basin, it is A BIG HARBOR. Boats range from ninety-foot goliaths offshore rigs to twenty-foot piss-pots. Each and every boat has a mast, and a set of poles. The far side of the harbor is lined with rickety old wooden docks. Each dock has two or three unloading winches strategically placed along them. Small multi-colored shacks are sitting atop the docks near the winches.

Wind, blowing through the open window and across my arm, is carrying the smells of mud flats at low tide, rotting fish, and the clean sweet smell of ocean. We're dragging Tom-Tom's dory behind the pick-up. My father's camper is in the bed of the truck. It is a full-size self-contained camper, with a fully stocked refrigerator and cupboards. Thanks to my mom, she stocked it for us. My Dad loaned us the camper for this Moss Landing albacore venture.

Once over the bridge, we pass the power plant. Hanging a right, we proceed into Moss Landing Harbor proper. It's my first visit to a working fish harbor. The harbor is a polyglot of confusing sights and sounds. New eighteen wheelers are backed up to rickety old fish docks, their reefer units running full out. Old wooden buildings line the left side of the one lane road. All are in varying states of disrepair. And, every building needs, I mean desperately needs a paint job. The smell of drying blood and rotting fish is pervasive. Bloody pools of stagnate water lie along the roadside. Rusty old pick-ups are parked next to brand new Mercedes Benzes, and small beat-up delivery trucks are parked beside Cadillacs. Two cats, jumping from a garbage bin continue their fight, while running across the road.

I felt I knew what it meant to be a fisherman, now I know, I don't know the first thing about fishing. This is a whole new world opening for me. A world where fishermen fish for a living, not for a summer. A world of tough looking men, who are on a mission. A world of big boats, big harbors, and big money. Gee, is this that real world, the one my dad told me about.

Pulling off the one lane road in front of Di Girolamo Fish Company, Tom-Tom slows to a stop. Slamming the door of the pick-up Tom strides away. Exiting the passenger door I look back. Tom's running partner, Steve, pulls up right behind us. Mike exits the passenger door of Steve's rig, looking around he's dazed by the sights and sounds, just like me. Steve walks off towards the little office/house that sits under the DiGirolamo Fish company sign. Mike and I saunter toward each other.

The rickety old dock is calling to us, *"Come and see. Come and see a real fishboat harbor."*

On the dock we feel like tourists, watching a troller unloading albacore. *Wow this is something.* Sauntering over we observe the goings on. A large square basket rises out of the fish hold, frozen albacore filling it to the top. A dockhand working the winch is resting his large belly over the handle. Swinging inboard, the bucket stopped over a large two wheeled cart. Pulling a handle on the bucket lets the bottom fall. The bottom is hinged, like a trap door. Falling albacore fill the basket. Four of them fall onto the dock.

Picking up the fish the dockhand throws them back onto the cart. The cart is rolled onto a large square scale.

A burly bearded man, standing next to the scale, is writing the weights down. He's the skipper. Next to the burly guy is a swarthy dark-haired man, dressed in expensive clothes. He's writing weights on a fish tag. Hogie he ain't, but he's the fish buyer.

The fisherman grinning is joking with the fish-buyer. The fish-buyer is laughing right back. They're both making money, this is a good transaction, and it shows.

Tom-Tom walks up between Mike and me, placing a hand on our shoulders. "Come on we can launch down the road. According to the fish buyer we can park in the lot across the slough. There are a few fish out fifty miles; we'll head out tomorrow and see how we do."

***

It's 4 A.M. Tom-Tom's dory is heading out through the jaws of Moss Landing harbor. Ocean swells are lifting the bow. The red flashing light on the end of the jetty gleams off the bow cowling. Peeking from the hood of a sweatshirt, Tom-Tom's face has a reddish hue. The wind blowing around the hood of his sweatshirt is also whipping his long hair around his ears and face.

This morning, like every other morning this summer, we're heading out without eating breakfast. There is no food aboard again. She's a hungry ship, this ship.

Heading out thirty or forty miles, in a twenty-two-foot boat has an element of risk. This better work out for Tom-Tom. I didn't know it before, but this is a lease boat. The boat, the Jeep, and the gear, it all belongs to someone else. Tom-Tom is working on a forty-sixty percentage deal. He's done well this season, but he didn't put any of it away. Now, we're down here on a do or die effort; get some money for the winter.

Since TomTom is broke I'm not taking any wages. This is going to be a hard winter; I don't have any money at all. It has been said; there are many biscuits to be found at my father's table. Besides security is a state of mind, not the state of your pocket book.

We're going to kill the albacore, after all; we have to. If we fail, I don't want to contemplate what this winter is going to be like for Tom-Tom and his family.

Opening up the six cylinder Volvo, we begin to fly. Wave top to wave top, the ocean we're heading out on is large rolling swells. Legs bending and flexing we jet toward the albacore grounds. That feeling of anticipation that comes with a hunt, rises from my belly, adrenaline flowing through my body, muscles tingle with excitement; the hunt begins.

Looking toward the sun, I guess; it may be around ten o'clock? Still no fish. Looking down south I spy Steve and Mike out on the horizon. Tom-Tom just hung up the radio mic they're carrying a skunk too.

"What are we going to do, Tom?"

Tom-Tom scratches his bristly jaw. The jaw sports mostly black bristles but gray is starting to dominate in some areas around the chin. "Well Ben, I just don't know, I just don't know?"

Tom-Tom saying he doesn't know, doesn't mean that he doesn't know. He is the only one out here who may know. Tom-Tom is saying that what we have tried hasn't worked, so far. It's fishermen code. Fishermen code for we're going even further offshore. So, we do.

It's a good two hours later when the first albacore hits, the line springing tight. Reaching for the line I start to pull. Looking over my shoulder at Tom, I grimace. "Wow, these fish pull a lot tougher than salmon."

Pulling; the line is slipping back half of every pull. I'm not use to this, from the onset of this fight the outcome is in doubt. The line digging deep into my palms, hurts.

Tom-Tom points at the nippers tucked under the handrail, "You need those?"

Looking at the nippers with longing, yet knowing, I can't let the fish back out. I pull, pulling with more force than one little old fish should require.

Tom-Tom points to a second line that just hit. "Big green water fish, lots of times the big lunkers will hang out in the colder water in shore, that's why we're here."

The fish pops to the surface, skiing along for about twenty seconds. Getting a look at this monster; yep, Toms' right. This lunker I'm fighting is thirty pounds, if he's an ounce. Oh there he goes, his head is down again; diving deep. Our battle continues, pull slip, pull slip, pull slip.

Finally arriving at the stern, the fish flops aboard. Reaching for the second line I stop in my tracts. My nippers? I ain't going to pull another lunker without some protection.

The innertube fits my hands nice and snug. A thin veneer of rubber may not seem like a lot of protection, but it is a big step up from no protection at all.

At the end of the day we, Tom-Tom and I, have twenty fish. About two-hundred and fifty dollars' worth. Mike and Steve have a few more fish than we do. Not bad not too bad for our first day. The next few days follow much as the first.

In too few of days, it is time for Mike to go off to college. Heading off too Humbolt State, Mike is going to study marine biology. Cool. He's going to be a scientist working on boats, diving all over the world. Even cooler. As Mike boards the bus in downtown Moss Landing, I wave him off. A sad little wave, with no heart.

Already, I'm missing him. Mike is the closest thing to a brother I've ever had. I don't know, I just don't know how or when I developed these feelings. Mike is a sardonic, crusty, and slightly dangerous youth. He would laugh at me if I told him how I feel. Ya got to love a guy like that.

***

We've been here three weeks. The fish were within striking distance for a few days, we did fine, just fine. Not great we didn't make winter money, but we were getting by. The fish moved offshore three days ago. At sixty miles off we get into a few green water lunkers, but it's just expenses, no payday. Albacore fishing just hasn't paid off. Today, we got into some Bonita tuna, they are a wild fast fish; getting hold of a Bonita tuna is like catching a wild cat. We got a couple of hump. They're only worth a dollar and a half per fish. It's gas money not much more.

The day is done; Tom-Tom is at the wheel. We're closing in on the Di' Gigamon dock. All the hoists have albacore trollers tied up under them.

A dockhand leaning against one hoist is lowering the bucket toward the fish hole; they're unloading. This troller has a ways to go before she's empty, she still lies deep in the waters. Tom swings us alongside another boat. This boat was just towed over, she's brand new, still under construction.

The new boat is light in the water. From the looks of her, she doesn't have any fuel, water, or maybe even an engine aboard. The water line is at least three feet above the water. Her name on the stern reads, Alley Cat, funny name that.

The deck of the Alley Cat is plugged with people. Readying a bow line, we bump alongside. Looking up, I make eye contact with a young man on deck. With a nod of my head, I pitch the line. Grabbing it in midflight, he ties us off. Tom-Tom throws up a stern line.

Jutting his chin at the office Tom-Tom mutters, "Hey Ben, I'm going up to the dock, be back in a bit. OK?"

Making an OK sign with my thumb and forefinger, I nod in agreement. "That's cool Tom-Tom."

Wondering back to the stern I lay down on the engine cover. Throwing an arm over my eyes, I try to ignore the party going on next door, especially the smell of burgers burning on the grill. Smoke drifting down to me is a punishment. My stomach rumbles forth in a violent growl, placing a hand on my noisy belly I concentrate on trying to sleep.

Lying there, I hear a voice sounding like Yogi the Bear, the cartoon. Its' unusual timbre intrudes on my rest. "Hey hey hey, the

Douggers, you cheap little bugger. Why don't you feed this here kid? I'm gonna go deaf from his stomach noises. He's got to… eat or move. What-do-ya-say, lets feed this here kid."

Under my arm I grin at the sound of some fisherman sounding just like Yogi the Bear. Does this guy know he sounds like Yogi the Bear? Moving my arm looking up toward the gunwale of the Alley Cat.

There's the guy; he's in a white floppy hat and a green workman's shirt. Peering down at me, he's a big guy, six foot one or two. An old guy, he's pushing forty-five years of age, big, round, old, and strong looking. No wonder he sounds like Yogi the Bear, he looks like Yogi. Broad sloping shoulders, a large grin, with the girth of a prosperous picnic basket stealing bear of a man.

A small man wearing a green baseball cap, a green work shirt, and Levi's walks to the gunwale. Taking a swig of beer, "Hey kid, would you like a burger? Come on aboard; we are having a launching party, Come on kid, have a coke, and a burger, heck... have a beer, I don't care."

Setting up, I smile at the two guys inviting me aboard. These are troller men, highliners, asking me onto their boat.

Stepping on the gunwale of the tuna troller I swing aboard. The little guy points toward a wash tub filled with beers and sodas.

"Help yourself. We're having an open boat today. I've invited everyone in Moss Landing to drop by, we'll be having people aboard all afternoon, until dark. Kind of a let everyone see the new boat party. Grab a beer, take a look around."

So, I do. Grabbing a beer, I walk forward. Looking in the double Dutch door at the impressive interior, stepping over the foot high threshold I notice the floor. The deck is covered with a soft thick sound absorbent plastic flooring. On the port side is the galley table. It's nice big and comfortable. The starboard side is all galley. A sink, a diesel stove, counter area for preparing meals, it's a nice galley. Just forward, on the port side, of the settee are two bunks. They're closed off from the rest of the pilot house. The bunk area has a chart table bolted to the ceiling. The chart table is hinged and drops down. It's big enough to hold a full-size chart. To read a chart you stand in the passageway outside of the bunk area. It's a good design.

The wheel is cool, it's three feet in diameter, wooden, with cool spokes. Just like an old time's ship's wheel. No electronics are aboard yet. The far port side on the wheel station has a neat-do pilot's seat. It's black Naugahyde with comfy arms and a foot rest. Sliding into the seat my head rests against the bulkhead. The pilot seat enfolds me in comfort. Kicking back, I begin daydreaming.

The bow is bucking into heavy seas, she cuts through the wave tops, in my mind, her bow riding high and dry, what a sea boat, what a captain.

The young man who took the bow line walks up beside me, "Cool boat huh?"

My head nods up and down in confirmation, "Really cool boat, how big is she?"

Placing a hand on a spoke of the wheel he muses. "She is fifty-two feet long; she's got sixteen foot of beam. She'll pack thirty tons, sixty thousand pounds of product. What a pay day huh? She's powered by a six-seventy-one GMC, screaming Jimmy. It's like real Cool?"

"Wow, you know a lot about the boat, is this your Dad's boat?"

"Naw, it's my Uncle Doug's boat. He is the guy that invited you aboard. That's Stormy on the deck with him. I've been fishing with Uncle Doug for three summers now."

"That's cool, he must have sold his other boat huh?"

"Not yet, it's still for sell. The Ardy it's a forty-eight-footer. We've caught a lot of fish on that boat."

"So, you looking forward to fishing on the Alley Cat?"

"Yea, but I can't this year. I joined the Navy, I just got out of Boot Camp."

Oh, that explains the short hair on this kid. The kid sticks out his hand, "Hi my name is Doug Junior."

No body, but no body, wares short hair, unless they're in the military. The chicks just don't dig short hair.

"Is there anything else on the boat I should, see?"

"Yea, come and see the engine room."

Doug Jr. waves me down a hatch next to the wheel. Half an hour later we start up a ladder that's in the fish hole. We can hear Stormy up on the deck, holding court. He has a crowd of five or six fishermen around him. This guy Stormy is the center of attention. Stormy is standing near the gunwale, his backdrop the old wooden piles, the rickety dock sticking about five feet above his head. Stormy's hands are flying around while he pours forth, with rapid sentence after sentence. My head rises above the hatch combing. Stormy stops in mid-sentence.

"Hey hey hey it's the kid. Where ya been kid? Douggers, why don't you feed this kid? It looks to me like he ain't seeing no hamburgers. Not out in that squirt of a boat he's on."

The little guy named the Douggers, walks to a Bar-B-Que grill, and flops one very small hamburger onto a dwarfed bun. Pointing to the small containers of condiments he says, "Help yourself."

Doug only places a burger onto the grill when someone asks for one. Or, if Stormy badgers him into it. He just must be forgetful, huh? After all, it's launch day, this is his first new boat.

Stormy pulls his dark glasses down on his nose, looking over them. "So kid are you Jake now, or what?"

Feeling confused, I stare at this guy called Stormy, the unspoken question plane on my face.

"Jake, kid. You know is everything Jake, like cool man. You know, JAKE?"

Stormy is looking me in the eyes, staring over the top of his glasses, waiting for me to respond.

Having a mouth full of hamburger I nod, giving Stormy a thumbs up sign.

Stormy turns from me back to his audience. Me, I'm not interesting enough to hold his fleeting attention.

"We're standing at the gate to "A" dock. My brother Freddy he was there. Hey hey hey, you know Freddy he is mellow, like cool man. The old man is there, crusty old coot that he is. Dave on the Warlord is hanging out. You know Dave, he don't ever just hang out.

Stormy, using his middle finger, pushes his sunglasses back up his bear-like nose. He shakes his waist back and forth. His girth gyrating like he's using a who-la hoop. Stormy is a wild man. He loves being the center of attention, and he is!

297

"There was a big bunch of us just a hanging out; shucking and jibing in the parking lot. The last few days they been making a movie here. The Choir Boys, it's a cop movie. We're standing right at the gate. This old beater of a car comes racing into the parking lots. Nothing unusual in an old beater driving in the parking lot too fast. Heck, it's probably some fisherman, running from an irate husband. Two cop cars flying into the parking lot after the old beater. Red light and sirens are just a screeching. It were like cool man.

We're all standing around, saying jake man, this looks like the real deal. You'd never know this is a movie. The guys in the old beater jump from their car. They got pistols drawn. One of them has a shotgun. There's four bad guys. Two cops jump from their cars they both got shot guns. The shooting and banging starts. It was like jake man. The cops are shooting at the bad guys, the bad guys shooting at the cops. We're standing real quite so we won't ruin the scene."

Stormy pulls his dark glasses down, piercing us with a penetrating gaze. Connecting with his audience eyeball to eyeball; he identifies with each of us on the deck. His head jerking around he looks over his shoulder like he's being stalked. Stormy seems surprised to see only the dock behind him.

My old man he is a shade sharper than the rest of us… he asks; "Hey where are the television cameras, and lights, and crew? You know; this may not be a movie?"

We're looking around for them. One of the bad guys makes a dash from his car to the dumpster we're standing by. He is hit in his leg during his run. He's jake man. Rolling behind the dumpster he keeps on shooting his shotgun. Like BOOM, BOOM. I tell the other guys; hey hey hey, this is like the real deal man. It's about this time that the light over the gate is shot out. Glass, from the overhead light falls all around us; tinkle tinkle tinkle. I tell um all; this is the real deal man?"

Stormy stretches and moves to the ice bucket full of beers, cheap ones. Popping the top, Stormy settles on the gunnel which is his original position; the center of our attention. Once again, Stormy lowers his sun glasses down his bear like beak; once more he gazes into the eyes of all.

"We all book-it for the gate. We want nothing more than to get back to our little boats, where it's nice and safe. Hitting the end of the ramp I pull on the gate hard enough to rip it off its hinges. The gate's locked. Bullets are ricocheting off the dumpster and all around us. At about this time a bullet pings off the gate.

The old man says, "Well gentlemen, this isn't quite low enough for me."

The old man vaults the handrail on the gangway lighting down on the rip-rap like an eighteen-year-old marine.

The old man is shrewd, so we follow his lead. We're down among the slimy rip-rap keeping our heads low. Bullets whizzing overhead like it's the Tet Offensive. Poking my head up I can see what's happening. The guy behind the dumpster is out of shotgun shells; he's using his pistol. Everybody is banging back and forth. When one of the guys at the car gets hit.

The guy at the car is screaming, "I give up, I give up!"

His buddy yells from his dumpster, "No you don't nobody gives up!"

The guy in the car yells back at his buddy, "Jamal, you can't tell me what to do. I quit."

"You can't quit!" To punctuate his point, he snaps off a couple at the car guy. His other buddies in the car start yelling back at the dumpster.

"Hey Sammy, you be careful, man. You could hit one of us."

Dumpster man gets all hot under the collar, "Screw you guys!"

Then he pops a couple of caps at the guys in the car. The Car guys fire back at the dumpster guy, shooting back and forth; it's a free for all. Everybody shooting at everybody, it was like cool man, real Jake."

Touching my shoulder Tom-Tom asks, "You ready to go?"

All caught up in the story; I don't want to leave it. It's hard to tell Tom-Tom I can't go yet because Stormy isn't through talking. Stormy ain't going to quit, not as long as anyone is listening. Shrugging my shoulders, I follow him back to the dory.

***

Tom-Tom swings up through the camper door. "Just talked to Ma, she says the boat's owner wants his boat and Jeep back."

"Oh?"

"Yea. We'll head back up north, tomorrow."

Scratching my soft blond beard deep in thought, "Oh well it looks like this show is over anyway." In reality I'm happy to be getting back to Oregon. Oregon has Debbie in it, you know?

"We'll drop by your home in Concord. Unload the camper, then head north and home."

***

Following Tom-Tom into our house I'm overwhelmed by aromas of home and my childhood. My mother has out done herself again. Stakes, one on every plate sits a-top our dining room table. Warm bread, salad, fresh corn on the cob, and homemade French fries complete the banquet. Setting out of sight, but not out of smell, is my childhood favorite. Homemade apple pie. Someday I'll travel the world over, tasting apple pies, just so that I can verify; my mother makes the world's best.

The dining room table is long and oval. It's maple wood with a natural finish. A solid maple captain's chair is setting at six places. Ahh home, Mom, Dad, Linda, it's nice to be home again. Tomorrow, we travel north, then what? I don't have a school to go to? I don't have winter money? What do I do now?

My father, always hungry for a new adventure has been contemplating just those questions. Long before I had any concerns beyond dinner he has been thinking.

Thinking, thinking on what I'm going to be doing, and how it's going to affect the family.

The plan proposed by Harry is simple and ingenious. While dinner is progressing, the plan unfolds. Tom-Tom and I are going to look for a troller. After we find a troller, we're going to buy it. Tom-Tom and I will fish it we'll put half the profits into a partnership account. When we have enough for a down, we'll buy another. I'll fish the second troller, Tom-Tom will fish the first troller. Half of all profits will go toward putting a down payment on a third troller for my mom and dad.

"Well? What do you think?"

The plan is fraught with uncertainty, fish, like the ocean comes in waves. The season for this year is over. Dad and I don't know this fact. I should, Tom-Tom may, but this plan is a way out of his financial woes. It just might work? Two boats paying for one, three boats paying for one. Yes! Why not? The new partnership is formed.

***

Leaving for Oregon, we're on a mission. The mission: find a troller and go albacore fishing. It goes without saying; we'll all be rich in a matter of days. That's the plan, anyway.

Driving day and night, we arrive on Saturday morning. Who should be home? None other than the beauteous Debbie. Even though it's rainy and cold, Debbie and I go on a "picnic." Funny; being away from one another built up a huge appetite for "picnic."

***

The next day Debbie follows us up to Tillamook in her car. Where we leave the Jeep pick-up and dory in a driveway. No note, no knock on the door to tell anyone, no thank you, or by your leave, just like a reverse repossession. Boom, you have your boat back. This fishing business is a funny business.

Scooting over from underneath the wheel, Debbie blinks a come-hither look. Debbie and I spent a lot of time alone on our little vacation. We used this time to good advantage, making love two, three, four times a day. Debbie and I have achieved a comfort level. As a part of our intimacy, we have developed a driving posture. In our driving position, we can cover mile after mile, and hour after hour of driving. Driving and fondling, fondling and driving, it's a small piece of paradise. By force of habit, we fold into our normal driving position. Which is anything but normal.

In my grandfather's words, once again; "She's laying up against me like a sick cat to a hot brick." Placing my hand comfortably between her thighs I back down the driveway.

Out in the street while changing gears from reverse to drive, I catch a look from TomTom's eyes. Tom's eyes articulate all. He knows. He knows his little girl is sleeping with me, his look becomes stern and menacing. Fear balls in my stomach, Tom-Tom maybe forty, but he's tougher than whip-leather and meaner than a stomped-on badger when aroused. His gaze wonders over at his little girl; she sighs contentedly. Tom's eyes soften; I'm safe. Saved by a sigh.

***

It's Monday, Tom-Tom and I pull my Mustang into the parking lot; we're in a Portland harbor. We're out trying to find a boat. Man, there are some real dogs for sale. We've been looking for boats all day. Down this gangway there's a huge boat lying at the end of the pier. She must be forty or forty-two feet long. She has a beam of twelve feet. No doubt about it, she's huge. Yep, she's for-sale too. Pretty boat, white with teal trim and in good shape. Walking up and down the length of her we're admiring her in her beauty.

My parading halts at her fantail. She exits the water in a graceful arc, "DUNA, nice name."

Tom-Tom joins me there, "Nice boat ah?"

Smiling and nodding I agree, "Beautiful just beautiful, love her lines."

"I'm going to call the number, see if the Skipper can come on down let us look her over."

"Sounds good."

Returning from the phone booth Tom-Tom relates, "The skipper can't come down until tomorrow. We'll have to hang out here in Portland tonight."

Tom jerks his head toward the Mustang, strolling in that general direction, Tom says. "Let me drive, I know where we're going."

About an hour later we're at a little house in a Portland suburb. It's Tony's. Tony is a mountain of a man; he's big, just big all over. Tony was a pro-wrestler in his youth. The TV kind. Tom-Tom road his motorcycle. Tom had been a Motor-cross racer, racing Tony's bike for him. Tony is telling all. Things I'm sure that Tom wouldn't want his P.C. friends to know.

"Yea kid, Tom-Tom would ride my bike for me racing. That was back in my wresting days. Saturday afternoons, Tom raced; he was balls to the walls.

Tommy remember that Saturday you flew off my bike? Why... you looked like a young eagle testing your wings. Up up up you flew, the bike soaring right beside you. Your arms out circling round and round, you were gaining altitude, for a while. But, as that old guy said a long time ago, what goes up must come down. Smack!"

Clapping his giant meat-hooks together, the tiny house shaking with the thunderous crack; Tony breaks up. "Ho ho ho ha ha, ol Tommy, my boy why'd you used your face to break your fall?"

Turning to me Tony lays a hand on my shoulder, "Believe it or not Tom-Tom here used to be good looking. Now look at him, would ya?"

Glancing over all I see is Tom-Tom not some guy who used his face to stop his tumble from thirty feet in the air, while traveling at fifty miles an hour. Looking closer I see the miss aligned nose, the scarring on his forehead and chin. His eyes have been wrinkled from years of squinting into the sun. Scar tissue around one eye, is masked by all the wrinkles.

Yep, Tom-Tom may have been good looking. Oh, that explains a lot; that's where Debbie got her beauty. Now he looks like a fisherman. Sunburned face, shoulder length hair, red work-hardened hands, scars here and there. I want the same harden exterior but it will take years. It will take years to look like an old fisherman, by then being old and wrinkled will not be so cool. Maybe… maybe it will be cool?

***

The sun shining in the front window of my Mustang wakes me. Stirring my legs, I'm trying to find a comfortable position. There just isn't one. We've been sitting in the parking lot since eleven last night, sleeping under our coats in the Stang.

Opening the driver's door, stepping into the cold Oregon morning, I need a cup of coffee. Up the road is a little restaurant it is calling to me.

"Coffee, I have coffee, come to me."

And, I do. In ten minutes, I'm back with two cups of the blackish, strongest, hottest, coffee on the west coast.

***

The Duna is as pretty inside as out. The wheelhouse is all varnished mahogany and stainless steel. The paint is sparkling white where it is white and is the prettiest teal bluish-green where it is not sparkling white. Lines are perfectly coiled they're hanging on the cleats. The poles reaching forty feet above the deck. Even the poles have been varnished. The electronics are of another era, old, but in fine shape, like the rest of the boat.

The skipper of the Duna is just what one would expect. The skipper is about seventy years of age. Standing six feet tall, that is, he would be, if he weren't stooped over. His bald head is graying on the fringes. The skipper's eyes are a deep blue and crystal clear. This old man is one hundred percent Norwegian.

He loves this boat; it's been a part of his life for twenty-five years now. It has made him a living, kept him safe in storms, and brought him home every year since nineteen forty-eight.

Now in his golden age he must watch younger men run their work roughened hands over his beloved lady. They fondle her wheel, they jump into her hole, they pop her hatch and poke her with undisguised delight. While all this is going on he must stand and smile. Smile as other men, younger men, contemplate buying her, taking her away from him. And, after they have touched, fondled, and poked every intimate part of his beloved lady, they feel obligated to deride her. Considering what we are doing; this old man is truly a gentleman.

We are standing just inside the pilot house door when he turns to me, "Veil young feller, vhat you tink?"

"She is a real beauty. Nice lines, well maintained, she is a real nice boat. How come you're selling her?"

The old skipper lifts a shaking hand to his eyes which have filled to the brim with tears.

Wiping his eyes, he smiles a wan smile. I find myself looking at the deck to keep from embarrassing both of us.

"Veil, you see my vife, she finks maybe I be a little bit old to be a-fishin' all by my lonesome. It's all cause of my friend Mandus. He vas tell my Vife about a little incident which I vas have up in Alaska. It vere last season ven it happened."

"What little incident did you have, sir? What in the world could make your wife tell you to quit fishing? After all these years you got to be good at it."

"Oh it vas nothing, but you know how dem vimmen get ven day get som-ting in dare heads. I'll vill tell you cause you von smart young feller.

It vas like dis. I vas fighting a big halibut fish. Maybe, tree hundred pounds? He vas a pulling I vas a pulling and he pull just pull a little harder dan me. Slip bang I'm in the drink, ha ha ha it shore-war-funny."

I'm not sure what would be funny about swimming in the waters of Alaska but it sure does tickle this old gentleman. Grinning at the skipper I shake my head in agreement, "There is no understanding women, that's for sure."

The old skipper sticks his hand out, "Veil you vone smart young feller dhats' all I got to say for sure. My name is Yohn, it vas goot to meet you."

John sticks his hand out and we shake. "My name is Ben, it's good to meet you too. If you don't mind I'll like to hear the rest of the story. You didn't just stay in the drink? What happened? How did you irritate your wife so much she'd make you quit fishing?"

"Veil, I'll vill tell you, although I yust don't tell lots of folks cause it vas kind of embarrassing. I tell you that I vas fighting a halibut right?

Nodding yes, I grin encouragement, "Go ahead I'm interested I've never caught a halibut."

I vwas trolling up in Peril Straights, fishing King salmon. Da fish, day vas way down deep, and on da bottom spread comes up dis big old halibut. I vas take it off da wire to put him on the fighting subber.

He vwas pulling so hard, I couldn't get him hooked up. Dare vas blood from the last smiley I yest landed in da gaff hatch. My old hoof, it hit dat blood, and it flies out from under me. Next ting I know me and dat halibut is swimmen for da bottom.

He is a pulling and I'm a hanging on, pretty soon, I figure out dat he vas going to vinn, dis time."

John starts laughing a deep infectious belly laugh. There is nothing to do but join him. We're hanging onto one another, laughing. He's being pulled to the bottom by a halibut that out weights him by twice. His boat is trolling away on auto pilot. If he don't drown he'll freeze. Something's are just too serious to take seriously.

Wiping his eyes John continues, "Veil, after a little while, I figure out that yust maybe I lose dis fight, and yust maybe it vas a goot idea to give up. So, I do, somehow I struggle to the surface. My friend Mandus he vas working da same bite as me. Ve al- vays run together. Mandus vas following me dis day. It sure vas lucky, cause he spotted me when I break da surface. Mandus, veil he stops his boat. He vere going to pull me aboard. You know, vee yust ain't as young as vee once vas.

He pull on my arm but I yust didn't yerk aboard. I vas getting mighty cold about then. Old Mandus, he is vone vorrie-wart, if you know what I mean?"

Shaking my head yes, "I know just what you mean. Marty's mother she's a worrywart too. We sank our boat one morning in the surf. She didn't want us to go back out later that day. Can you believe that, some people?"

John and I have a common concern. Concerned people, they're such a pain. He smiles at me showing strong white teeth then continues his story.

"Mandus, he go into da house, and calls on da radio. He yust come back on deck, and he vas tell me dat no vone wants to break off fishing.

Mandus, he tell dem other fishermens; he needs a little help over here. A couple of guys asked vhat vas a problem? Mandus, he vas tell dem; he show dem vhen day come over. You know; he didn't vant to tell da whole fleet dat I had fallen overboard. You yust don't tell everybody dat your best friend isn't smart enough to stay on his boat, and is swimmin around Peril Striates. Mandus, he tells me to hang on goot. Mandus, he goes back in da house. I can hear him talkin' to dem guys. Da-guys, dey keep asking him vhy, vhy he needs them to pull their gear? Vhat kind of help he needs?

Mandus, he yust keep on telling dem he vould show dem why he needs dem, vhen day get here. But, he needs some help, pretty badly. And, if he didn't get it pretty soon, he vasn't going to need no help no more. Then he told dem that dey would be sorry if someone didn't come right quick.

Yea, veil after a while dis new guy, he pulled his gear, and come on over. I tink maybe he yust want to see what all the fuss is about. By dis time I keep going to sleep. Mandus he yust kept on hanging on-to my arm and holding my head out of the vater. Mandus he is a goot friend.

Dat guy, which come on over, he yumped aboard and got all excited. He yelled at Mandus, and then he yelled at me to stay awake. Veil I was trying to stay awake I had to chase down my boat. Veil didn't I?

But, I sure vas cold. After they get me in the house next to the stove this new guy and his deck hand vent after the Duna. Chased her down, and the deck hand yumped aboard her. Ya, dem guys brought her back to me. I decided to call it a season it vas late in da fall anyway.

Da-vife, she heard dis story... she got all emotional. You know how dem Vimmen can be. Now, she tinks I'm yust to to old to fish anymore.

The tears spring to John's eyes again. A tear rolls down one cheek. "You know I tink maybe, she right this time. It is getting a little harder every season now.

A little later John and I are working together. Unfortunately, I get an object lesson on why his wife is so worried. I'm down in the lazurite John standing above me. He decided that he should move the hatch for me. I'm not sure why the hatch needed moving. I didn't know it, but it did, apparently? Picking up the hatch he dropped it on my head. Whack! The hatch is built of two by fours tongue and groove. It's very, very hard, when falling from six feet. Cracking me a top my head, it drives me further into the lazurite. Falling backwards, while rubbing my head, I stare up into the blue sky and the blue of John's eyes. Dazed and confused, but I am probably not any more confused than John. My remembrances are interrupted by…

CHAPTER SEVEN

The sound of flopping tuna is deafening. There must be twenty of them slapping the bloody water a-wash on the deck. The din from their beating tails is annoying; although, not as annoying as the bloody froth they are creating. Bloody froth fills the air around me; creating a pinkish haze blowing past. Yuck!

The lines are hitting one after another. I just can't keep up, but it sure is fun trying. I'm only taking short lines right now. They're five fathoms in length. Six pulls and another fish joins the chaos behind me. Flinging the jig down into the water another fish strikes it, sounding for the bottom. Then the fish's return to the open ocean is abruptly stopped by the snubber rubber.

Going to the next line, I continue my frantic activity. The Douggers, calls to me from the Dutch door, "Go Ben go! You keep gettin-um. I'm going to put the boat in a circle."

Looking around toward the door I nod but, not in the affirmative. The Douggers is gone. He is gone and I am doomed. Soon we'll be going round and round in fifty mile per hour winds. Well, at least, in a situation like this, you know you're alive.

Yep, there is no doubt about it; this is no dream. The flopping fish ringing the steel deck loud enough to deafen a crowbar. The bloody mist, caused by the fish beating out their death knell. Water is constantly awash over the deck. Cold, cutting wind whipping past me at fifty miles an hour. The spray constantly soaking me. This is sure no dream.

Landing another fish, spinning in the gaff hatch, I run my hand down the line toward the shaking hook. Glancing up from the fish, I watch the Douggers leave the pilot house, making his way aft. Leaping a bin board, the Douggers foot slips on the bloody deck.

Up, up, up, into the air, his feet fly up, until they are even with his head. And then, he begins to fall. The boat is descending on a swell. Douggers is descending toward the deck, accelerating. The boat hits the bottom of the swell as Doug hits the bin board with the small of his back. Time stops.

Then; in disbelief, conjuring up the thought, "The Douggers is dead? His back is broken."

Douggers lays there, his only movement caused by the pitching and rolling of the boat.

Staring Finally, he lifts his head for a brief moment, all the color has drained from his face. he is ghost white and his eyes seem to be glazed over. The Douggers is hurt. Hurt bad. Jumping from the gaff hatch, I charge to his side, arriving there gently kneeling.

His back maybe broken? He could have internal injuries? He can't move, and he is ghostly white. Doug's eyes are taking seconds to focus on me. Finally, he sees me; sees who I am. His mind comes to himself and he speaks. I expect to hear a plea for help. Maybe a whimper from a broken man.

"I'll be fine, get back to the fish. Get the fish, get the fish!"

"Doug you're hurt, let me help you. I'll help you into the house get you in a bunk."

"No! No, get the fish, get the fish!"

Returning to my duties in the gaff hatch, dejected and sad, I glance over my shoulder. I only wanted to help? I've got to remember; my job is to, "Get the fish." If the Douggers wanted a nurse-maid; he would have hired a nurse-maid.

Every time I land a fish, I glance forward. Douggers is sitting now, his back against the gunwale. He hasn't moved from this spot and every time the boat circles he is blown by wind, hit by waves and spray. It can't be comfortable for a hurt man. But me, I'm getting the fish. It is my job after all?

Time drags, watching the Dougger's misery, but it does drag along. After about an hour we have drifted off the fish, or caught them all? I don't know which.

Quietly, slowly, the Douggers rolls to his knees grasping the gunwale with both hands he rises. Rising but not quite to a standing position, he's bent over like a hunchback with a hernia. The Douggers crawls pulls and staggers into the pilot house.

Watching in dismay I can't keep from wondering, '*will we head to Coos Bay! Ah, maybe? Getting into an Oregon port. A few days off while Doug recoups?*'

I wonder, '*is Debbie still dating the guy from college she dropped me for? Would she want to see me again? Do I want to see her again? She broke my heart. She sent me into a cold Oregon winter night to sleep under a bridge while she slept with her new bow. Na. I don't think I want to see her. But; I love her so?*'

Hopping and jumping from bin board to bin board I make my way toward the pilot house. Doing precisely what the Douggers was doing before he bounced off his two by twelve board, using his back to break his fall.

Once in the lee of the house I wipe the blood and sea water from my face and slip my rain jacket off. The bottom of the Dutch door squeaks open and I step inside.

Moving forward I'm bouncing port and starboard off tables and cabinets. The chart table is down taking a quick gander I see we're just south of Coos Bay. My little heart skips a beat. I can already see Debbie lying back on our blanket in our meadow. Lust perks me right on up. I'll ask the Douggers about going in.

"Douggers, how you feeling?"

Doug is laid back on the pilot seat, his face a ghostly white. Doug turns to meet my gaze; eyes hooded not quite focusing, groaning he pulls himself up; setting a little straighter.

"I'm moving a little slow right now, but I'll be fine."

"We're off the fish right now. Thought I'd head back into it."

Holding his side, Doug groans out, "Sounds good, if we get into the fish come forward; put the boat in a circle."

The Douggers must be hurting if he can't even throw the boat into a circle. This is an opening. I'll ask about going into Coos Bay.

"Doug? Maybe we should head in? If-in you're a hurting that much."

"Ben, there is one thing about fishing you have got to learn. The fish are out here. This is where we make our money. We have to do a years' worth of work in four months. Sick, hurt, bleeding, you stay. You stick, you stay, you make it pay! Or, go get a shore job."

"I know Douggers, but, if you're really hurting? You could be injured?"

If I start spitting up blood, we'll think about going in. This is where we make our money, this is where we stay."

Standing at the wheel I'm putting the boat back on to a northerly course. Our bow rising to an on-coming comber. The comber breaking over the bow, our anchor disappears into the foaming white water. The bow fills with: sloshing, foaming, gyrating, boiling, water. It crashes into the pilothouse windows covering them. White, foamy white, is all that can be seen. Water sliding down the windows, clears our view. The bow is draining to the back deck. It's just another day in the sunny Pacific Ocean.

Moseying to the back door I lean on my two elbows. Soon I'm staring out on the chaotic ocean behind the boat. Waiting. Waiting for another fish to strike; it's just too painful to daydream of Debbie right now. The memory of that cold, cold night, is just too sharp. It was a drizzle of ice fog flowing in and around the bridge bents. I shivered in Mike's old sleeping bag he loaned me; I thought about crying, I was going to get laid this night. I had a true love of my life two hours ago, now I have a an 'X girlfriend', not much money, and a long ass thumb ride home. What am I going to do now, find another woman that is for-sure.

There is a life after Debbie; and this is it. How did I end up on this boat anyway?

***

It's a cold clear day in January. The gate down to, "A" dock, pushes open. Squeaking on rusty hinges and then banging against the handrail, the gate slams close behind me. Glancing around I'm locked in; oh well? It seems, it takes a key to get in; it also takes a key to get out.

315

Sauntering down the dock, hands jammed deeply in my pockets; the jacket zipped snugly up. It's cold, dang cold. There's no one around on this cold clear Saturday. A ghost town a-float is what we have here. Looking from pilothouse window to pilothouse window, I'm looking for; For-Sale signs. If the boat is old, if the boat needs a paint job, if rust stains her sides, if she has all the lines of a plank, she'll bear a For-Sale sign. If not, she won't.

Glancing down a skinny finger I spot an old codger of a fisherman. Standing in his gaff hatch, a hydraulic line is filling each hand. The male and female fittings are leaking oil onto his deck; his eyes open wide in dismay. The oil spreading across the deck is inexecrable creeping toward the waters of Moss Landing Slough. The old codger's eyes meet mine. The question posed in them is plain to see. *What do I do?*

Trotting down the finger, I skid to a stop on the icy float. Reaching over the gunwale for a rag I'm straining against the handrail. The reddish lightweight oil flowing over the deck, is following the camber. Swabbing and knocking at the oily mess I'm spreading it around like a mad woman's dung. It's a mess, but the oil is better off being rubbed into the wooden deck than in the water. In the water it will cost this old codger five thousand dollars. This old guy probably didn't make five thousand dollars his whole season. That's my guess by the look of his boat, anyway.

The old codger holds the hose ends up a little higher. The leak peters out to a slow dribble, my rag is saturated.

"You got another one of these?"

"Well, young feller just look under the galley sink in the house."

Grasping the pipe-rail I swing lightly aboard. My hands are covered with hydraulic fluid. Everything I'm touching is shining with a red oily residue. Inside the troller's pilothouse it's warm and comfy. The diesel stove gives off a marry little glow.

Glancing forward I notice electronics. Nice, very nice. This old codger makes a lot more than five thousand a year. Under the sink are three new rolls of paper towels. Grabbing one, I head out the door.

On deck, I get down on my hands and knees continuing to swab. Looking up from my work the old codger is watching me.

He grins at me showing perfect white teeth. "What's a young feller like you doing down here on a day like this. It's Saturday you should be off chasing the girls. You're only young once you know."

"I like boats. I want to be a fisherman."

"Well it's OK to like boats, but you shouldn't like them better than girls."

"Oh I don't, I like girls just fine, It's just that my father and I are down here looking for a boat to buy. You see, I'm a fisherman."

"Oh you are? How long have you been fishing?"

"About seven months now."

"Oh? You a deckhand on a boat around here?"

"Naw, I fished a dory up in Oregon... Salmon out of Pacific City, I announce pridefully, we're down here looking for a troller."

"We? You down here with a partner?" Clarence nods, a knowing look at the man.

317

"Well, my dad. He's wanting to see if we can go in together. Be able to make a living fishing."

The old Codger stretches his hand out, "My name is Clarance."

Reaching over the big oily spot we shake.

"My name is Ben, good to meet you."

"Let me plug this little weep. Then, I should buy you a coffee so we can talk.

Being a fisherman is not a direct route to fame and fortune. Being fore warned is being fore armed."

Maybe I should tell this old guy about the five months I just spent fishing. No, he means well. The house is warm. A cup of coffee in a warm house, he just might be worth listening to?

In the time it takes to brew a cup we're ensconced at the galley table. Steaming coffee wafting its aroma up toward me. The hot cup grasped in my frozen fingers. Clarence is a genteel present in his pilothouse. This old man has been around. He's too comfortable in his own skin not to have been.

"Now there Ben; you warning up?"

"Yup."

"Well winter fishing halibut up in Alaska you wouldn't be in a nice warm house. You'd be shoving three-inch hooks into frozen bait. About half the time a hook would be buried in one hand or the other. Heck, guys up in Berring Sea fishing crab, they have to break ice off their rigging with a five pound sledge.

Tuna fishing it's nice and warm. But weather. Two three hundred miles off shore. Weather comes up and you just got to tough it out. Does any of this sound fun to you?"

"Well Clarence, as a matter of fact, it all sounds good to me."

Clarence shakes his head. "It all sounds like adventure; adventure can kill you son."

"I know. It's not adventure, if you are not pushing the ragged edge of disaster. If the chance of your own death isn't part of the gamble? What have you wagered?"

"My boy, that is fishing in a nutshell, a man bets everything he own, and his ass against a chance of filling up his boat. Then, that same man must know when enough is enough. One fish too many. The boat, his catch, and him, all go to the bottom. Remember that my lad."

"That's a good point. It sounds like you know a lot about fishing. You been at it your whole life?"

"I've played at fishing most of my adult life. Both my boys own big boats. Me I'm out here for my wellbeing. I get a chance to read a good book. It's a good life."

"Your boys own boats hum?"

"They certainly do. The Flag Ship. That's Freddy's boat. Stormy, he owns the Hornet."

"I passed both of those boats. They're huge! Massive albacore boats. Guys doing that well, they should have helped you out a little. You know, help you get a little bigger boat."

Clarence laughs, running a cold, work hardened hand over his face, "Ben, that is mighty nice of you. However, United Airlines sends me a little check every month. I'm retired from United, they treat me dam good."

"Oh yea? What did you do for them?"

"Oh, I mostly flew their Airplanes, I was going to Harvard after the war, you see? The Big War, the First World War, the war to end all wars, had just ended. I spent two years in a trench looking up at planes, wishing I was up there. You're last night on earth should be spent between a set of sheets, not atop freezing mud.

But anyway, I made it home. My folks gave me tuition for college, Harvard. I went to an airport and plunked down my tuition money on flying lessons. Flying is what I wanted to do.

So, I went down to the local field, and dropped it all.

Two months later, I was working as a pilot on a mail run. The day I soloed I got a job flying the mail.

The Company merged with a bunch of other small mail carriers. They came up with a new name; United Airlines. I flew planes for them for thirty-nine years. We bought a little stock along. The stock has done all right too."

"Wow, that must have been a good deal for you."

"Lucky is better than good my boy."

"Ben, if you don't mind me asking how much are you and your dad willing to spend on a troller."

"We're thinking around fifty grand."

"Fifty grand, you can get yourself a pretty nice little troller for that."

"I know a guy who has a nice fifty-footer. It's on "C" dock, you should take a quick look at it. It's sure one nice little boat."

Meeting the guy who owns the Arty is weird. It's that Douggers guy. He fed me a hamburger when I was fishing tuna out of Moss Landing, he remembered me.

The Arty was a very nice forty-five-footer. She has the high bow and low stern of most trollers. So her lines are good. The price is about right, but Doug informs us that someone else has earnest money up on her. Douggers was very helpful on information, and we spent a lot of time with him. At the end of the day, Doug offered me a job pulling albacore if getting a boat did not work out for us.

As Dad and I drove home… we mulled over the offer and it seemed like a good idea to learn a little something about the business that we are about to spend my folk's lifesavings on.

Doug asked if I was interested in helping him this winter putting together the Alley Cat. I was.

***

The deck is wet from dew. Standing here, I'm wondering; where the heck Doug is. It's eight O'clock. The sun is rising to the east, burning the fog off in its ascent. Plopping down on the hatch, I wonder, does this fish company have coffee? Will they be friendly like Hogie's? Heading up the ladder, I figure on standing around until someone offers me a cup.

Strolling into a small shed on the dock, this place is rough. Bare un-painted one by twelve's standing upright make the walls. A board works as the counter. Behind the counter is that coffee urine I'm looking for. The guys standing around don't look like

Oregon fisherman. They're swarthy. I feel like I just stepped onto the set of "The Godfather."

A big guy asks, "So, kid? What's you up-a too?

"Just looking for a cup of coffee. I'm waiting for Doug."

A little Chinese guy hidden in the corner pipes up, "Ah is so. Doug troll me he have new kid coming soon."

The little Chinese guy looks like a Tong Chieftain. One eye cocks to one side and is hooded.

Everyone here has a gritty quality. I'm nervous. Three or four dark swarthy men eye me suspiciously. The feeling that I just stumbled in while they were planning to rob the local bank over whelms me.

Maybe all fish companies don't have free coffee for their fisherman. I'm considering backing out the door. I have to be around these guys every day. Do I want to tuck my tail and slink away? Yea I do.

A flash in the corner of my eye causes me to turn. There's a real big guy, his large nose filling his face. Strands of long gray hair are swept across his large bald head. Looking down on me, his ham of a hand is reaching for me. God, what have I walked into?

"Here. You want cream or sugar? It's right behind you."

His ham of a hand opens to reveal a tiny Styrofoam cup of coffee. His voice is rough, from deep in his throat.

Controlling the shaking of my own hand, I take the coffee. "Gee, thanks. Yea, I need everything. I'm a real wuss."

Deciding I belong on the boat, I go there.

The Douggers talked to me about what needs doing. I'll be working in the engine room for about two weeks. Then, we'll be building the fish hold. That's going to be my job. Doug is partners with Stormy on a urethane foam machine. What's a urethane foam machine? After we foam the hole, then we're going to fiberglass it. Stormy and Douggers have all the equipment. It'll be cool.

A hundred dollars a week, wow! That's what Doug is paying me. All I've got to do is work ten hours a day, six days a week. Then... when we start fishing, I'll get ten percent off the top.

Living in my dad's camper, across the road from a hippie boat, I'm in-um. All kinds of women are coming... and going, there are some guys too. They're a cult, or so I've heard. The girls sleep with anyone on the boat. It's kind of cool. I wonder, could I land a job over there? It don't matter. The Pacific Ocean is my backyard, and it includes a sandy beach that runs from Santa Cruz to Monterey. A big brand-new boat to work on. Life is good... life is very good.

I've been living here for a few days now. My dad's camper is parked next to the fish company's office. There's a real big guy next door. He's the one that gave me a cup of coffee at the company. Man, his little trailer smells. It smells to the high heavens.

Aromas pour from his hovel like he's running some kind of five-star restaurant. He looks like a man-mountain, but boy can he cook. I think?

My shower accouterments flung over my left shoulder I glance into the door of that smelly little trailer I stride past. A ham of a hand pokes out, his arm taking up half the door.

"Here kid, want this?"

"Excuse me?"

"This glass of wine, I poured two by mistake. You wouldn't mind drinking it for me, would you?"

"Why no, not at all. If you poured it by mistake, I'll be glad to help you out."

"Thanks kid."

The ham of a hand sticking out of the door opens just a little. This huge ham reveals a water tumbler filled to the brim with a cheap vin-rose' wine. Reaching for the tumbler of wine, aroma from his cooking pot makes me weak in the knees.

"Wow, what are you cooking in there?"

"Oh; just a little dinner. You wouldn't mind helping me eat it would you? I've made a little too much spaghetti sauce. Used a little fresh fillet of sole as the base. Some Italian sausage for the spice. Lots of fresh garlic of course. It would be nice if you could join me."

I've been eating TV dinners next door, fried. Could I join him? Of course I could join him.

"Yea, that'd be cool."

"Go ahead and grab a shower, I'll put together a little Caesar salad, heat the French bread, we'll be ready by the time you finish."

Taking his wine glass to the shower,' *I'm in-em; this is good, real good. Good food, good wine. Dinner? It just don't get any better than this'.*

Stepping out of the rotting shack where the fish company shower is I'm weaving from side to side. Not much wine is needed to get me drunk. One twelve-ounce tumbler and I'm blitzed.

Pulling myself up into the smelly little trailer, the man-mountain hands me another glass filled to the brim. Same cheap wine as before. Oh boy oh boy?

The smell in the trailer mingles most of the spices known to man. The big guy has filled his hand; not engaged in holding a tumbler of wine, with a huge knife. The knife is chop, chop, chopping a gargantuan hunk of garlic. He points the knife at me.

"My name is Russell, but, everyone calls me Unk. My nephew fishes with me most summers; he calls me Unk, the name just stuck after that first season, we fished.

"Well Benjy, it's good to meet you… hurry up and drink that wine, the wine is getting warm setting out like that."

The one-gallon wine jug is sitting on the table beside me. The wine in my tumbler isn't chilled. Unk just wants my glass empty. To oblige him I empty it promptly, he refills it. He must be a sales rep for Gallo when he's not unloading fishboats.

Dinner! Yes, yes, I know I'm drunk, but? Dinner this is the best Dinner I've ever eaten. Who'd of thunk it? Sole, in fresh cooked spaghetti sauce, I do mean fresh cooked. This spaghetti sauce has more vegetables than one of my mother's salads. Caesar salad, mmuumuu good. It takes Unk a half an hour to make a salad. But, what a salad. He sure doesn't use anything out of a can or bottle. I've never seen anybody like him. He's a real Chef.

"Wow, how in the world did you ever learn to cook like this?"

"There's a little school, back in New York. They give you the basics. From there, you just use a little creativity. It helps to get your guests good and drunk first of course." Unk smiles at me.

Then I moved to the Four Seasons as the Sauce Chef.

"Why'd you quit cooking? You obviously like it?"

"I fished as a kid. Once a fisherman always a fisherman. Working ashore? It's relentless. Five days a week the same place at the same time. Week in week out I just lost it one day. It was seven O'clock on a Friday night. The kitchen was chaos. Everyone yelling in three different languages. The Head Chef came to me complaining about a marinara sauce. In French. He was all hot and bothered. You don't talk to a boy raised on the docks of Eureka the way he talked to me. I decked him. Short little squirt. I do believe that was the first time that Frenchman had ever been hit. He hit the floor like a sack of potatoes. I stepped over him and took the first plane back to the west coast."

It's past eleven O'clock. Eating has taken all evening. I've got to stand up. Somehow; I've got to stagger back to my little hovel. Then... somehow, I've got to get up in the morning. Man, life is good, but in may not be tomorrow?

***

They call me Benjy here in Moss Landing. Unk referred to me as Benjy twice. That's all it took. I kind of like it. If the guys from Pacific City ever hear about my new name I'll never live it down.

Stormy is coming today. We're going to foam the hold. Hold is another name for the fish hole. The two names are interchangeable around here. Whichever it is, hole or hold it's my project. Boy, I'm looking forward to getting down there and going to work.

Doug and I are down in the engine room. We're wrestling the power-take-off unit into position. A thunderous bang on the deck announces Stormy's arrival. It sounds like he jumped from the dock to the deck, a drop of ten feet or so. The bang is followed by Stormy using his Yogi the Bear voice.

"Hey hey hey, Douggers you cheap little bugger. Where are you? You'd better buy me lunch today you cheap little bugger. I ain't eaten no peanut butter sandwich put together by your old lady. You're buying me lunch you cheapskate."

Stormy throws the engine room hatch open. His bear shaped head appears upside down peering at us as though we're up to no good.

"Hey hey hey, there you are. I got the urethane gun you're a going to love this thing. It squirts foam like there ain't no tomorrow. Give me your Benjy kid and we'll get the gun down here. Come-on kid we got us a hole to blow."

An hour later, Stormy and I have his equipment on deck. Along with two fifty-five gallon drums of urethane foam, parts "A" and "B". That's a lot of foam. I mean it's a whole lot of foam!

Donning coveralls Stormy and I descend into the hole. The little air compressor is put-put-pntting away out on deck. Hissing air, leaks from every fitting on Stormy's rig. But, we're ready. Stormy holds the gun like contraption in his right hand. His left hand held out flat, measuring his canvas. The fish hold.

Pulling the trigger Stormy shoots; the two-part foam mixing in midstream. The chemical reaction beginning even before the

327

stream splatters onto the steel plating. The mixture expanding to thirty times its original volume.

Stormy squirts, foam grows, Stormy squirts, foam grows, foam grows and grows. Raking the gun back and forth over the steel Stormy covers it. Again and again, over and over the same area, squirting his squirts. Each pull of the trigger brings a smile to Stormy's eyes. His mouth and nose are covered by a fresh air delivery system. Stormy's eyes crinkled, his sunburned wrinkles revealing his contentment at the chemical reaction.

His blue eyes bright with happiness. He's a mad man. A happy mad man, but a mad man all the same. I've got to admit this is fun. Watching the foam grow is mesmerizing.

Gun in hand, Stormy shoots and shoots and shoots. The fish hole is filling up. It's filling up with foam. It doesn't strike me that someone is going to have to take out the excess foam. It doesn't strike me that, that someone is me. Had I known the work involved in trimming that foam I would have killed Stormy right there.

The sun is shining into the hole. It must be straight overhead by now. Stormy and I have been having such a good time down here that we haven't notice the morning slipping away. The hole has a good three or four coats of foam, everywhere. Each coat is two to three inches of foam. Stormy pulls the trigger one last time. Nothing but air shoots out. We've used our one hundred and ten gallons of liquid foam in a thirty-ton fish hold. Wow.

Stormy climbs the ladder ahead of me. His coveralls overlaid with foam drippings of varying thickness. Me too it seems; it's cool. I can feel foam enveloping my clothes and hair. On deck we strip to street clothes.

I'll have to cut the foam from my hair tonight. I'm going to look kind of funny, I think? It's the seventies; hair is the most important asset a young man has. They've even written a musical, called Hair. Foam is down to my scalp in places. This is going to be Ugly.

The barrels being empty, Doug suggests lunch. Well, he suggested lunch for Stormy. Standing here, my feelings are hurt, a little… anyway. Gee, I'd like to go to lunch too.

Pushing his dark glasses up onto his nose, Stormy opines. "Douggers, you cheap little bugger, you better buy my helper Benjy kid something to eat."

Having gotten an inkling of just how conservative Doug is I volunteer. "That's OK, I'll buy my own."

Stormy tosses in. "You little tightwad, you've got a boat worth two hundred thousand. Benjy is working for nothin'. For nothing. The least you can do is buy the kid a burger."

"Oh course Ben is coming to lunch. I'll just deduct it from his wages."

Stormy and I stare at the Douggers aghast at the unmitigated gall of the man. Then the Douggers grins an evil little grin. Doug likes getting Stormy's goat just to watch him perform.

The Whale Bone Cafe is one un-whale of a place. It's little, it's crummy, and it's slow. It's also the only place to eat in Moss Landing. Which makes it the lunch spot for every fisherman in the harbor. The Whale Bone is run by a little Jewish woman who lived through the holocaust. She is one pisst-off little old lady. Friendly don't buy you nothing with her. Shut up and pay your bill, that's all she wants.

Sitting at the back booth Douggers and I are watching Stormy perform. Stormy's hands are flying in big round circles as he completes his story. His story involves a charming fisherman/Hells Angel, a lady lawyer, and a parking space in Monterey. An argument over a parking space ends up with an invite to dine at a local drinking establishment. The dinner ended with the lady lawyer leaving a tuna boat well after sun up. It was kind of a three-day one-night stand. Boy, if this particular lady lawyer knew that the albacore fleet knows all about her. And, I do mean all about her. She'd move to the mid-west. Ignorance is bliss.

A swarthy man in clean clothes enters the cafe. The slamming screen door drawing our attention. His nice clothes, almost a suit kind of, sets him apart from the fishermen, shoving his hat back on his head Stormy waves at the man.

"Hey hey hey, Johnny-boy." Slipping from his Yogi the Bear voice, Stormy, continues in an Italian accent. "Ay you-a one gomm-body. We had-a some good-a trip, you and me-a and your gomm-bodies. You-a put-a them sheet-a-heads in the right-a mind in Las Vegas."

Stormy slips from his Italian accent, and I hear his natural voice for the first time. "Loved, absolutely loved, seeing you put the squeeze on those casino nerds. I've never seen anyone come to heel so quickly. Telling them that you're from the Monterey Goom-Buddy Club sure scared them, huh? Why, you'd think we're in the Mafia or something."

A grin spreads across Stormy's face; he just loves pushing the envelope. Johnny is the Mafia here.

The grin transfers to the fish buyer's face, "Yea, you'd think that some of us are in the Mafia. Wouldn't you?"

John shakes hands with Stormy, then Doug; he's a respectful man. A very respected man, proceeding to another table John takes a seat with two other fish buyers.

Scrutinizing me, Stormy says, "A bunch of us went to Las Vegas a few weeks ago. The best of everything. Nice. The fish buyers put it on for a bunch of us. You should go next year."

Next year? I'm going to have enough money to go to Las Vegas next year? Man, this albacore fishing must be good bucks.

Stormy is on a roll again, "We had one little bump. Or, rather the casino management had a little bump. We had us a show to see, part of the package. We showed up a little late and they didn't have a table for us. Some casino guy told us to wait. When they got us a place set up. Ho-man, it were bad.

We was so far back we couldn't see the stage lights much less the stage. We didn't have a column in our way, we had a whole coliseum in our way. It was just bad. John and two other fish buyers from Monterey had a little conflab with the Casino nerds.

At first the Casino nerds blew John and his good-a-bodies off. I saw them shrug their shoulders and point at our table. Telling them go sit down, and stop bothering important people. That's when our good-a-buddy, Johnny, let them have it.

First, he pulled the manager off to one side. Then they spoke in earnest to him.

The kind of talking that lets someone know, how the hog ate the cabbage. Every once and a while he'd point to the mirrors at the ceiling. The ones that the big bosses look through. Twice he pointed at our group. Just once he closed his hand real slow in a choking motion, there was a power to his body language. Even though we couldn't hear the conversation, we knew that pressure was being applied.

Soon, another boss-man showed up. The thousand-dollar suit wearing type of boss-man. Five-hundred dollar shoes adorned his size twelve clod-hoppers. His watch cost more than my truck. He and Johnny spoke at our table in Italian. He spoke with respect to Johnny. Johnny waved at us, using the Italian word for fishermen. And, he said we'll stop deliveries coming across our docks. He said it in English, just so us guys got his message. Somehow, I don't think he was talking about salmon. If you get my drift."

I got it, that is for sure, Johnny is a member of the family. He allows certain people to unload certain cargoes in Moss landing. Those people show respect to Johnny. They show respect by giving him money. If they don't show respect, they end up floating out of the harbor with the flotsam and jetsam. Stormy is giving me a whole new insight into this little world I've just joined. Everything is not what it seems.

Does Unk do jobs for Johnny? He's big enough to be a leg breaker. But a leg breaker that cooks spaghetti sauce with fillet of sole as the base? Naw, no way, it just couldn't be, could it?

Stormy is getting into his story. He's beginning to gyrate again. His seat sways with his bulk as he wiggles. Stormy's hands go into story telling mode. Flipping and flying around too fast to be seen.

"Douggers, Benjy, I'm telling you. You should have seen it. It were beautiful. Here little Johnny is standing there looking up. The big I-tie in the silk suit is crumbling like a wedding cake during the brawl at an Irish wedding. The big guy's chin drops to his chest. He holds both hands up in a sign of surrender. The show was put on hold. Put on hold mind you. New tables were brought out."

Returning to his Yogi the Bear voice, "Hey hey hey, like we were in-um man! They parade the bunch of us front and center. It was Jake man. Cool. Taking a seat at this long ass table, we take a bow. Cool man. Nobody was closer to the stage than us dirty old fisherman. Ya gotta love it. We could see the sweat dribbling between dancing girl's jugs. Yea! It were like jake man. Cool. Stormy has both hands raised in the air, fist closed; thumps extended.

I'm enthralled. Sweat dripping down and around the breasts of dancing girls is something I can wrap my mind around. Yes sir-ree. The restaurant is dead still. Everyone is watching Stormy. No one is eating, or talking, or drinking, we all sit there looking at Stormy. He loves it. Johnny picks up a glass of wine and gives Stormy a toast.

***

Hands in my pockets I'm sauntering down the dock. It's around six in the evening. A man in a high-pressure captain's hat strides purposefully past me. He has a face that is red from sun and booze. The expression residing on his glowing oval is sour. His rights have been usurped and he is going to set things straight. If there is any one thing that marks him as, not a fisherman, it's the hat.

Sea going men on this coast never wear nautical head gear. A cap with the letters CAT prominently displayed is what the cool fisherman is wearing. This guy's hat has more scrambled eggs on the bill, than an admiral deserves. Hanging a left, he pounds up the ramp. Grabbing the gate the angry stranger pulls and nothing happens. He needs a key. Turning on his heel he stomps back down the ramp; where he runs into Stormy and Freddy.

At this point it's important that you know something about Moss Landing Harbor. Fishermen built it. They own the harbor. The fishermen run it. The Board of Trusties answers only to the boat owners here. The Board are all fishermen. They are as independent as a hog on ice.

Moss Landing was a smuggler's cove in the twenties. Rumrunners brought offshore booze to this little inlet. They unloaded into the slough. Moss Landing has retained the feel of a smuggler's cove. The men who fish out of here are just a little over the line.

To defray the cost, during the fishing season, the harbor master lets out slips. Boat owners come in and take an empty slip.

Then they check in with Whitey. If someone makes a reservation Whitey may even send them a confirmation. Owners feel confident with their little letter.

Whitey, the Harbormaster, even gives them a slip number. The admiral here, has one of those little confirmations. They aren't worth the paper they're written on.

The admiral holds his letter in the air. "Someone has taken my slip. He's got to move that boat. I don't understand how some jerk can just take a person's slip? It's mine, this just will not stand!"

Stormy reaches for the letter taking it from the waving hand. Unfolding the letter Stormy reads aloud. "Ah, here it is. 'Slip C-27 is reserved for you, April 24, 1973, through April 25,1973 and it's signed by Whitey, Harbor Master.'

Well, there you go. Whitey has written, it's got to be so."

The Admiral takes the letter back, flourishing it. "There, you see? That boat is in my slip he'll just have to move."

Warlord John walks up to our little gathering; he knows wherever Stormy is, that's where the action is. "So, what's happening Stormy?"

Stormy shoves his sunglasses up his large bear like nose, using his center finger. Performing his one finger glasses adjustment while staring straight at the irate admiral.

"Well Cap, how big is your boat?"

The Admiral waves down the dock with his confirmation letter. "There it is, the Robin's Nest, she is sixty-eight feet long."

Shuffling around each other, and craning our necks, we shift positions to get a look at her. Yacht! Big yacht! Antennas litter the pilothouse. She looks like a spy ship. She is gleaming white, a speed boat worth twenty thousand sets a top her deck. The yacht under the speed boat would go for a couple of million bucks. She looks like a queen coming to inspect the poor house here in Moss Landing. Two deck hands stand on her deck, watching the owner gam with these dirty old fishermen. The yacht fills a slip built for a fifty footer; twenty foot of her stern pokes out, into the channel. Both sides touch the fingers. She fits, but just barely.

The admiral waves his confirmation at her again, "Well you see we can't stay there. My hull is being marked."

Stormy just naturally drops into his Yogi the Bear mode. "Hey hey hey, Booboo, you better stay where you're at. Ya see little buddy; you want Sea Lion Bob's berth. Sea Lion Bob, he ain't moving. Not for you, not for anybody. Bob... Well Bob, he's a Norwegian. He just ain't going to move because you tell him to. They're like that Booboo, a Scanda-hoven don't take bossing to pretty good. Hey hey hey, you got a spot. Be happy, you're like jake man."

Stormy's Yogi the Bear voice and his reference to this high-powered business man as, Booboo, seem to be rubbing the Admiral the wrong way. I can see the Admiral is getting irritated by all this fall-de-rall. Stormy, he loves it. Pushing people's buttons is an avocation with Stormy.

The Admiral's face takes on a brighter glow of red. His sour, circular head somehow becoming stern. "He'll move. He's in my berth. He is going to get his happy ass out of my berth or he'll be in big shit-in trouble!"

By this time Sailor Bill and Vince, Bill's deck hand have joined the scene. Sailor Bill owns a fifty-seven-footer named the Betty-Anne. Sailor Bill is a retired Chief from the Navy. Somehow calling Bill, Betty-Anne Bill, just don't work. So, he's Sailor Bill. Vince is a Hell's Angel. Vince is Bill's deck hand; he has been for three years now. Stormy has been telling me stories about him. Vince is cool. Mean, but cool. Behind his back Vince is called Vince-E-Pooh. Because he is so damn tough and mean looking. He is built like an anvil. His arms are massive. He wears his three-patch vest with pride; and a Bowie Knife whenever he isn't working. He looks dangerous and he is.

Along the way we've picked up Clarence, and Jack off the Velma-Kelly. It's such a large group of fishermen it looks like we're having a meeting. The crew off the yacht can't stand watching from afar anymore. Hopping from the bow they join us.

The owner's eyes brighten; all these rough looking men are making him nervous. If his crew hadn't joined us maybe he wouldn't have made his next mistake. But this guy has been bossing people around for years, so maybe he would have?

"I'll tell you smart-aleks one thing. That guy is going to move that big ugly boat I'll bet a thousand dollars on it."

Silence follows this bold statement. No one moves, no one comments. He has made his brag. All of us are too dumb founded to speak. Until...

Pulling his wallet from his pants Stormy thumbs ten crisp new one-hundred-dollar bills into the air. "I'll take a thousand of that."

Seeing an easy thousand dollars is to be made; Freddy also holds out a grand to the Admiral.

The Admiral looks these two grubby fishermen in the eye. "Why you think you're smart? I'll, I'll cover you, that's just what I'll do."

Sailor Bill also keeps a couple thousand bucks on his person. He pulls a grand out joining in on this easy money.

"What about me? Can I get in on this? I've never made a grand so easy. You going to cover me too?"

Now the Admiral is looking a little worried. But he's a millionaire and a proud man, also just a little drunk right now. "Yea yea, you're covered too!"

Vince pulls three hundred and forty-two dollars from his wallet that is hanging on a chain. It's all the money he has until he goes fishing next month.

Hey Admiral, how about me, I could use an extra three hundred and forty bucks? It's all I got. If you want to take my bike as collateral, I'll bet you ten grand, Sea Lion Bob; won't move his boat."

War Lord John pipes up. "Hey stay right here I've got a couple of thousand stashed on the boat."

The Admiral is starting to figure out that maybe, these dirty old fishermen may know something he doesn't. He raises his finger as John strides back to his boat. "Ah ah, I don't know..."

To late John is jumping the rail of the War Lord, he'll bring back his money and then what. The bet is over six grand, and growing. The Admiral turns to his task. His task, make Bob give up his berth. No big deal for a high-powered executive, right?

Striding down the dock we halt at the end. The Sea Lion is an end tie.

She is sixty-five feet long. She's a Long and narrow slab of a boat, white with red trim. Fire engine red is her trim, high gloss white paint covers everything else. Her bow is sticking up in the air sixteen feet. The top of her bulwarks are a full five feet above the dock. The Sea Lion is massive. Even with her proportions, the pilothouse is tall; I mean real tall. Bob built the Sea Lion to his own design and specifications; Bob stands at six-foot-five-inches and his house gives him plenty of head room.

The Admiral knocks on the hull, standing there he looks up. Gazing up at the door, we're waiting for it to slide open. The door slides aft. A large bald man ducks his head as he squeezes through the large door frame. Yep, there's Bob.

Bob was a prize fighter in his younger days. One of those giants that takes on all comers at the County fair. Not an easy life, so he took to commercial fishing. He's a Norwegian, who built the Sea Lion on the sand spit just west of here. Each and every timber was hand hewn by those hams hanging at his side. His continence is pleasant; a big grin spreads across his face when he sees all his visitors. Not a lot of guys come by and visit Bob.

The Admiral has to ruin this visit for Bob. But, he's just the man for the job.

"Mr. ah ah Bob, you've got to move your boat, this is my slip."

"Ha ha ha, You one funny feller. Why? Why you say I got to move my boat. I don't get joke. Tell me how it funny that I move my boat?"

The Admiral wipes his nose. Taking his hat off, then he wipes his face. "No no, this isn't a joke, I have a confirmation from the Harbor Master. This is my berth for today and tomorrow. You better just move on out."

These high pressure negotiations aren't going so -well. Are they?

"So, if you'll start your motors, and just move on along. That way, we won't have any trouble."

I don't got to move my boat; dis is my slip. I built dis here finger. I run the pile driver, driving every pile on dis here finger. Look, look behind you! Look at dem piles. Have you ever seen any-ting prettier?"

Looking around, I see exactly what Bob is looking at. The piles are vertical. A perfectly vertical pile takes talent. They're in almost perfect alignment. Straight piles in alignment, is an almost impossible feat. Bob has skills that shore men just wouldn't understand.

"I think it'll go easier on you, if you leave now. I DO mean NOW!"

The rich executive makes a shooing motion with his hands. He looks like he is herding chickens. At the shooing motion this entourage of fishermen burst out laughing.

"Ya, dis is my berth I tink I'll yust stay right here." Bob's accent is becoming stronger in frustration. He can't get this dunder head to understand he ain't moving.

"Stormy, you vone smart feller like dis guy. Stormy, you tell him dis is my berth and I ain't movin."

With that said, Bob steps backward into his pilothouse closing the door for good measure.

Stormy gyrates his body in his Yogi the Bear motion. "Hey hey hey Booboo, you lose."

"I'll call the police! I've got a letter from the Harbor Master, the police will deal with this ruffian."

A snigger runs through our little group. Clarence, is the elder statesmen here. Stepping forward he explains the facts of life.

"One; you're in a harbor, not a town. There are no police that work here. This is a harbor, no City Hall, no police station, no nothing. Two; that is a documented vessel. Only a U. S. Marshal can board her and make an arrest. Three, unless you are a lot more important than I think you are, Bob hasn't broken any federal laws here. Bob has an agreement with the harbor of Moss Landing, giving him the right to use that berth all year. That agreement, supersedes your letter. Therefore, it is my opinion that you sir, are screwed. Now the only question that remains, is, will you do the honorable thing and pay your gambling debts?"

"I haven't given up. We'll see about this. The admiral pushes through us heading back to his yacht. Again, laughter of dirty, poor, fishermen fill his ears; in his defeat.

"He better pay up or some night me and my brothers is going to pay him a little visitation." Vince stares at the departing millionaire with disgust. He wanted that three hundred and forty two dollars.

About thirty minutes later, the big yacht fires up both engines. Leaving Moss Landing harbor at eighteen knots. Her wake is a good four feet high. A lot of boats sustained damage at her departure, a vessel is responsible for any damage her wake does. Just guessing, I'd say that grand exit cost the millionaire about forty thousand dollars.

As Marty would say, "What goes around comes around. It's like karma man."

***

The clunking on the deck is intruding on my concentration. I can't take too big a bite or the saw will never get through it. You have to keep the end poking through, or friction kills you. At least it's not itchy. Sweat dribbles off my nose and onto my belly; the way I'm leaning back here. Arched over backward I'm straining every muscle fiber standing in this awkward position.

Doug's voice intrudes even more on my concentration.

"This is the fish hole."

The foam cracks... Then snaps off. Falling over backwards I hit in two feet of foam chips.

"Hump."

Foam chips swirls into the air, displaced by my body. As the foam dust settles I can see six faces gazing down on me. Three, no four of the faces belong to chicks. Wow, where did the Douggers get four girls?

"And that... is my deck hand, Ben."

Brushing foam from my body I climb the ladder trying to look cool. Had I thought of my hair, I wouldn't have bothered. My hair has been hacked to pieces by me and Unk. Some blobs of foam are still stubbornly clinging. I know because my comb won't go through it. I just can't see them, to cut-um out.

Emerging from the hole I scan the scenery. It's nice. Very nice, of course I haven't seen a girl up close since I came to Moss Landing.

Doug gestures toward the middle-aged man with a beer belly. "Ben this is ah ah... I'm sorry I don't remember your name."

"Jackson's my name, I own the boat tied-up right over there. This is my crew; girls say hi to Ben."

Glancing over toward the boat he spoke of; I'm taken aback. The boat Jackson is pointing at; looks like a cabin-cruiser on steroids. It's about fifty feet long. The whole deck is lost to cabin. The pilothouse has dozens' of windows. Large plate glass picture windows cover the entire house. Picture windows, on a tuna boat? It looks like a damn site-seeing boat. I don't know what that thing is; but, it's not a sea boat.

Jackson inserts for public consumption. "We're building a tuna boat too. A lot of work building a tuna boat, I had no idea."

Douggers nods in agreement. "Yea, I'm lucky, Ben offered to help me work on this one.

"Come on in I'll show you guys the house and engine room."

Douggers leads Jackson, and the ladies off toward the pilothouse. Following along just to watch the sway I'm impressed by Jackson's crew. This is that hippie cult; the one I've been told about. These ladies are everything I've been told, they span the spectrum of white chicks.

Following Jackson through the Dutch door is a young thing. She's a little over six feet tall with proportions to match. Her top comes to a ragged end about a foot above her belly button. Wow. Firm young breast, hard enough to poke a hole in your chest, distort the faded words on her top. Double wow. She bounces away giving me an imperious glance while spinning on her heels. She doesn't like the way I cast my eyes on her. Heck it ain't my fault. I didn't tell her to wear that blouse.

The next babe to step into the pilot house is a woman of about twenty-five. Small, a little over five feet tall. Skinny without much figure, until my eyes find her bottom. Her legs and bottom are all female. Soft, supple, firm, downright lovely. The hair falling down her back is as soft as the last rays of a sunset, the highlights of her red mane catching my eye. Her smile is friendly as she turns away. Scrutinizing her I decide, although not the prettiest, she is by far the sexiest of Jackson's harem

The girl with black hair and flashing eyes doesn't even make eye contact. Her waist length hair whips around as she turns her back on me. A beautiful face sets a top her perfect little body. Must be about twenty-two or so. I don't have to worry about my ego getting out of hand here. The only young women I've met here have let me know that I'm nothing special.

The last girl on deck is a little too round but in shape. Her sun burned shoulders a little too brawny. Her hair has been sun bleached until it is brittle and frizzy. Freckles cover her cute little nose. Short cutoff jeans reveal strong looking legs. The pockets of the jeans hanging below the strings left by the cut. She's not a bad looking babe. That is, if she wasn't surrounded by all these bona fide beautiful ladies. It's all a matter of perspective. As Einstein said, "Everything is relative."

The last blond swishing into the house leaves me with a decision. Do I follow or do I return to work? Work? Follow? Work? I'll follow; Doug couldn't blame me, could he?

After crowding into the engine room, rubbing and bumping into each other for ten minutes or so we've gotten to know one another, a little better anyway.

Jackson has one hand on the ladder up the dock. Looking over his shoulder he invites. "You guys come on over sometime take a look at my boat."

Doug answers for us both. "Sure, we'll drop by next time we're in the neighborhood."

Neighborhood? Neighborhood? There is only about fifty feet separating the two boats. How much in the neighborhood do we need to be, to drop on over?

My hair is still wet. I'm staggering back from the shower. There is one of the ladies I met today. She's trapped outside of the gate trying to get down to her boat. Trotting across the road I'm waving my key in the air. The young girl smiles demurely at me and steps aside to let me at the lock. Unlocking the gate my heart is pounding.

"Would you like me to… to ah help you with that?"

"Cool man."

The blond with the fit body, hands over her clean laundry. She pushes through the unlocked gate. The rickety dock twisting side to side and bouncing up and down with each step. Striding the unstable platform her balance is impeccable. The leg muscles working under her smooth brown skin in wonderful unison. We halt at the cabin cruiser on steroids. Her deck is a full five feet above the dock.

Real sea going boats have a low profile. A sea boat will have as much as two thirds of the boat below the surface. This boat couldn't even get into Moss Landing if two thirds of her are sitting below the water-line.

The young lady and I are looking across the deck. Standing on the step above me, shaking her blond hair at me, she smiles. "I'd invite you aboard but I'm, I'm... I'm just moving aboard today, you know? You know how it is?"

Disappointment showing on my face, "Yea I know. I know how it is?" Turning, placing my hands in my pockets I amble away. I'll go by and get a glass of wine from Unk. I don't want to visit with four babes on a boat, do I?

You know; I don't get women? Debbie was going to visit me over spring break. She was that is, until I found out about her new boyfriend. Strange? She was going to visit me when I didn't know about her new man. After I found out about the new guy she wouldn't see me. Why not, the only change was I would know she was cheating on someone, if not me then she was cheating on him?

On this here boat, right here, there are four girls living with one ugly, pudgy old guy. He's cheating on these girls, with these girls. I don't get women.

Pulling up into the smelly little trailer I flop down. Unk flips one of his special plastic twelve-ounce wine tumblers at me. Reaching up and catching it one handed I settle the tumbler on the table. Picking up the gallon wine jug he adds about four good gluggs of wine, to the sauce he's cooking.

"Unk what do you know about women?"

"Bad for the fishing. Seen more good fishermen miss a season over a bad woman than a shot engine. Women will cost you fish and money, mark my words."

"Not all women. Not like those women down on that, that...cabin cruiser?"

Unk pulls my glass over to his side of the table and gluggs four more good gluggs of wine into it. "The cult boat? Yea. Now there are some fine up standing models of woman hood? They got some real good virtues hanging all over them. Don't they?"

Pulling my glass to me, "I like those hippie chicks, they're nice."

Unk stirs the sauce with his giant wooden spoon, pulling the spoon from the sauce he shakes it in my direction. "You watch those chicks they'll suck you into that cult. Do you want to be running drugs for Jackson? I don't think so. You got potential, but man. Those women will suck you dry."

"If I ain't going to go for hippie chicks; what kind of woman should a fisherman look for?"

"The best kind of woman to have, is the wife of a buddy. Preferably one that is off fishing. Give him a call on the radio every night. That-a-ways you'll know when he is coming back in.

It's a good idea to have your boat iced and fueled. Iced and fueled all the time.

When your buddy comes in; you head out. Safest that-a-way."

"That's just sick Unk. Who'd cheat with some other fisherman's wife? Especially while he was out to sea? It don't seem fair."

"Fair is in the eye of the beholder. About half the fleet cheats with the wives of the other half. It assures genetic diversity. Once a woman marries into the fleet she is never divorced she's just on hold. You ever notice how many of the kids around the dock looks like Freddy?"

"Yea? No. I mean Freddy is blond; most little kids are blond. You can't mean that Freddy? I mean, oh come on now."

"For you boy it's either the wives, or the hookers."

"There aren't any hookers around Moss Landing."

"Oh you've been looking, have you?"

Crimson flushes my cheeks, "No, but look around, you don't see any girls, much less girls of the night."

Unk shoots half a glass of wine. "Do you want the number of a hooker? Is that what all this is about?"

I have no idea how this conversation got onto hookers. All I know is that I want it over. "No. I don't want the number of any hookers."

"Wives? You want the number of some wives then?"

Man oh man all I wanted to do was talk about them girls down on the giant cabin cruiser. Unk is giving me a bad time about all women. I wonder; has all his experience been that bad with women? He's lumping wives and hookers together. He wouldn't even do that with bottom fish. Whoever taught Unk about women sure wasn't gentle. Not gentle, not at all.

I like women. I kind of figured they're all like my mom. Good clean women. Just good. Is Unk telling me there are other heart breakers out there? If so, the one Debbie gave me, may not be my last? "Well... them's the breaks."

***

Coffee cup in hand, I'm staring out my door. The fit blond girl, from the cult boat swishes by. "Hi. Like a cup of coffee?"

"Oh cool, I'd love a cup. It's like nobody is up over there. They are like screwy with time. You know what I mean?"

No, I don't know what she means. But, talking to a female is a joy. She places a hand on her hip and hunches it toward the south. Her short hair is tasseled from the night. Sexy is the word that comes to mind. Stepping into my camper she sprawls onto the settee; her low-cut top revealing cleavage enough to belong to a grown woman.

"You been working for Jackson long? On his boat... What do you do?"

"No, I don't know what I do yet; yesterday was my first day. I surf. Last summer, like when school was back in session... I like? Well, hanging out on the beach is cool. School is like a drag man... and some of the best surf is in the fall."

Placing a mug in front of my guest I pour fresh brewed coffee into it. "Yea, surfing is cool. Down in Australia every night after work I'd go surf for an hour or three, I loved it."

Her long, lovely legs, naturally crossing into the Indian setting position. "Ah, catching a wave it's like the coolest man. A good ride is like good sex. It's all body, no mind. Don't you think?"

"Oh, yea; No mind?" The crimson of last night is nothing compared to the crimson of today. My face is burning. This seventeen-year-old surfer girl is a lot more worldly than me. Wow, think, think? What would someone cool say? They sure wouldn't say, "No mind?", would they?

The young surfer girl overlooks my inaptitude, smiling at me she continues her monologue. "My Mom she parties with Jackson. If you know what I mean? She was getting all kinds of grief from the school. The high school was like all hot and bothered that I didn't come last year. So, her answer was to send me down here. Jackson, he is like, taking care of me.

Sex, sex, sex, that's all he wants. Like man, I feel like saying cool it you old pervert. You know what I mean?"

Surfer girl takes a big swig of coffee. She wipes her mouth with her arm.

"You don't want sex all the time, do you? I mean like, you look almost normal. Except for your hair man. What did you do get in a fight with an Indian?"

Laughing uproariously, she sputters coffee all over my table. "He sure as hell won. Hey like bend over here, I want to take a look at that haircut."

Placing a hand on the seat and table bending into her voluptuous breast I bear my head to her. Running both of her hands through my hair she's pulling at the congealed foam. Soft hands running through my hair has an effect on my excitement level. As long as her hands are doing their roaming I'm not moving. Time escapes us.

The Douggers steps into my little abode. Clearing his throat, "Ah-hum, oh well Ben?"

Lifting my head from the soft breast it's buried in I look into the Dougger's confused eyes. "Oh Douggers, ah-hum, well Doug?"

"You are a little late. Thought I'd come on over, see what was keeping you. Are you all right?"

"I'm good, real good. Thanks."

"Well go ahead with what you were doing. Don't let me stop you."

Giving a little wave Doug backs out the door. He disappears a funny little grin appearing on his face.

***

"Hump." Pitching the second bag of foam cuttings onto the deck twelve feet above me, I reach for another. The hole is half filled with large garbage bags of foam. Each thirty-gallon bag of foam weights less than a pound. Pitching bags up the twelve feet to the deck is a cake walk. Even after a full day of shaping foam, the lite oversized bags fly from my hands.

Climbing onto the deck; bags are scattered everywhere. Glancing down south I catch the surfer girl looking this way through a set of field glasses. Maybe I'll drop by there tonight; do a little visitation?

***

Looking across the shoulder high deck, looks expansive. This cabin cruiser on steroids is wider than the Alley Cat. She is almost half as wide as she is long. Not good proportions for a woman and no good for a boat either. Mounting the ladder I hail the house.

"Hello, the Warlock."

Jackson's head appears from the light-weight galley door. The door has the look of being salvaged from a housing project. The back of the house has a large plate glass window. Man, oh man, I sure wouldn't want to be punching into a heavy sea in this teacup of a boat?

"Hi kid, come on aboard."

"I came over to take a look-see of your vessel."

"Yea, well come on in we'll give you the twenty-five-cent tour."

Jackson's voice has a New York, south Jersey nasal quality. The fringe of hair around his skull hangs to his shoulders. There's a tuff of hair up front swept to one side. The rest of his head is skin. A large gut over hangs his belt buckle. I just can't figure out what all these women like about him.

Striding across the deck Jackson extends his hand. We shake. Gripping my hand, he slides his palm down one side; grasping it in an upward motion he's twisting his wrist in a weird way. I'm trying to follow the secret handshake but failing miserably. Seeing the confusion in my eyes Jackson takes pity on me and drops my hand. I've failed the first test. He invites me in anyway.

The house is nice? The walls are kind of an off-white paneling with vertical black lines. The galley table is a sheet of plywood; a settee wraps around it. A red velvet material covers the settee, looking like it has been salvaged from the Whale Bone Cafe. It all works, in kind of a cheap gaudy fashion.

The small red head is already ready for bed, setting in her skimpy nighty. The nighty is a see-through muslin; a couple of little flowers are embroidered in strategic spots. Now, that is nice, oh yes, very nice. She smiles in a friendly manner gracefully sipping from a cup of tea, hazel eyes blink in a come-hither way.

I blink back in a daze.

My eyes sweep to port where the dark-haired beauty stands. Her mini skirt and knit top are a lovely lime green. She matches right down to her go-go boots. Black waist length hair shines in the florescent light. It's the soft shiny hair that a man just wants to run his fingers through. Her body is perfect. And, I do mean perfect, seeing my lust she departs below. She reminds me of Claudia, except Claudia liked me.

My surfer girl bounds up from where the dark-haired beauty descended. Funny thought, my surfer girl? She belongs to Jackson her mother gave her to him.

Surfer girl is bounding across the deck, her large breasts undulating in unison as she speeds toward me. Skidding to a stop she crashes into me. Wrapping her strong brown arms around me, she hugs.

My arms are trapped by my side. I'm nervous. This is one of Jackson's girls. I want to be hugged, but, but... She's got no reason to be throwing herself at me, does she? What's Jackson going to think? He'll think I'm trying to take advantage of one of his women, oh well, it's the truth.

Surfer Girl squeals, "Oh, you're just so cute I want to eat you up."

Funny... when this was happening to Albert it was really funny. Somehow this doesn't seem so funny now. Maybe, I'm losing my sense of humor?

Blushing beat red, "I, I, oh come on now, stop teasing me."

Jackson adds his opinion to the mix. "Boy, I don't think she's joking."

Surfer Girl gives me one last squeeze. "Come sit down we'll make you a cup of tea, or roll you a joint."

Rocking back on my heels as she releases me from her grasp. "Let me see your boat first, that's what I came for."

Jackson leads me below, where the dark-haired lovely is. Following him through a beaded curtain, I'm in the red-light zone. Yep, that's right, his lights below decks are all red. Below decks is the bedroom. The floor has one huge pad where everyone sleeps.

There are no walls, beaded curtains give what little privacy is allowed. Wow, I wish I was Jackson. It must be fun being him at bedtime.

The beautiful brunette, with the perfect body, is standing next to one of these colorful beaded light deflectors. She is nude, full-frontal nudity. Holding a long see-through robe in one hand she's penetrating me with her gaze. Brazenly daring me to stare at her; I don't. The only girl I've ever seen nude is Debbie. That was different. I do so wish I could look at this grown woman's body, but my raising forbids me my desires.

Catching the hatch for the engine room out of the corner of one eye I dive for it. Bonking my head in the process. Below, I'm in the dark, my head throbbing. What did I run away from; no one but me seems to care? I could be up-stairs, looking at the most gorgeous naked woman I've ever seen.

I want to go back up and see what I'm missing. But, it's just too embarrassing.

Poking his head through the hatch Jackson has a flashlight in hand.

"Here take this light. We haven't put lights below yet. No need to, we ain't got no engine. That's next."

Lucky he ain't got no engine. It would fall through the bottom of the Warlock. If he takes this boat out through the jaws, he'll die. They'll all die! Other than that, Jackson has got it made.

What the hell is he thinking? Why did he buy this boat? I'm dumbfounded by how flimsily she is built? She's got one by four ribs set on five foot centers. Five foot centers, for God's-sake? It has two by eight stringers to put the engine on. Large sheets of plywood warp between the ribs from the water pressure. I'm nervous, this thing could pop a sheet of plywood just setting here. She'd go the bottom in a heartbeat.

The Cap Armstrong, which is a real wooden troller, has four by six ribs, set on twelve-inch centers. It's the difference in strength between a concrete block house and a cardboard box.

One thought keeps invading my brain. "Tell Surfer Girl not to go to sea in this crate."

Finding enough nerve to go back upstairs, I'm remembering what my Mother taught. *If you can't say anything nice don't say anything at all.* Arriving in the bedroom I'm kind of relieved, and kind of disappointed. There aren't any nude women in here, anymore… what a shame.

Mounting the three steps to the pilothouse, I pause. *Say something nice.*

"Nice bedroom Jackson." *Then it just slips out, I don't know how, it just slips out?* "Are you going to put some sisters in her as time allows?"

Jackson's face becomes quizzical, "Sisters? Sisters? You know some sisters you want to turn me on to?

"Sisters? I don't know any sisters? Oh... Sisters. No, by sisters, I mean put more ribs in her. You know, for strength?"

Jackson rubs his bald spot, "Naw, she don't need no more strength. Her hull is half inch plywood. The Warlock is built like a brick shithouse."

The little red head, still holding her teacup, opines. "What are you saying? This is the best boat in the harbor. She can go anywhere in the world. We're taking her to Mexico or Columbia once we get a motor."

The story of the emperor's beautiful clothes floods into my mind. *What's wrong with me? Can't I see his beautiful clothes? I don't have the heart to rain on their parade more than I already have. Besides, what little sense a man has; goes right into the drink when he sees the boat he loves. So, what do I know?*

"You're right she has some of the best lines here. I like her bow, great bow."

The babe with the black hair pokes me in the ribs. She pushes a joint at me. Her face is contorted with the effort she is making to hold her breath. Having smoked pot only once before; I'm not sure of the pot smokers etiquette. Do I puff, or do I pass it on? Is this thing for me? The only other time I've done this is with my best friends. Not knowing what to do I stand here holding this tiny little joint between thumb and fore finger.

Surfer Girl comes to my rescue by singing, *"Don't bogart that joint my friend, pass it over again."*

Swaying up to me she bends her head to the joint, and sucks. Air is flowing past my fingers as she expands her chest. The air stirring near my fingers is stirring my nether parts. However, these two lady's faces are turning red from holding their breath. Their gaze is holding mine, a question in their puffy cheeked expression. Are you going to take a hit, or are you a nark? I puff. The room visibly relaxes. I'm cool, I smoke dope. Passing the joint on I cough the smoke into the cabin.

Setting down at the table we have tea. After some mindless conversation, I take my leave of Jackson and his four winsome mostly un-dressed Lovelies. Sauntering back to my camper I'm still trying to understand women. What is it that Jackson's got?

***

The Rodrick-Due bumps alongside the dock, "One fish Bob is in."

Douggers looks up from where he is working. "Old, one fish. He's been at this dock for as long as I can remember. One fish Bob...I don't know, I just don't know; how in the world does he eat?"

Shaking my head, "Well he's a friendly guy, anyway."

"I don't know how he makes it. It can't be easy when winter comes."

"Heck Doug, it can't be easy making it during the summer on one fish a day."

"One fish is thirty forty dollars, after turkey day he don't make nothing. And I do mean nothing."

"It don't make any sense, why not blow some ice, take a trip, go catch some fish?" Looking up from the wires he is soldering, Doug replies. "It's work out there on that ocean, fishing salmon you got to stand anchor watch half the night. Up at four, pushing hooks through frozen bait, cleaning Jellyfish off your lines half the day.

Fishing albacore, you're laying adrift getting up four or five times during the night. Laying beam-to in a big lump, running all night long every other night.

It's a lot safer and nicer tied alongside of the dock. Of course, the fish ain't alongside the dock; unless they belong to someone else. Come on let's go to Moss Landing Marine Hardware store. I need some parts, and you need a break from the hole."

Grabbing his hat, the Douggers leads me out the Dutch door.

***

The Store is cavernous. Taking up half a city block it's filled top to bottom with stuff. Fishing stuff is falling out into the aisles. It's stacked to the ceiling. I've never seen such a store. How do they use all this junk?

My neck is hurting from all the looking up I'm doing. At first, I tried to follow the Douggers, but I've lost him. Now, wondering the store, I'm lost and stumbling over all this junk. About to call out; I run into Surfer Girl. She is also wondering about the stacks of gear, looking a little lost herself.

Glancing down her top, I ask. "Hey, what are you doing here?"

"We're all here, Jackson is ordering some junk for his boat. I didn't know that Douggers guy ever let you out of your hole. Like cool, man."

"Yea, he didn't tell me what he wanted. We just came. I don't know where he went."

"Like cool man. Have you ever seen a place like this? It's outrageous. What do they do with all this stuff?"

Pondering the question, I gaze around looking for something that I know how to use. Seeing nothing... but, wanting to impress Surfer Girl I scan the high walls. Ah, there's some net. I've seen draggers working before.

"That's a drag net. Boats use doors to keep the net open. Then they drag up bottom fish."

"Oh." Her mouth forms a perfect oval, her eyes a picture of confusion.

Smiling at me, "Well I'm certainly glad you explained that, I never would have known what a net is for. Me, I was just wondering if there is any rope in here, rope can be used to tie someone up? Now that's sexy."

"Tie someone up? Tie someone up?

"Yea, you could use dock line, say half inch."

Trying to sound cool and knowledgeable, "I guess, but, why would you tie someone up?"

"You've never been tied up? Where have you been your whole life? Oh, man you like got to try it!"

My mind is going through every conceivable reason that someone would like to be tied up. Nothing comes to mind, now I'm as confused as she was, during my explanation about drag boats. There is just no good reason to be tied up.

Our conversation is a little uncomfortable.

"Let's go to the front of the store. We'll find our skippers."

Glancing at the pile of netting Surfer Girl says, "That looks kind of comfy over there. But, if you would rather work? Then, well OK?"

Burning beat red my face could power the Moss Landing power plant. Oh, maybe being tied up has something to do, with sex? How would that work?

Arriving at the front of the store we find both the Douggers and Jackson. Jackson is ordering an engine for the Warlock. Twelve thousand dollars plus, for a turbo charged GMC "Jimmy" V-8 diesel engine. It's a lot of money but it's a lot of engine. The skipper of the Warlock pulls a money clip from his pocket. A two inch thick wad of hundreds fills the clip to capacity. Jackson begins counting.

"One," laying down a hundred. "Two," another hundred is placed on the counter. "Three," this hundred joins the first two.

Some white powder stubbornly clings to the bill. Jackson wipes it on his shirt sleeve. There are a couple of other fishermen watching Jackson count his cash. After a good long time, he's still counting.

"One hundred and eighteen," the stack of bills is closing in on two inches high.

"One hundred and nineteen." Licking his thumb with a flourish He puts the last bill on the stack, "One hundred and twenty-four. There you go, cash makes no enemies."

Reaching across the counter pulling the bills toward himself Leonard smiles. Ringing it up, the amount is impressive. Twelve thousand, three hundred and ninety dollars and eighty-nine cents $12,390.89. Man! Jackson's wad of hundreds in his clip is still two inches thick.

Some fishermen keep a grand or two on their boats for emergencies. But, twenty some odd grand? That's, well, somehow over the top.

Poking me Douggers jerks his head, in a; let's go motion. Turning I wave to Surfer Girl, a fingertip wave. She waves back. Shrugging, I follow the Douggers to his little Toyota truck.

***

Bumping alongside the Spirit's engine is making a racket. She's backing down, full bore. The prop wash pushing the Alley Cat hard against the dock. It's salmon season. Boats are beginning to unload. Making my palms itch to get out there and join them.

Stepping from the pilot house Sonny hands me a bow line. Leading the line through a hawser I lay the eye over a cleat. Fisherman etiquette requires the eye end of a line be handed to the boat you're tying alongside. In that way the crew of the boat tying up will do most of the work.

Walking side by side we parade to the stern, Sonny pitches me a line. After laying the line over the cleat I ask the one question any fisherman can ask another.

"So, how'd you do?"

"We got-them, pretty good, two hundred king salmon, even got a few silvers."

"Wow, two hundred kings; that's a good trip."

"About half are spliters."

Sonny is about forty. A ten-day growth of beard adorns his cheeks. Sandy hair hangs to his shoulders gray streaks showing at the sides. He looks tired, dead tired. The crows-feet around his eyes are deep; a net of white lines surrounded by wind burnt red. His eyes are a piercing blue surrounded by a web of red. Like I said, he looks tired.

Hauling on the stern line Joe grunts. "Hey, you guys are getting it together over here. She's looking more and more like a fishing boat."

"Gee, thanks Sonny. We're working our butts off, but we're latching her together all right."

"You know my name, but I don't know yours."

"Ben, Ben is my name. They call me Benjy around here."

"Benjy ah, your name is Benjy? Well, I'll be drowned."

'A cold shiver runs down my spine. How could a fisherman use such a saying, calling out his own death?' Shaking off the curse I grin back at Sonny.

He's a well-known highliner. Sonny built the Spirit on the sand spit just up the beach. She is forty-five feet, steel, a Monk design. One tough little sea boat.

"Doug's got a Benny? Well, that's just great. I had me a Benny. When I built the Spirit. God, what a great old guy Benny was."

"Is he still around, you don't meet that many Bennys?"

"No... old Benny died." Sigh. "Benny named the Spirit. I had the keel laid, I was trying to stick the stem up, I was balancing the stem on the keel. The stem's a piece of one-inch-thick steel plate cut in the right shape. Must have weighed five hundred pounds. I needed the stinger, to tack the stem. Couldn't reach it. Suddenly, there is a set of hands above my head holding the stem in place. Without looking up I grab my stinger, and started welding away."

Sonny's eyes have a far-off look to them. He's looking out on the horizon, not at me. A tear brims in one eye, but he refuses to let it roll down his cheek. His voice that had been light and airy is somber.

"Turning around, and looking up, I see a skinny old man. Skinny but rock hard. Gray hair hung down to his shoulders. His shirt was falling apart. His pants were being held up by a rope. I grew up poor, but man, he was poorer. He says to me, "The Spirit sent me." After that... that old man would come to the boat every morning. He would spend all day long helping me, I'd feed him, got him a sleeping bag, gave him money, mind you not too much. If he got to much money he'd get on a drunk. My old friend Benny; he slept on the beach the whole time we were building the Spirit.

Every morning he'd show up and say, "The Spirit told me to do such and such."

Then, Benny would do just that. Whatever the Spirit told him that's what he'd do. Finally, I figured out that was the name of my boat. Spirit. After all the Spirit told old Benny how to build her."

Wiping his red rimmed eyes; Sonny gives me a wan smile. Nodding he glances at a tangle of fishing gear. "I've got work to do."

Sonny turns from me, dropping into his gaff hatch. "You know Benny died right here in the hatch. After we finished the Spirit, he fished the boat with me. Sometimes the Spirit would tell him where we should fish. The Spirit was never wrong you know. Benny, Old Benny, what a good friend?"

***

A knock on the door pounds into my sleep filled brain. Feeling around I find my watch. *One thirty two? Who the hell?*

Rolling from my bunk I stagger to the camper door. About the time I arrive Surfer Girl swings it open.

I never lock it; I don't have a key. Being in my underwear I think of retreating. OOPS to late, she's coming in.

"Mind if I come in? I can't get down to my boat, the gate is locked. Would you mind if I crash here?"

"No... that's all right you can sleep on the table. Oh; wait a minute, I have a key to the gate."

Silence nothing but silence. There are not many nineteen-year-old men who'll turn down a girl that wants to stay with him. It has to be a new experience for this young lady. In my own defense I did just wake up.

"Ah, I don't ah want to wake everyone up over there. You know, we all sleep together."

"Gee... that's really nice of you. How come you're coming home so late?"

I went home, did my laundry. Now, I'm just coming home. But, I don't want to go home tonight. Can I stay with you?"

"Yea sure. Do you want to sleep on the... table?"

Surfer Girl pulls her shirt off as she makes a bee-line for my bed. Gee, she must be tired? Stopping at the bed; Surfer Girl strips down before crawling up into my bunk. Her bare bottom disappearing beneath my sleeping bag. What to do? What to do?

***

The fish hole is shaped-up, it's a thing of beauty. I've thrown bags and bags of foam onto the deck. Foam that I've cut, and hacked, and hewn, out of the hold. Sawing, using a knife at times, grinding, ripping with my hands, anything and everything that works. Shaping the foam into smooth sides with rounded corners. When I started the rough sides held up to four feet of foam. Now after two weeks of work the foam is kind of a uniform thickness. At about a foot and a half thick at the bottom of the hole, and six inches thick at the top, all transitions are nice and smooth. I'm proud of my job.

Stormy's Yogi the Bear voice breaks into my ponderings. "Hey hey hey Benjy. Like is everything jake man? Hey hey hey, we're a gonna glass us a hole. It'll be a blast kid-o."

Looking up at Stormy I offer, "I've never ever fiberglass before. Boy I am looking forward to it. I've been thinking that if I like working with it maybe I'll build a boat. You know out of fiberglass, it can't be that hard."

Stormy smiles his big bear of a grin, "Hey hey hey Benjy, I'll tell you a little secret, this is my first time too. We'll both lose our cherries on the same job."

Stormy and I exit stage... up to the dock. We have equipment to transport. Stormy is the proud owner of a chopper gun. Chopper gun and all the paraphernalia needed, must be brought down. An hour of the morning is lost to transport of Stormy's equipment.

The chopper gun pulls strings of glass from a big spool. Chopping the glass, it shoots it onto any surface you want. You spray resin out, then glass onto the resin, it's a major labor-saving device. The glass is rolled smooth; becoming a shiny finish. It's just the perfect material. Strong, watertight, lightweight, easy to work, it's just the perfect material, except for one thing, it falls.

Stormy and I are in coveralls. This time: one of Doug's hats is perched on my head. Learning a lesson from the last time we blew the hole. It could be that a little of the glass may over spray, and get in my hair.

"OK kid-o, this is how it's going to work. Hey hey hey, I'll wet everything down with the gun. Good and wet, you got it Benjy?"

Nodding in agreement, I got it. Stormy is going to wet everything down. "Yea yea, I got it."

"Then, I'll shoot a little resin on the glass."

"Yea, OK, yea, sounds easy-peasey."

"You roll like hell, with this."

Stormy hands me this little, tiny, itsis-bistsy device. It's a tube with ridges that rotates. The roller is about three inches long. I've have to roll the whole fish hole with a three inch roller?

Raising the little-bitty roller into the air, "Yea, I've got it?"

"Hey hey hey little buddy, it's you and me against the hole."

Stormy raises his chopper gun into the air, the gun joining the little bitty roller hovering over our heads, a sure sign of victory.

Down in the hold it's a small corner of hell. The kicking resin is overpowering. We have a fresh air delivery system, but it's not working too well. Burning eyeballs weep tears down my cheeks. About every fifth breath my throat and lungs burn with the intensity of an acid bath. Stormy is in about the same condition.

Stormy started on the walls and overhead. He's blowing a four-by-four-foot section, then I roll like my life depends on this glass staying where Stormy put it.

About a quarter of the hole is glassed. I've decided that I don't want to fiberglass as my life's work.

It is an easy decision when engaged in a fight of the fish hold.

The roof above my head has just been saturated with fresh resin. I'm rolling like a mad man. Straightening up, I glance at Stormy's eyes. Terror is reflected in the wide-eyed look on his face. What? What can be wrong? I'm rolling the glass like I've been doing for the last three hours. Have I been screwing up? Stormy didn't say anything.

Turning I look at what has Stormy's attention. In the far back corner, where we started, the roof is un-raveling. Glass is hanging by a thread. A gaping hole has developed between the roof and the layer of glass. OOPS. Big OOPS!

Tripping over air hoses I charge toward our breach. As soon as I get to it; I'm rolling for all I'm worth. My hard work, is not working. Using my free hand, I'm pushing and patting at the glass. Pushing on one part dislodges another. Resin and glass are raining down around me. Not good, this is not good at all.

The collapse of the roof is under way.... Stormy seeing what is happening turns and scuttles out from under it. Assessing the situation as hopeless. Stormy retreats up the ladder. The collapse is total and complete. The only part of the roof, still on the roof, is under my hand. A goodly part of the roof is resting on my back and shoulders.

Covered with wet glass I'm trying to determine the best course of action. It seems best to me to remove my hand from the roof. My Chicken Little like attempt to hold the sky up has been an utter failure. The glass from the roof sticks to my hand. This isn't going so well, is it? All the glass is either on the floor... or on me.

Knowing that glass hardens I bend over and begin cleaning up the mess. Stormy throws a cardboard box at me. Piling the glass into the box is a disheartening act.

Mounting onto the deck I'm feeling a little guilty. Maybe I didn't roll fast enough, or hard enough, or long enough? But, one thing is for sure, fiber glassing is not my life's work.

Once I'm back on deck I take a seat on the gunwale. The sun kicking the fiberglass is burning my back and chest.

Stormy, seeing a chance to increase my pain, rubs it in. "Hey hey hey, Benjy? Like what happened man? We was a blowing and a going... then, our whole hold fell apart. *It* was like jake man; like it was a raining glass."

"I know Stormy. I was right under the fan when the shit hit it."

Hey hey hey, I told the little Douggers here that there was only a fifty-fifty chance that you'd make it out. You were so covered; I thought the glass would kick and that'd be it for Benjy. Douggers might have to stack fish up against you."

"Well, we sure didn't get the job done."

Douggers sniffs at my glassy smell. "If I were you Ben, I'd go over and get a shower. You're covered with glass and resin. I think maybe your clothes are... maybe shot, when that stuff dries."

That's a big admission for the Douggers, he don't allow that anything can't be repaired.

As a parting shot Stormy opines, "He was just about shot himself when that roof came a caving down in on us. He would have shown a lot more brains if-in he'd a run and hid. Like me."

In the next few days we hire a real glass man, to man the chopper gun.

With him at the helm, the three of us get the hole blown. It goes well, but I still don't want to be a real glass man when I grow up. That is if I ever do?

***

It's Sunday morning coming down, a dreary fog covers the harbor. Everything outside is wet and cold. I'm kind of lonely, and there's no work today. Surfer Girl is tied up with Jackson. I hope she is not actually tied up, but nothing is certain.

Think I'll take a little walk to the Whale Bone Inn, have a good breakfast. Ham and eggs, wow, something besides cold cereal, that'd be good. Throwing a shirt on, and some water on my face, I head out the door.

A water pipe, three feet in diameter, crosses the slough right next to the bridge. Just for fun I use the pipe to cross on. Making the bank on the far side I head along the sandy road to the Whale

Bone. Beside the restaurant is an old two pump service station. The service station guy has four or five junk cars out back.

A short cut to the back door takes me through the junkers. Striding through the cars; a small, still voice speaks to me. The small still voice, coming from deep within, whispers, "HEY, WATCH YOUR ASS!!"

Turning I catch sight of a pit bull charging me from between two cars. Not a sound leaves his ferocious mouth as he surges at my groin. I consider running, then scan the litter strewn path before me. Naw, that won't work. Fight or flight, flight isn't available, it's fight. The pit bull is closing on my crotch, drool dripping from the large canine teeth his head turned for the bite. My leg snaps from the knee in a kick, the ball of my tennis shoe connecting with the bottom of a gigantic canine jaw. The jaw snaps together on the dog's tongue. The pit bull whimpers in pain as his head collides with my upper thigh. If his jaws hadn't been kicked closed, I'd be missing a pound of flesh right now.

The dogs' been hurt I've been scared; so far, the fight is a draw. Old pit bull backs off and then charges again. I kick. Once again, the old hound dog draws back. We work out this little dance, he moves toward my leg and up it snaps in a kick. Every time his massive jaw snaps close, I can hear the click of teeth. He's serious and I'm scared. As I kick old hound dog backs off, then he moves in again for the kill. Blood is dripping from his mouth. At least it's his own blood. Backing toward the kitchen door the dog is driving me from the pile of junkers. Once clear of the junkers, the fight is over. The old hound dog barks happily once, and wags off toward an old and fading camp trailer. Man, that was close.

Spinning on my heel I enter the back door of the Whale Bone Inn. The grouchy old lady that runs the place frowns at me. That's her greeting for everyone, so I shrug and ease past her.

The kitchen drips grease. Next to the words, "Greasy Spoon", in the dictionary there's a picture of this place. The kitchen leads to the wrong side of the counter. A greasy dirty swinging plywood door opens to let me on the right side. Sliding onto a stool at the counter I plop down. Plopping on the stool I eyeball a babe. She's with her hubby at a table near a window. They're a couple of about thirty. Their window seat gives them a wonderful view of highway one, and the parking lot. They're an attractive couple, nicely dressed and obviously deeply in love. I think it's their honeymoon.

When you have been broke a long time you always check to see if you really have money. Pulling my wallet out I glance into it. It's no problem pay day is Saturday. Yesterday was Saturday so I'm rich. OOPS, no I'm not. Doug wasn't at the boat yesterday, he went to San Francisco, I didn't get paid. All I've got is two dollars, and that'll have to last me until Monday.

Getting up to leave, the aroma of pancakes rivets me to my stool. Stomach muscles spasm in protest to the message my brain is sending them. Leave? Hell no we ain't leaving. My stomach tells my brain to blow the two bucks on a short stack. Checking my pockets I've got another seventy-five cents, that's enough for a tip. So, here I sit.

The old lady comes to the counter. She spent World War II in a concentration camp. Life's been tough on her and I want to be nice; but man, she makes it hard.

"Hi, how you doing."

"Vaht you vant, ah?"

Double checking the menu to make sure I have enough money; I order. "Could I please have a short stack? Please?"

"You damn deck hands always vant not-ting but pancakes. You damn deck hands spend all your money on beer and got not-ting on breakfast."

Mumbling about what a loser I am, she departs to make me a couple golden brown griddle cakes. Least ways that is my hope.

The love bird couple gets their breakfast first. Ham, eggs, toast, hash browns, the works. It's a thing of beauty, watching those plates float-by resting on the old lady's hands. Sipping coffee and glancing around, I wait my time with patience. Breakfast will come.

We three, are the only customers of the Whale Bone; pancakes have to be next. My coffee cup sits empty for the next ten minutes. Nothing happens, there is waiting, while more nothing happens. Time passes, oh so slowly. Aroma, wafting out into the dining room, turning my stomach into knots, it's a digestive engine. Ah at last, here they are.

The old lady lays the plate before me, "You vant more coffee, I guess?"

"Well, that would be nice, yes please, I'd love another cup." I sound like Oliver Twist begging for more gruel.

"Huff."

The pancakes are black. Not just burnt on the edges they're charcoal black. Charcoal black on all four sides. It wouldn't be bad if they were cooked. But they're not. Inside of the pancakes is a white goo. The combination is uneatable. Bad, these are the worst pancakes I've ever eaten. Rather the worst pancakes I can't eat.

While working on my third bite, I'm contemplating complaining. The words are forming in my mind. I'll be nice, but firm. I paid for these pancakes; I have the right to complain. They're really not eatable.

The handsome, charming groom steps to the cash register. Slipping a hand into his pressed chino jeans he opines. "That wasn't the best breakfast I've ever eaten."

The old lady wipes away a drip of snot from her nose. Her brown eyes pierce this young groom on his honeymoon. I watch him shrink away from her as though she had a gun. The dining room is completely quite. A wall clock ticks off five seconds as we wait. This is going to be bad.

"You fink I give a rat's fuck?"

"No, no, I don't think you do."

He turns and strides to the door where his bride is waiting. Arm and arm they leave, never to return.

The complaint I have been forming, withers in my gut, along with the uncooked goo that I'm trying to masticate. The groom was right; this isn't the best breakfast I've ever eaten.

***

Monday morning, back to work, So, this is what it must have been like. Being a sailor that is, hanging out on a yardarm trying to tie a knot and not fall to the deck. Right now, I am about thirty feet above the deck; my right leg is wrapped around the crosstree on the mast. One hand is hanging onto a one-inch line that I have been told to splice, my other hand is just hanging on. God, if it is this scary up here in a dead calm harbor, what must it be like at sea?

When the boat is rocking and rolling it must be a small piece of hell.

The Douggers wants me to do a clove-hitch splice for the pole rigging. I told him no problem I can splice in my sleep... but man? This is sure as heck not a dream.

I have the clove hitch tied, now all I have to do is the splice. Somehow, I have to cut this end off and tape the three-braids of line, and then splice it, somehow? I can use my one hand and my teeth everything else is hanging on.

KA-BOOM! Spinning my head toward the explosion I catch my nose on the two-inch diameter pipe I am balanced on. "What the hell was that?" I moan out while rubbing my nose. Then I spot it, a torch is burning in the ocean. Just past the bell buoy a huge torch is flaming away. What would cause that? The ocean is not just going to blow up and catch fire. Is it?

Then it hits me the torch is a boat. A fishing boat just blew up outside the harbor. Still holding my nose, I yell down at the Douggers on deck.

"Doug, Doug, a boat blew up. It's flaming, just outside the jaws."

Clarence: coming alongside the dock, has been at sea on a ten-day salmon trip. The Harmony is in hard reverse and closing with the dock. The Douggers calls out, "Clarence, come along side... Quick, a fish-boat just blew-up, We got to go look for survivors. Quick, get your ass in gear."

The Douggers changes the direction of his yelling, he lifts his face toward me and instructs. "Ben, take a bearing mark the point of the explosion, where is it from the buoy? You got it?"

"Yea, yea I got it. It's a quarter of a mile south of the bell buoy."

"If you got the place marked then get your ass down here, we're on a rescue mission."

Pushing myself back down the crosstree my left foot finds a ladder rung on the mast.

"Oh, that's better," I sigh.

Both feet on the ladder I squirm into a vertical position and drop toward the deck three feet at a time.

With my feet on the deck, I turn to see the Harmony sliding by next to the Alley Cat's gunwales. Already on her back deck, The Douggers is waving at me to get aboard. I make a mad dash toward the departing Harmony, hitting the top of the gunwale I leap at the receding target. Both tennis-shoes plant on the deck just forward of the gaff hatch. I am aboard, we're on a rescue mission, and I'm in on it. God, I love an adventure.

Walking into the pilothouse I can hear Clarence talking on the radio.

"X-Ray Papa Alph 16-42 to the Monterey Coast Guard. X-Ray Papa Alph 16-42 to the Monterey Coast Guard. Coast Guard Monterey do you copy."

"Monterey Coast Guard back to X-Ray Papa Alph 16-42, go ahead Captain."

"Yes; Monterey, I want to report an explosion off of the Moss Landing jetty. A fishing boat has just exploded we are on our way to the boat right now."

"Copy that, you are reporting an explosion, is there a fire onboard?"

Clarence looks over his shoulder at me with an unspoken question in his clear

blue eyes. Man, here I am, on a rescue mission, and people are asking me questions. Wow, this being a grown up sure is a lot of fun.

"Yep, lots of flames, they must have been forty-to-fifty, feet in the air. Lots of smoke too."

Clarence has enough info; he turns back to the radio. "Monterey Coast Guard that is an affirmative. Lots of flames lots of smoke."

Clarence has the Harmony in the channel, so he pours the coal to her. The Boat squats and pushes a bow wake out in front. Clarence has her at full tilt-boggy we are doing about twelve knots, that is fast for a troller.

Still squatting, the Harmony rounds the jetty and heads toward the bell buoy. The fire is out but the smoke continues to column up. We boil out toward the last of the smoke. The boat bucks into the steep swells pitching and swaying.

Douggers orders, "Ben, go aloft, look for bodies, look for anything that looks human. They may be burned, covered with oil, or... well it could be ugly. Just look."

Clarence has ratlines up to his crosstree, I don't know why a man in his seventies has ratlines up his mast, but he does. Here I go, I get to experience thirty feet up, in a bucking sea, well at least I don't have to splice.

Swinging onto the gunwale I start up the ratlines, the boat rolls heavily and I am leaning backward over the sea. Stopping my climb I just hang on, when the boat rolls back I climb again. Yep just like I thought it would be, it is downright scary. At the crosstree I throw one leg over the two by six, that is the crosstree. My left hand is wrapped around Clarence's anchor light. Looking down I notice it is held to the top of the wooden mast by two very small screws. It ain't much of a hand hold, but it is the only one up here.

"Hey the deck, just to starboard I see debris we're at the outer edge."

Doug is on the bow; he glances up and then points out the direction to Clarence. I begin my job in earnest, looking for a body, or maybe, even a swimmer. The boat has slowed down to six knots the big bow wave has disappeared. We enter an area of oily water, splintered and chard plywood. The mast sways in a large uneven circle never following the same path twice. The wind blows through my flannel shirt chilling in its cut.

We plow a straight line through the debris; there is a bottle to the north, dead ahead is part of a bunk cushion. Here there and everywhere are parts of someone's life. Some fisherman like me, coming home; and he's lost his boat, his livelihood, maybe his life. He made it home, then at the jetty, on a calm day and for no reason he's lost it all.

It strikes me, *Look, look for a swimmer, look for someone covered in suet and oil.* I hang on to my anchor light and roll around the sky searching the sea.

Time, like the oily water under Harmony's bow, slides by. As the sun sets into the Pacific the first Coast Guard Cutter plows onto the scene. As the Cutter slows to a search speed, Clarence steps onto the back deck.

"Ben, Ben come on down. The Coast Guard has ordered us out of the area. They don't want us in the area screwing up their search pattern. Come on down now Ben, they don't want us here."

I kick my legs over the crosstree and find the first ratline down to the deck. Soon I stand in front of Clarence, he places a hand on my shoulder, "Let's go home they're not going to find anything here but a body. We were here when it counted. If there was anything to find, we would have found it. Come on in the house, you look as cold as you did the day we first met."

"Ok Clarence, I sure could use a cup of your coffee. Why did they kick us off the search we've been here for hours. I've seen the same bottles, gas cans and burnt chunks of wood for five hours now. Why don't they want us here, we know this area better than any Coasty."

Doug pats me on the back, "Come on guys let's head in I'm cold. The Coastys don't want us here watching them making fools of them self."

Walking into the house Clarence says, "When we get in I'm going home I'll sell my fish tomorrow, I'm bushed."

The next day we heard through the gossip network that is links ever port in the world to one another what happened. The boat was a little thirty-footer, and she was headed in from a five-day salmon trip. His running partner said the whole trip the boat had been having carburetor problems. Unlike most fishing boats this one had a gas engine. The carburetor kept flooding and would leak into the bilge. He also had a stern gland leaking. Water was dripping into the bilge where the shaft goes through the keel. Drip drip drip, hour after hour, it becomes gallons. What we surmised was that the automatic bilge-pump came on, a spark from the switch ignited the gas. The bilge was a bomb awaiting that spark.

I make a decision on that day; I'll never own a boat with a gas engine.

***

It's only been a week or so since Surfer Girl spent the night. She's been coming by every morning for... "Coffee." Most mornings I'm only half an hour late for work, after our, "coffee".

Not too bad, not really.

Then the D-E-A shows up. Stepping outside, looking for her; a guy in a blue jacket motions me over. Coffee cup in hand I wonder up to him. His blue jacket has a big D-E-A on the back.

Mr. D-E-A asks me, "Hey kid, you got a key to the gate?"

"Mr. Deeaah, do you have a boat down here? Only boat owners or their crew are suppose to be on the docks."

"Kid, give me the key, then get back."

Scratching my three-day growth, I dig in my pocket. "Ah here it is."

The gate key brings out more Mr. D-E-As. They're all in suits, lots of suits. Moss Landing has never seen so many guys at one gate. Let alone a whole bunch of guys in suits wanting to get in. It's some kind of traffic jam. Seven of us at one gate, wow. I like being helpful, and they're all dress nice. Why would all these guys dressed up in suits steal junk from an old fish boat? They wouldn't; they just wouldn't.

Holding my key in the air I lean past Mr. D-E-A and slide it into the lock. The click of the lock is some kind of signal. It's like opening Pandora's Box, only in reverse. Every Mr. DEA on the outside of the gate shoves, pushes, shoulders, bulldozes and rams past me to the inside of the gate. I'm a little offended here. Being propelled halfway down the ramp I'm left in a quandary.

At the bottom of the ramp the suits start pulling guns. Opp's, big Opp's. What should I do? I don't want to get any of Pandora's problems clinging to me. So, I back up the ramp and away from all this hubbub. The suits converge on the Warlock their guns at the ready. This may cause a passal of problems for old Jackson.

A hand slaps my back and Stormy's Yogi the Bear voice breaks into my thoughts.

"Hey hey hey Benjy, what'd you do? Why'd you sick all the cops on our boy Jackson, and the babes. If-in you wanted to get rid of Surfer Girl you could have just given her away."

"Stormy, I didn't sick the cops on Surfer Girl, I just opened the gate for them guys. They're not cops, they're DEA."

"Benjy, do you know what DEA stands for?"

"No. Should I?"

Laughing at me Stormy places a large paw on my shoulder, "Drug, Enforcement, Agency."

"Oh."

"They're going to throw Jackson and everyone of those lovelies he sleeps with in jail."

"No, not Surfer Girl. Please not Surfer Girl. She's only seventeen."

"Hey hey hey Benjy, them's the breaks."

"Stormy, I didn't want to get Surfer Girl busted. 1 didn't know they were cops, all the cops I know wear blue and sport big badges."

"Hey hey hey, it don't matter what you wanted. You turned the coppers lose on her, and her other honey. She ain't a going to be comin over and rockin your camper, not this morning."

"Damn, you're right. What am I going to do?"

"Might as well watch the fun, then you can go back to work." Grinning in delight Stormy continues, "The Warlock is surrounded. Hey hey hey, she's a gonna have to surrender."

Two of the Mr. DEA's jump onto the deck. Running across it they crash into the flimsy door. Splinters explode from their shoulders like they hit a load of kenneling wood. The door is gone; it's just gone?

Moaning, "What have I done? What have I done? I'll tell you one thing Stormy, that's the last time I open a gate for anyone in a suit."

"Hey hey kid-o, never have anything to do with a suit. Suits never did you no favors, trust me on this one kid."

Nothing much has been happening since the door splintered. Finally, two DEAs propel Jackson onto the deck. Appearing on deck in handcuffs, he's almost immediately surrounded by his bevy of beauties. The young ladies are in varying stages of undress.

Two or three other fishermen have joined us by now. Sonny, captain of the Spirit, is one of them. Gaping at all the long luscious legs protruding from skimpy sleep wear; he sums up our thoughts in one succinct word. "Wow."

Stormy nods in agreement, "Sonny, you never spoke a truer word."

The mostly undressed women; hop, and jump, and leap to the dock. Nighties pillowing in the air during their descent. On the docks, raised arms are ready to catch Jackson, in case he falls. The lovely arms raised in the air reveal even more of these beauties. Jackson is making motions at getting off the boat. With his hands cuffed he's dithering about the deck, making a big deal of jumping off the boat. We don't mind. It's quite a spectacle, lifted arms, lifting their nighty.

After a bit, Jackson is safely ensconced in the back of a white ford. Suits start to bring up their finds. The guns come first. Nice guns, lots of guns. Guns fill the trunk of one car and spill over into a second.

Stormy bobs his head at me, in a come this way motion, foolishly I follow. With me in tow Stormy wonders up to a car. Sauntering around to the trunk we peer in at the weapons. While we're admiring the guns a D-E-Aer shows up with another load, his arms filled to the brim.

Pulling dark glasses down his bear like nose, Stormy's eyes merrily crinkle. "Hey hey hey, what'd you need so many guns for. Jackson's whole gang is made up of girls. They wouldn't hurt you, not unless they gave you some kind of disease. The kind like my little buddy here is going to get. Anywhos, I could think of worse ways to get an on-the-job injury. Getting a little disease from one of these babes, you'd be doing your duty."

The D-E-Aer shoves past us, "What are you talking about?"

"The guns why'd you need so many?"

"These aren't our guns."

"They're not huh? Mind if we take a couple? A man can't have too many guns you know."

Mr. D-E-A's expression is running the gambit; it's gone from mild interest, to surprise, then incredulous, too blatant suspicion. The arm load of arms are getting heavy and Mr. D-E-A drops them in the trunk.

"What? You want these guns? Are you some type of deranged prankster? You can't have any of these weapons, they're evidence."

"Hey hey hey, evidently... you got all the evidence you need. I wouldn't want you guys to have too many guns, you might get hurt."

"Get back! This is a crime scene. You God-damned nut."

Gyrating his girth in a circle, Stormy's middle finger pushes his dark glasses back up his long bear like nose. "OK Mr. Ranger, we ain't gonna steal no pic-a-nic baskets, honest Mr. Ranger."

Easing back from the trunk, I can't help but ask, "Stormy, why are you screwing with these guys heads? They may be dangerous."

Pulling his sunglasses back down his bear of a nose, Stormy peers over the top of them. His eye's still glowing in a marry blue. "Hey, hey hey, Benjy me boy. When ever a suit is around, mess with-em. If-in you don't... they'll mess with you. I don't give advice to anyone about anything, but hear me on this. Mess with the suits. Right now that guy is trying to figure out if I'm crazy, stupid, or making fun of him. No matter what he decides, we won't be called as a witness. You and me, we won't be bothered having to make some court date in the middle of an albacore season. Never trust a suit, always screw with a suit, a suit is trouble."

The procession of drugs starts up the ramp. All six of the DEAers are carrying big garbage of grass up the ramp.

Poking me in the ribs Stormy asks me, "What is that stuff?"

"Grass. I think?"

"Grass? Last time I looked the Warlock didn't have a lawn."

"Not lawn grass, smoking grass."

"Oh, is that what that funny smell was coming out the back door of the Warlock?" "Smells like hay burning, don't it?"

The car, that the drugs are in, is guarded, that car, is guarded big time. The procession of drugs continues until two trunks are full and back seats are being filled with more bags. Then a bag of white powder is marched up the ramp. Wow, they were into drugs over there. Lots and lots of drugs. I'll bet they were selling them.

Stormy, impressed with the volume of drugs queries, "Why would anyone take this kind of risk? Having all those drugs, it just don't make any sense."

As Stormy finishes his thought, the money starts emerging from the gate. Stacks and stacks of money, bags of money; money money money.

Smiling, his marry eyes gleaming, Stormy voices his understanding. "Bags of money; well I guess that explains the, *WHY.*"

***

Light slanting into the hatch reflects off the white gelcoat, blinding me. I'm applying the finishing touch to the hole. It's the shaft alley; the covering plates need to be bolted down then; that's it. Doug has tasked me with the hold and I've done it. It's a nice feeling. Neoprene strips are laid out and the plates are ready to be bolted on.

The ladder scrapes on the hatch twelve feet above me. What's up? What's up is; Surfer Girl coming down the ladder. Her mid-rift blouse is being held out by her sizable female endowments. Staring up, I'm enjoying her luscious breasts as they bounce down the ladder with her. Surfer Girl is followed by the sexy red head, Sharon.

Hugging me, Surfer Girl sobs, "Did you see what happened?" Wailing, "They took Jackson, the money, the drugs, everything. He's in jail, they took him to jail."

Gee, from what Surfer Girl said, she didn't even like Jackson, now all these hysterics? No matter what she said, she really did like him. I just don't understand women.

Surfer Girl, is sobbing and hugging around on me, Sharon patting her shoulder. The Douggers sticks his head over the hatch he's wondering; what's all the trouble and noise. Looking up at him I roll my eyes, trying to show him; that this isn't my idea. Pulling his head back from the opening, Doug retreats from the chaos. He wants no part of this.

Breaking into hysterics, the sexy red head says, "Ben... Ben I know that this isn't any of your concern... But? Would you mind? Could you help us?"

Emotions tug at my heart. I want to help these lost souls. Besides needing my help, they are two young beautiful, sexy, luscious, women. In addition, they're rubbing themselves all over me. Of course I'll help them, they're my first set of crying females.

"What do you need? I'll do anything I can to help."

"Can you, that is would you ah. Loan us your car, sniff, sniff?"

My Mustang? She wants my car? Other than half of the Bloody Wog, which ain't much, all I own is my car. A half a million in; drugs and money and guns hauled off and now this gal wants my car. They are both rubbing me, and touching me, and well, you know.

How would Unk, who doesn't like women handle this? How would Stormy handle this? Doug? How would the Douggers handle this?

"Doug, Douggers"

The Dougger's head reappears over the hatch, "What is it Ben?"

I don't know what to say; I don't even know why I called him.

Digging in my pocket, I haul out my keys. "Sure, you can borrow my car."

The Dougger's face drops into a serious frown. OOPS maybe I shouldn't be so free and easy with my car. Well, too late now.

Slipping my keys from my hand the sexy red head pecks my cheek. "Thanks. Can we borrow some money? We're going to see if we can get Jackson out of jail."

My wallet comes from my pocket. Out comes a twenty, one fifth of my weekly take home. Handing it over to the girls, they bounce up the ladder. Doug shakes his head at me. Oops, I guess I shouldn't have done that either.

***

Time, it's a relative thing. A few days later, Surfer Girl's mom picks her up from the Warlock. When she comes by to say goodbye, I ask, "Can I come up to Santa Cruz and visit you?"

Hugging me she shakes her head into my chest, "No, Mom doesn't like me seeing boys. Not unless she's getting some too. I wouldn't like that, not with you."

We hug one last time and she walks from my life, forever. It's a sad thing she's a free spirit; I'll miss her.

***

We've been busier than a one-legged man at a butt kicking contest for the last two weeks. That's all right; nothing is free. This adventure will be worth the hard work. Right now, I'm on a tour of the harbor, paying my respects. Rapping on Unk's door, I step into his dirty little smelly trailer. Dinner is on the stove and another five-star meal is being prepared.

"Well, Unk, this is it. We're on our way out the jaws." Sticking my hand out in a farewell gesture.

Glancing at my hand, Unk ignores it, "You're acting as though you won't be back. You'll be back, you're hooked. I'll see you in Coos Bay or Fort Brag. We'll see you up the line."

Extending my hand a little further, "See you up the line then."

We shake and I back out the door; I'm going to miss these five-star meals. Unk is the first guy to be-friend me here. Every time I offered him money for dinner he turned me down. Poor, proud, and generous, that's Unk.

Moss Landing is five hours of running time behind us. Santa Cruz head is about ten miles inside. A sizable swell runs under the Alley Cat's bow about every two minutes. Leaning into the hatch, I'm peering through a droplet encrusted window. It's good dark, and fog swirls past us at eight knots. Not a light mist, not just fog, but FOG, thick heavy cut with a knife FOG. The radar sweeps a ten-mile radii every thirty seconds telling us what's up ahead.

The Douggers, kicked back in the pilot seat, the Alley Cat is on autopilot. Droplets of moisture running down the glass is all three inches from my nose. Perched in the hatch to the focsel; I'm considering going to bed. In another two hours it's my watch. That's when the Sea Monster reaches up out of the ocean to eat us.

Long, slimy tentacles reach from the sea, grabbing our bow. Stopping the Alley Cat in her tracks, our bow is being pulled under by the monsters' arms. The prop whipping a froth, because it's been jerked from the water.

"HO, MAN!" Running down the passage way. "What the hell is that?" About five feet from the window, adrenaline is pumping through my veins at light speed. I've never been this scared before, not at sea.

The Douggers is at the wheel trying to wrestle control of the Alley Cat back. He's fighting a game but losing battle. Throwing the boat into reverse he revs her up. She lays there and waddles in the swells. Throwing her forward; she does the same.

Shouting over his shoulder at me, "He's got us! This critter is going to eat us, boat and all."

The sea monster's long tentacles wave in the air; they're slapping at the house and holding our bow down. In and out of the fog tentacles wave, lashing our windows. He's trying to break into the pilot house. The Douggers has changed strategies. He's got her at full-tilt boogie; trying to run over the sea monster. It ain't working. The sea monster is holding onto us like we're dinner; which we are.

Backing down the passage way I find myself in the galley. Digging through the fork and knife drawer, I pull out our salvation. Brandishing my weapon, I crow, "I'm going to cut a tentacle off. That'll make him turn us loose."

Meat cleaver in hand I run forward. Pulling down on the latch for the water tight door I slam my shoulder into it. Popping open all of two inches the door pops back close. The sea monster is holding the door, not letting me out. God this guy is smart. What are we going to do? Shouldering the door, hard, all I accomplish is the bruising of my shoulder. If I'd had my fingers in there, they'd be gone. Wow, we're up against one smart monster here. He knows what we're thinking.

The tentacles keep lashing at the pilot house. Sliding across the windows, soon he'll break a window then we're done for. He is making a low growling noise, like wood being ground to pulp as he climbs aboard.

Adrenaline has the Douggers and me pumped up. He's gone back to revving the motor in forward then reverse. Doug shouts, "The back door, try the back door!"

Plunging aft, I raise my cleaver ready to attack, crashing out the Dutch door I stop. Back here it's a very nice night, a calm night, droplets of fog are dropping from the rigging to the deck. The deck lights reflecting the gray mist, a halo of rainbows running through the shrouds. It's too nice of a night to be fighting sea monsters.

Rounding the corner my courage begins to waver. Tentacles wave at me in a come-hither motion. Tentacles sling in and out of the fog, I'm afraid; this may be the monster's plan. Screwing my courage up, I charge.

Charging into harms way I scream, "Aahhh!"

A large tentacle whips at me, knocking me to the deck. Wow this guy hits hard. A lot harder than I figured he could. Getting to my knees I crawl to one of the larger tentacles. Hack, grabbing the tentacle, hack hack hack. This don't seem right?

The tentacle is splintering? Splintering; cant' be… Wood? Wooden tentacles? I don't think this is a sea monster. Maybe we should slow down here? See what we got? Standing I grab another tentacle. It's hard, slimy but hard. This thing can't be alive. I hack again this time as an experiment. Yep, it's wood.

Walking into the pilothouse I'm all smiles. "Douggers, Douggers."

Doug is back to spinning the wheel port and starboard. He is still all pumped up.

"What happened? Hack another tentacle! He's backing off… a little."

"Douggers, I think we caught a stump."

"A stump, a stump? What do you mean a stump?"

"We snagged us a stump. It's the roots that we're seeing, roots and some seaweed. Some seaweed got hung up on roots; that's what's waving around out there. Roots and seaweed, but it sure looks like a sea monster."

"It's a stump?"

"Yep, a God-awful big stump, but a stump."

"Well, all right then, let's go see what we have."

The stump turned out to be a tree, a eucalyptus tree ninety feet long or so. The best we can figure; it washed out of a levee up in the delta somewhere. There were floods last winter. It probably fell into the river during high waters. It apparently spent some time in a kelp bed. A lot of bull kelp is hung up on the roots.

We hit the root system head on. Our anchor is caught on a root. Taking a hand saw forward we're cutting roots off. Every time we cut one root another root catches the anchor. It looks like we hit the tree at the bottom of a swell. That's why it is pulling the bow down so hard.

Once free of the stump, we cruise by our sea monster. Ninety feet long with most of the limbs still attached. If it had been a sea monster we'd be dinner by now.

CHAPTER EIGHT

Shut down. It's good dark; I just put the gear away. Flood lights are casting long shadows across our deck. There's a hundred or so fish to put below; the afternoons' catch. Once they're below decks, I've got to put all the fish to bed. It'll be an hour or two, then I can go to bed myself.

Carefully dropping the last fish below, I start down our ladder. Our ladder, even for a deckhand, our ladder is a piece of work. Stormy thought he had fixed it for me but I had to fix it back. The ladder is some redwood two by fours, with old pieces of broken pallets as rungs. It's crap, but deck hands are cheap.

Back when Stormy and I were blowing our hole Stormy broke out some rungs on the ladder.

His answer to the broken rung, was to break out every rung. Leaving the broken pieces in the fish hole. Then, Stormy took me to the Whale Bone for a hamburger. Off buying parts and pieces, Doug returned to the boat finding his ladder splintered and is gone. A normal guy would have assumed one of us was hurt. A normal guy, not a tightwad, would have gone to a hospital in the area to see. Not Doug, he brought his sack lunch into the Whale Bone and sat down at our table.

"Hey-hey-hey, you tight little tightwad. You come down here to buy us lunch?" "Can't afford to. Someone broke my ladder, now I have to replace it." "Hey-hey-hey, you tight little bugger, did you at least go to the hospital, at least check?"

"Didn't have to," Doug takes a large bite of sandwich and chews, talking around the food. "Unk told me that you guys were both up right when you left. I know you, Stormy, you don't work without food."

"Hey-hey-hey, at least you'll have to buy a new Ladder, for the Benjy kid."

***

After Stormy left that day, Doug sent me to the scrap pile to find new rungs for our ladder. Doug, he's thrifty. The rebuilt ladder is the same one I'm using today. Descending from the bottom rung I step into three hundred gallons of sixteen-degree brine. Freezing water sloshes up and down my boots, coming precariously close to over topping them. Fish are lying in the brine freezing into solid chunks. The water spraying from the piping overhead dribbles to a stop. The Douggers just turned the spray system off. At least the brine won't be raining down on me tonight.

"Hey Douggers, can you throw me my gloves?"

The gloves float down to me, snagging them from the air I slide them on.

There are a couple of hump to put to bed. The fish need to be spread over the entire hole. We don't want any hot spots. In the last three days we have done well. There are two feet of fish in the bins. Today's catch will add another foot. By the end of this trip, we'll have been off shore for thirty days, and the fish will be stacked twelve feet high.

Picking two fish up from the brine I place them in the aft bin. Bending I grab two more, sixteen-degree water swirls around my gloves. This will take a while.

After an hour in the hole; the warmth of the fifty mile an hour wind feels nice. Drifting like this, the weather doesn't seem so bad. Standing at the back of the cabin I strip my foul weather gear off, and slip from my boots. Stepping into the pilothouse the heat from the stove almost knocks me over. Radios squawk and squeal at me there's no relief from information on a fish boat. The deck vibrating beneath my stocking feet hums with the throb of the diesel engine. The Douggers is at the stove.

Looks like we're having Campbell's chicken soup, and a piece of toast. And I do mean "A" as in one piece of toast. Doug told me once that he use to make his sons split a candy bar. One son would cut the candy bar; the other son got first choice. That is tough, heck it's double tough.

Setting down at the table I want to lay my head down. It wouldn't be right so I just yawn. After all I had three hours sleep last night. What do I expect?

"Doug? Are we going to run tonight?"

Smiling at me Doug asks, "Why, you tired?"

"Well just a little, but if you want to run... I'll take the first watch."

"Naw, we did all right today. At least as well as anyone else. No need to run to no more fish than we got."

"That's good. I am a little tired."

"How many did you put down at shut down?"

"A hump plus three."

"That gives us two hundred and twenty-six for the day."

"How much is that in dollars?"

"We're getting a grand a ton, takes about a hump and twenty to make a ton.

Rubbing my tired eyes with a fist, "We're doing pretty good, think we'll plug her this trip?"

"Hope so, we better. To have a decent year, we need to plug her twice. That'd be about sixty tons; your take home would be six grand. Not bad ahh?"

The Douggers doing a straddle legged walk carries two bowls of soup toward the settee. The Alley Cat is sliding sideways down the face of a wave.

The deck is on a slant, but Doug spills nary a drop. That'd be a waste of food.

"Tell me something Ben, what in the heck has kept you distracted all day?"

"Well Doug, I'm trying to figure things out."

"Figure what out?"

"Well... I don't know what I'm doing out here. How come I'm on a fish boat a hundred miles off shore? My buddies are all in college."

"Look at history. All throughout time the world has needed men like us. Or rather, men like us have needed jobs like this. In the seventeen-hundreds, we would have been fur trappers. The eighteen hundreds... we'd be buffalo hunters, or gold prospectors. Fishing it's a cross between hunting and prospecting. You, me, we're not built to punch a time clock. Fishing is a respectable way to be disreputable. Just look around Moss Landing, you'll see what I mean."

"Yea, like Vincey Pooh."

"Vincey Pooh takes disreputable to an extreme; don't go that far. But yea, anyone who stays in the fishing business just don't give a damn."

Taking a slurp of soup, "I think you're right. People think we have a job, but we don't. We don't have to be anywhere at any particular time. We work until we fall in our tracks, or we don't. It's kind of good."

Doug sits back in his seat, giving me a wan smile. "What we do is tough, hard and dangerous, but you can't call it work. For one thing we don't know if we're going to make any money when we throw the lines off. For another if I decide to sleep-in, in the morning, we'll do just that."

A little thrill runs through me, sleep in, wow, but I know Doug is not serious.

"Hey Stormy's deck hand... you know the other night, complaining about weather?"

Sniggering at the memory, Douggers says. "Complaining doesn't change a thing. Except it makes it worse."

Noticing my soup, I fall to devouring it. When you get two meals a day, you eat both of them. Slurping with gusto, I contemplate my lot in life. I'm a fisherman. I want other people to know what being a fisherman is like. It's different. Maybe someday I'll write a book. Let me see now; I'll start by describing a wave busting over the bow.

The foam the bubbles are all white. The lights reflecting the red and green of the running lights. Yea that's good. How cool fishermen are in bad weather. Oh, oh, sea monsters... Write about sea monsters...

AFTERWARDS

This book was written some twenty, now thirty years ago, as a way to remind myself that I was not always an engineer living in suburbia. I left the fishing business at thirty-eight years of age. By this time, I had a wife and a son. I missed going to sea, and writing this tale gave me a reason to remember how it was.

After I finished my book, I gave it to close friends and other men that had gone to sea. I was told to hide my work as my dyslexia made me look like an uneducated dunder pate. For years, the few copies of my manuscript sat unmolested in the hold of my boat. Once in a while, I would let someone read my work… but I always received no encouragement to proceed with my writing.

And then, in my seventies, Mike, my old partner, called me out of the blue and said he had re-read my manuscript and that the story was good, it just needed to be cleaned up. So, for the next couple of years, I tried to find someone to edit my work. I failed to find anyone to do the work that I could not.

Then I found out Word can read. Word would read to me my book; and at that point, I understood why no one would take on this project. But I think there is a story to be told here. So; I listened to my manuscript and wrote what I had meant to write years ago. I listened to the book several times, trying to make it a little better with each review. At this point I give it to you, the reader, and hope you are not wasting your time with my little story.

benwalkabout@yahoo

www.ingramcontent.com/pod-product-compliance
Lightning Source LLC
Chambersburg PA
CBHW070900120626
46546CB00001B/81